PRAISE FOR THIS BOOK

"Dr. Brown more than fulfills his promise to provide an accessible summary that describes and integrates new facts and perspectives on ADHD. The book is comprehensive, current, and engagingly written. It will be a terrific resource for parents, educators, and clinicians as well as for patients themselves."

F. Xavier Castellanos, *MD, Brooke and Daniel Neidich Professor of Child and Adolescent Psychiatry, Professor of Radiology and Physiology and Neuroscience, and Director, Center for Neurodevelopmental Disorders, New York University Langone Medical Center Child Study Center*

"Brown presents a comprehensive case for comprehending this disorder in terms of a wide range of executive functions, rather than on the basis of behavior and attention alone. Loaded with up-to-date research findings and synthetic in scope, this work is bound to challenge assumptions and pave the way toward new paradigms."

Stephen P. Hinshaw, *PhD, Professor of Psychology, University of California, Berkeley, and Editor,* Psychological Bulletin

"Tom Brown's book is placing cognitive changes at the heart of ADHD and drawing out the implications for clinicians and researchers. It is a welcome corrective to the overemphasis on disruptive behavior and it is written so clearly that it can be recommended to everyone who wants to understand the nature of this serious problem for adults and children."

Eric Taylor, *FRCP, FRCPsych, Professor of Child and Adolescent Psychiatry, Institute of Psychiatry, University of London*

"A very intriguing read. Dr. Brown skillfully examines the diverse nature of executive functions, ADHD, and their overlap."

Timothy E. Wilens, *MD, Associate Professor of Psychiatry, Harvard Medical School, and Director of Substance Abuse Services, Massachusetts General Hospital*

"Professionals and lay people looking for a synthesis of our current understanding of this condition will find Dr. Brow~~'~ ~~~~~~~~~ understandable, and very readable contribution."

Gabrielle A. Carlson, *MD, Professor of Psychiatr~ Child and Adolescent Psychiatry, Stony Brook*

"Dr. Brown presents a science-driven and cohesive way of re-conceptualizing the disorder, revitalizing the central role of executive functioning impairment in ADHD. This book translates recent advances in ADHD science into understandable words not only for mental health professionals, but for all those interested in this very prevalent disorder affecting individuals across the whole life cycle."

Luis Augusto Rohde, *MD, PhD, President of the World Federation of ADHD, and Professor of Psychiatry, Federal University of Rio Grande do Sul, Brazil*

"Tom Brown's newest book pulls from the latest research in ADHD to present a new explanatory paradigm. Research results are distilled to debunk myths and offer sound guidance on evaluation and effective treatment. This book is a must-read for any education, health, or mental health professional who encounters children or adults with ADHD. Its direct and clear language makes the explanations and conclusions accessible to parents and adult patients, too."

Mina K. Dulcan, *MD, Osterman Professor of Child Psychiatry and Head, Department of Child and Adolescent Psychiatry at the Ann & Robert H. Lurie Children's Hospital of Chicago; Professor of Psychiatry and Behavioral Sciences and Pediatrics, and Director, Child and Adolescent Psychiatry, Northwestern University Feinberg School of Medicine*

"This book presents a highly useful and current summation of the major findings concerning ADHD and the role of executive functioning in it. Clinicians, students, and laypeople will find here much valuable information on the disorder, its assessment and diagnosis, and its management."

Russell A. Barkley, *PhD, Clinical Professor of Psychiatry and Pediatrics, Medical University of South Carolina*

"Thomas E Brown has produced a comprehensive reference. It extends our understanding of the impact of Attention Deficit Hyperactivity Disorder as that diagnosis assumes new borders in DSM 5."

Martha Bridge Denckla, *MD, Professor of Neurology, Pediatrics, and Psychiatry, Johns Hopkins University School of Medicine, and Director, Developmental Cognitive Neurology, Kennedy Krieger Institute*

"Tom Brown is one of the true pioneers in our growing understanding of ADHD. Both a clinician and a researcher, he continues to deepen and enlarge our knowledge of ADHD. Dr. Brown is a dedicated doctor who's written yet another brilliant book."

Edward Hallowell, *MD, author of* Delivered from Distraction *and* The Childhood Roots of Adult Happiness

A NEW UNDERSTANDING OF ADHD IN CHILDREN AND ADULTS

For over 100 years, ADHD has been seen as essentially a behavior disorder. Recent scientific research has developed a new paradigm which recognizes ADHD as a developmental disorder of the cognitive management system of the brain, its executive functions. This cutting-edge book pulls together key ideas of this new understanding of ADHD, explaining them and describing in understandable language scientific research that supports this new model. It addresses questions like:

- Why can those with ADHD focus very well on some tasks while having great difficulty in focusing on other tasks they recognize as important?
- How does brain development and functioning of persons with ADHD differ from others?
- How do impairments of ADHD change from childhood through adolescence and in adulthood?
- What treatments help to improve ADHD impairments? How do they work? Are they safe?
- Why do those with ADHD have additional emotional, cognitive, and learning disorders more often than most others?
- What commonly held assumptions about ADHD have now been proven wrong by scientific research?

Psychiatrists, psychologists, social workers, and other medical and mental health professionals, as well as educators and those affected by ADHD and their families, will find this to be an insightful and invaluable resource.

Thomas E. Brown, PhD, is Associate Director of the Yale Clinic for Attention and Related Disorders and Assistant Clinical Professor of Psychiatry, Yale University School of Medicine. He is a Fellow of the American Psychological Association, developer of the *Brown ADD Scales for Children and Adults* (Pearson), and author of the prize-winning book, *Attention Deficit Disorder: The Unfocused Mind in Children and Adults*. Dr. Brown is also editor of the textbook, *ADHD Comorbidities: Handbook of ADHD Complications in Children and Adults*. Visit the author's website at www.DrThomasEBrown.com.

A NEW UNDERSTANDING OF ADHD IN CHILDREN AND ADULTS

Executive Function Impairments

Thomas E. Brown

Routledge
Taylor & Francis Group

NEW YORK AND LONDON

First published 2013
by Routledge
711 Third Avenue, New York, NY 10017

Simultaneously published in the UK
by Routledge
27 Church Road, Hove, East Sussex BN3 2FA

Routledge is an imprint of the Taylor & Francis Group, an informa business

Library of Congress Cataloging in Publication Data
Brown, Thomas E., 1942-
A new understanding of ADHD in children and adults : executive function
impairments / Thomas E. Brown.
pages cm
Includes bibliographical references and index.
1. Attention-deficit hyperactivity disorder. 2. Attention-deficit disorder in adults.
3. Mental illness--Classification. I. Title.
RJ506.H9B7652 2013
618.92'8589--dc23
2013001384

ISBN: 978-0-415-81424-9 (hbk)
ISBN: 978-0-415-81425-6 (pbk)
ISBN: 978-0-203-06753-6 (ebk)

Typeset in Garamond
by Saxon Graphics Ltd, Derby

The untangling of the complexity has barely begun... But even at its early stages, the whole business of the matter of the mind requires a global view if we are to get anywhere.

Gerald M. Edelman (1992)
Bright Air, Brilliant Fire: On the Matter of the Mind

Perhaps the most indispensable thing we can do as human beings, every day of our lives, is remind ourselves and others of our complexity, fragility, finiteness and uniqueness.

Antonio R. Damasio (1994)
Descartes' Error: Emotion, Reason and the Human Brain

CONTENTS

ACKNOWLEDGMENTS

To my wife, Bobbie, with deep gratitude and love for all you are, all you give, and all we still share together. You are the light of my life! And with much appreciation to our family, Liza, Dave, Nancy, Abel, Noah, and Simone for your generous love, encouragement and continuing sunshine. I am also grateful to Philipp Reichel who served as my research assistant throughout this project; he provided not only research support, but also many helpful suggestions.

Thanks also to George Zimmar, my publisher, for his generous encouragement and support of this project, to Rob Brown for co-ordinating production, to Lorna Hawes for her careful copy editing, to Sally Beesley for the attractive cover design, to Jennifer Sefa-Boakye, for coordinating marketing, to Christopher Tominich for his management of countless details, and to all the others in the team at Routledge/Taylor and Francis who helped to complete the project and make it available to readers.

T. E. B.

INTRODUCTION

The disorder currently identified as Attention Deficit Disorder (ADD) or Attention Deficit Hyperactivity Disorder (ADHD) has been described in the medical literature with a variety of different labels for over 100 years. (In this book, the term ADHD is used to refer to Attention Deficit Disorder with and without hyperactivity). Throughout most of those years, the emphasis has been on behavior problems of young children who were seen as being overly active and not listening to others. The term "attention" as a central aspect of the syndrome was not introduced into diagnostic criteria until 1980 (American Psychiatric Association, 1980). Until recently, this syndrome was classified in the diagnostic manual as a "disruptive behavior disorder." That old model of ADHD is now outdated. Rapidly it is being replaced by a new understanding of ADHD as a developmental impairment of the brain's self-management system, its executive functions.

This book describes that new understanding and the recent clinical and neuroscience research that supports it. Here the reader will find, in clear and accessible language, information on how scientific research on functioning of the human brain has created this major shift in how ADHD is now understood. This discussion describes and elaborates many concepts and research findings about ADHD not included even in the description of ADHD provided in DSM-V, the most recent version of the psychiatric diagnostic manual. It moves beyond a simple listing of behavioral characteristics of those with ADHD and provides a more integrated understanding of the complex problems of brain development and cognitive functions that underlie the disorder at various points in the lifespan. Moreover, this volume offers a working definition of ADHD that highlights characteristics of this developmental impairment of the brain's management system, its executive functions.

The purpose of this book is to provide an accessible summary that describes and integrates new facts and understandings of this disorder which have been developed by a number of researchers and clinicians working at the cutting edge of the study of ADHD. The integrated understanding provided here is not new in the sense of totally original or never before seen. Concepts in the working definition proposed in this book are not the creation of any one individual. Much of the research and most of the key concepts have been disparately reported in many scientific journals, books and conferences by a number of researchers and clinicians over the past 15 years. What is new in this publication is the integration of these fragments of emerging research data and perspectives into an updated and readily understandable paradigm with a working definition for this complex syndrome.

Findings from neuroscience, brain imaging and various forms of clinical research have made the old understanding of ADHD as essentially a simple behavior disorder no longer tenable. A new paradigm has emerged to conceptualize this syndrome. This new model is not yet fully refined. Its language of executive function is barely mentioned in the description of ADHD provided in the most recent version of the official diagnostic manual. Yet this updated model increasingly is being recognized and used by many professionals in psychology, medicine, education and related fields.

This new paradigm can provide a useful way to put together many of the not yet integrated pieces of research on this puzzling syndrome which causes some children and adults to have great difficulty in focusing and managing many aspects of their daily life, while they can focus and manage a few other tasks or activities quite well. This new understanding provides a useful way to more readily recognize, understand, assess and treat this complex syndrome which impacts about 9% of children and almost 5% of adults.

Further research and increased clinical experience will eventually provide even better ways to conceptualize this disorder, its assessment and treatment. In the meantime, this book offers a new and, hopefully, helpful understanding for primary care physicians, psychologists, child and adult psychiatrists, pediatricians, advanced practice nurses, clinical social workers, and other medical and mental health professionals as well as educators, disability service providers and interested patients and family members who struggle with the complexities of ADHD.

Research has made it increasingly clear that ADHD is not essentially a behavior disorder and not limited to childhood years. The working definition offered in the second chapter of this book asserts that this syndrome known as ADHD is a complex developmental impairment of the brain's self-management system, its executive functions, which may emerge in boys or girls during early childhood, but often is not recognized until the affected individual encounters the challenges of adolescence or adulthood. For some, impairments of ADHD diminish considerably as their brains mature over the mid to late adolescent years; for others, the disorder persists as a chronic impairment throughout their lifespan.

This book begins with a review of multiple widely-held, but mistaken assumptions about ADHD; it also presents scientific facts from research findings that contradict those myths. It then offers and explains a new working definition of ADHD based on the emerging facts and paradigm. The four chapters following that description describe and explain in more detail the nature of the disorder, how it can be effectively assessed, how it can be effectively treated, and why many learning and psychiatric disorders often co-occur with ADHD.

Chapter 1 presents 35 commonly held myths about ADHD that are challenged by findings developed from scientific research. Listed after each of those myths is a brief summary of facts that contradict that mistaken assumption and citations to specific pages of this book where more detailed information on relevant research can be found.

Chapter 2 proposes and explains a working definition of the new paradigm that is based upon facts of ADHD developed in research. It also highlights the developmental nature of the disorder and the puzzling fact that individuals with ADHD all tend to have a few specific activities and situations in which they have no difficulty deploying those executive functions in which they are usually significantly impaired. That chapter also describes similarities and differences between the old and new models and summarizes findings regarding the prevalence of ADHD in various age groups.

In Chapter 3 are reviews of research describing specific ways in which individuals with ADHD at various stages of life tend to be impaired in brain development, cognitive functioning, and their self-management for many activities of daily living. Recent findings on differences in rates of brain maturation, brain structure, and functional connectivity of brain components are included to address the question: "Is the ADHD brain structured or wired differently?" This chapter also describes research on the role of emotion and motivation in ADHD. It explains why ADHD impairments are found among persons along the full spectrum of IQ, including some who are extremely bright. A concluding section reviews genetic research seeking to explain the very high rate of familial heritability for ADHD coupled with information about environmental factors that can also impact this disorder.

Chapter 4 presents research findings on how impairments of ADHD understood in this new model can be adequately assessed and diagnosed at various points across the lifespan. It challenges the assumption that impairments of ADHD can be adequately assessed with traditional neuropsychological "tests of executive functions" and explains how clinicians can use clinical interviews and rating scales to assess ADHD as it is now understood in this new model. It also points out limitations of some ineffective assessment methods in current use.

Chapter 5 reviews research on the uses and limitations of approved medications and various psychosocial treatments for ADHD. It reports research regarding how medications for ADHD can improve brain function and describes the ways medications can affect various aspects of the self-management system of the brain. It also summarizes scientific findings regarding possible side effects to medication treatments for ADHD and reports on which psychosocial treatments for ADHD are helpful for various cognitive and behavioral functions in different age groups.

The sixth chapter of the book describes research showing how and why most individuals with ADHD suffer also from one or more additional learning or psychiatric disorders. It argues that executive function impairments of ADHD underlie and are foundational to dyslexia and other learning disorders, anxiety and depressive disorders, bipolar disorders, oppositional defiant and conduct disorders, obsessive-compulsive and hoarding disorders, substance use disorders, and Autistic Spectrum disorders. It suggests that ADHD is not like having a problem with one software program that interferes with only one type of functioning of a computer. It presents ADHD as more like a problem with the operating system of the computer, a broader, more foundational impairment that impacts a wide range of cognitive functioning.

35 MYTHS ABOUT ADHD AND WHY THEY ARE WRONG

This book describes a new understanding of ADHD (Attention Deficit Hyperactivity Disorder) based upon facts demonstrated in empirical research. This new understanding is summarized in a new definition and model described in Chapter 2. It challenges a number of widely-prevalent myths, mistaken assumptions about ADHD, that are still held by many lay people and some professionals. This chapter lists 35 of those assumptions, provides a brief summary of science-based facts that contradict each of these myths, and refers the reader to the more substantial evidence in Chapters 2 through 6 that challenges each mistaken assumption.

1. A person who has ADHD always has difficulty with executive functions such as focusing on a task and keeping things in mind, regardless of what they are doing.

Clinical data indicate that executive function impairments characteristic of ADHD are situationally-variable; each person with ADHD tends to have some specific activities or situations in which they have no difficulty in utilizing those executive functions that, for them, are significantly impaired in most other situations. Typically these are activities in which they have strong personal interest or where they believe that something very unpleasant will follow quickly if they do not take care of this task right here, right now (Chap. 2, pp. 32–33). Research findings indicate that intra-individual variability in performance from one context or time to another is the essence of ADHD. Multiple studies have shown that performance of persons with ADHD is highly sensitive to contextual factors, e.g. reward, nature of the task, and internal cognitive and physiological factors (Chap. 3, pp. 58–63).

2. Everyone has impairments of executive functions; those with ADHD are just like everybody else.

Although everyone suffers from executive function impairments sometimes, only those individuals who are significantly and chronically impaired by this syndrome of impairments qualify for the diagnosis of ADHD. Epidemiological research in the U.S. indicates that about 9% of children aged 6 to 17 years, 8.7% of adolescents aged 13 to 18 years, and 4.4% of adults qualify for an ADHD diagnosis under current diagnostic criteria. A pooled estimate from 102 studies of children up to age 18 years in diverse cultures around the world yields a more conservative estimate of 5.29% (Chap. 2, 40–41). Comparisons of individuals with ADHD versus matched groups in multiple aspects of brain development, brain structure and brain functioning have demonstrated significant differences between those who have ADHD and those who do not (Chap. 3, pp. 63–70).

3. If a person with ADHD really wants to focus and work effectively on a task they can make themselves do it. Using executive functions is just a matter of "willpower."

Because persons with ADHD can typically exercise their executive functions very well on specific activities or tasks that interest them or which cause them to fear some very unpleasant outcome quite soon if they do not accomplish that task, it is easy to assume that individuals with ADHD can exercise those same functions equally well in other situations which they or others consider important—if only they will exercise a presumed internal force called "willpower." This new model of ADHD challenges that assumption on the grounds that most operations of executive functions are unconscious, not in the psychoanalytic sense of repression, but in the more modern sense of "automaticity."

From this view, most operations of these executive functions are not under conscious control any more than is erectile dysfunction. Research on motivational influences impacting decisions of "Will you do it and, if so, how and when?" has shown that such decisions result primarily from complex and dynamic interactions of memory-influenced emotions with inborn patterns of reactivity that operate instantaneously with relatively insignificant conscious input, despite our assumptions to the contrary (Chap. 2, pp. 33–37).

4. Anyone who has ADHD will show clear signs of it during early childhood and will continue to have difficulties with executive functions for the rest of his/her life.

For decades ADHD, under various names, has been seen as essentially a disorder of childhood; DSM-IV (Diagnostic and Statistical Manual of Mental Disorders-IV) diagnostic criteria stipulated that, for diagnosis, at least some of the symptoms must be noticeable by age seven years. More recent research has shown that many with ADHD function quite well during childhood and do not manifest any significant symptoms of ADHD until adolescence or later when greater challenges to executive function are encountered (Chap. 4, pp. 77–78). Over the past decade research has shown that impairing symptoms of ADHD often persist well into adulthood (Chap. 2, pp. 29–31; Chap. 3, pp. 46–51). However, longitudinal studies have also shown that some individuals with ADHD during childhood experience significant reductions in their ADHD impairments as they grow older (Chap. 3, pp. 52–55).

5. Impairments of executive function are best assessed by neuropsychological "tests of executive function" administered by a neuropsychologist.

"Tests of executive function" used by neuropsychologists are not useful for assessing impairments of executive function associated with ADHD. Some with ADHD do poorly on a battery of such tests, but many who clearly meet diagnostic criteria for ADHD perform adequately or even quite well on such measures, despite their impairments of executive function (EF). The most effective measure for assessment of ADHD is use of a normed ADHD/EF rating scale in the context of a semi-structured clinical interview done by a clinician experienced with such disorders. These measures should inquire about how well the individual is able to manage relevant tasks of daily life as well as assessing for other possible causes of the symptoms and for possible comorbid difficulties. Unlike neuropsychological tests that attempt to infer dynamic patterns of functioning from just 5 to 20 minutes of behavior in an artificial laboratory setting, rating scales inquire over much wider time frames in a variety of settings and tasks (Chap. 4, pp. 88–92).

6. Persons with high IQ are not likely to have executive function impairments of ADHD because they are smart enough to overcome such difficulties.

Intelligence measured by IQ tests has virtually no systematic relationship to the syndrome of executive function impairments described in the new model of ADHD. Studies have shown that even extremely high IQ children and adults can suffer impairments of ADHD which significantly impair their ability to deploy their strong cognitive skills consistently and effectively in many situations of daily life. Clinical observations indicate that often high IQ individuals with ADHD face lengthy delays before they obtain a correct diagnosis and appropriate treatment. This is due largely to uninformed teachers, parents, clinicians, and patients themselves assuming that high IQ precludes ADHD (Chap. 3, pp. 70–72).

7. Modern imaging techniques such as PET and fMRI scans or computerized tests can provide objective evidence to diagnose executive function impairments associated with ADHD.

Many claim that "objective" measures such as positron emission tomography (PET), single photon emission computed tomography (SPECT)or functional magnetic resonance imaging (fMRI) scans can determine whether an individual has ADHD or not. Although these measures are useful research tools, they are not sufficiently developed or normed to make them useful or valid for assessment to make or deny an ADHD diagnosis for any specific individual. The same limitations apply to computerized "tests of attention" and to quantitative electroencephalography (EEG) tests. All of these measures provide only snapshots of brain functioning in brief moments of time and do not adequately capture the wide situational variability in functioning characteristic of most individuals with ADHD. This complex disorder can be effectively assessed and validly diagnosed only by a clinical interview that assesses longer term patterns of functioning in multiple contexts. This task requires a clinician skilled and experienced in this field (Chap. 4, pp. 94–95).

8. Executive function impairments of ADHD usually are outgrown when the person reaches their late teens or early twenties.

Some children with ADHD gradually outgrow their ADHD-related impairments as they get into middle childhood or adolescence. For them ADHD is a variety of developmental lag. Most often hyperactive and/or impulsive symptoms improve as the individual reaches adolescence while the broad range of inattention symptoms persist and sometimes get worse. Often the most problematic period is during junior high, high school and the first few years of university; that is the time when the individual faces the widest range of challenging activities without opportunity to escape from the ones in which they have little interest or ability. After that period some with ADHD are fortunate enough to get employment and a life situation where they can build on their strengths and find ways to work around their cognitive weaknesses; others are not similarly fortunate (Chap. 3, pp. 52–55).

9. Modern research methods have established that executive function impairments are localized mainly in the prefrontal cortex.

Executive functions are complex and involve not only the prefrontal cortex, but also many other components of the brain. Those with ADHD have been shown to differ in the rate of maturation of specific areas of the cortex, in the thickness of cortical tissue, in characteristics of the parietal and cerebellar regions, as well as in the basal ganglia, and in the white matter tracts that connect and provide critically important communication between various regions of the brain. Recent research has also shown that those with ADHD tend to have different patterns in functional connectivity, patterns of oscillations that allow different regions of the brain to exchange information (Chap. 3, pp. 63–70).

10. Emotions and motivation are not involved in executive functions associated with ADHD.

Although earlier research and diagnostic criteria for ADHD gave little attention to the role of emotion and motivation in this disorder, more recent research has highlighted their critical importance. Some research has focused solely on the problems of many with ADHD in regulating expression of their emotions without sufficient inhibition or modulation. However, research has also demonstrated that a chronic deficit in emotions that comprise motivation is a critically important aspect of impairments for most individuals with ADHD. Studies have shown that this is related to measurable differences in the operation of the reward system within the brains of those with ADHD. Those with ADHD tend to have abnormalities in the anticipatory dopamine cell firing in the reward system; this makes it difficult for them to arouse and sustain motivation for activities that do not provide immediate and continuing reinforcement (Chap. 3, pp. 55–62).

11. Impairments of executive function occur only if the person has inherited ADHD.

There are many ways in which executive functions can become impaired. Traumatic brain injuries, strokes, and Alzheimer's dementia are just a few of the many ways in which some individuals with previously adequate executive functions can become impaired in those functions. ADHD impairments of executive function are different. They are highly heritable, and they are *developmental* in the sense that they do not unfold and "come on line" for the individual in the way that occurs for most others of the same age. A number of imaging studies have demonstrated that children and adolescents with ADHD tend to show a lag of three to five years in the development of the brain infrastructure for executive functions relative to their peers. For some, delays in development of some specific aspects of the brain continue into adulthood (Chap. 2, pp. 28–31; Chap. 3, pp. 63–66, 72–76).

12. Usually executive functions of ADHD are problematic only while a person is in school. Once they get out of school, executive function impairments are not much of a problem.

Impairments of executive function associated with ADHD are often noticed first in school because academic and behavioral requirements of the classroom are difficult for many children with ADHD to meet in an age-appropriate way. Some with ADHD manage to meet these requirements quite adequately during the early years of school, but later find that their executive functions significantly interfere with the increasing demands for self-management and more complex learning and academic output in upper grades, especially during secondary and post-secondary education. However, studies of adolescents and adults with ADHD indicate that long after school years, many continue to have significant problems in their work, social relationships, sleep, family life, household management, driving, and many other aspects of daily life (Chap. 3, pp. 49–55).

13. The new model of ADHD as developmentally impaired executive function is completely different from the older model of ADHD.

The new model of ADHD differs in many ways from the earlier model of this disorder as essentially a cluster of behavior problems in young children. The new model is truly a shift of paradigm for understanding this syndrome. It applies not only to children, but also to adolescents and adults. It focuses on a wide range of self-management functions that are not limited to readily observable behaviors; functions included are linked to complex operations of the brain. However, there are still substantial and important points of overlap between the old and new models. The new model is an extension and expansion of the old model. Most individuals who meet diagnostic criteria for the new model will also meet the diagnostic criteria for the older model. The old model is no longer tenable not because it identifies individuals with a totally different disorder; the old model is no longer tenable because it does not adequately capture the wide breadth, complexity and persistence of this syndrome as it is found across the lifespan. (Chap. 2, pp. 39–40).

14. ADHD is a problem that occurs mainly in males and rarely in females.

On average, about three boys are diagnosed with ADHD for every one girl. This higher rate of ADHD among boys may be due to greater likelihood of behaviors that disturb teachers and parents during childhood and adolescence, prompting more referrals. Among adults, the ratio obtained in epidemiological studies is 1.6 males for every 1 female. In clinics providing assessment for ADHD in adults, the ratio of males to females tends to be more equal. ADHD is neither rare nor insignificant among females. Girls identified with ADHD in childhood or adolescence have been found to suffer from ADHD impairments fully comparable to those found among boys. It is not yet known whether the prevalence ratio will change if epidemiological studies of ADHD employ a model similar to that described in Chapter 2 for studying both genders at various ages. Since the new model is focused primarily upon cognitive impairments rather than on disruptive behavior, it seems likely that the ratio of males to females will be found to be more equal. Some rating scale studies of executive function impairments in adults have shown little significant difference between overall scores for the two genders (Chap. 2, pp. 40–43).

15. If a person with ADHD is hyperactive and impulsive during childhood, they are likely to continue that way into adulthood.

Many individuals with ADHD never manifest excessive levels of hyperactivity or impulsivity in childhood or beyond. Among those with ADHD who do tend to be more "hyper" and impulsive in childhood, a substantial percentage tends to outgrow those symptoms by middle childhood or early adolescence. However, symptoms of impairments in focusing and sustaining attention, organizing and getting started on tasks, managing emotions, utilizing working memory, etc. tend to persist and often become more problematic as the individual with ADHD gets into adolescence and adulthood (Chap. 3, pp. 47–48, 52–53).

16. ADHD-related executive function impairments are due primarily to a "chemical imbalance" in the brain.

The term "chemical imbalance in the brain" is often used to explain impairments of ADHD. This suggests that there are chemicals floating around in the cerebral spinal fluid that surrounds the brain that are simply not in correct proportions, as though there were too much salt in the soup. This assumption is simply wrong. Impairments of ADHD are not due to a global excess or lack of a specific chemical within or around the brain. The primary problem is related to chemicals manufactured, released, and then reloaded at the level of synapses, the trillions of infinitesimal junctions between certain networks of neurons that manage critical activities within the brain's management system. The brain is essentially a huge electrical system that has multiple subsystems that need to communicate with one another constantly to get anything done. This system operates on low voltage electrical impulses that carry messages from one tiny neuron to another in fractions of a second. However, these neurons are not physically connected; there are gaps at each point of connection. To get messages from one neuron to another, an electrical message needs to jump the gap. Arrival of the electrical impulse causes tiny "micro-dots" of a neurotransmitter chemical to be released. This works like a spark plug to carry the message across the gap and further down the circuit. Persons with ADHD tend not to release enough of these essential chemicals, or to release and reload them too quickly, before an adequate connection has been made. Medications used to treat ADHD help to improve this process (Chap. 5, pp. 99–104).

17. There is no real evidence of significant differences in brain development and functioning in those with executive function impairments of ADHD compared to those without ADHD.

Modern imaging techniques have provided a lot of evidence of differences between persons with ADHD and those who do not have ADHD in their processes of brain development and functioning. These include evidence that while most aspects of brain maturation in children with ADHD are identical to typically developing children, there are several specific areas of brain that tend to take three to five years longer to mature in the brains of most children with ADHD; those specific areas of brain are especially important for age-appropriate executive functions. Other areas of difference include thickness of cortical tissue, global reductions of gray matter, atypical development of white matter connections across various regions of the brain, less efficient communication over white matter circuits linking various brain regions, and differences in rates of oscillations critical for linking communication from one region of brain to another. There is also evidence of differences between persons with ADHD and those without in their ability to suppress and sustain suppression of default-mode oscillations when necessary to facilitate sustained attention (Chap. 3, pp. 63–70).

18. For some individuals with ADHD, prescribed medications can cure their ADHD impairments so they do not need to keep taking the medication.

Medications for ADHD cure nothing. They are not like antibiotics that may cure an infection if the medication is taken consistently for a few days or weeks. ADHD medications are more like eyeglasses that may improve or even normalize a person's vision while the glasses are worn, but the eyeglasses cannot fix the problem with the person's eyes. When the eyeglasses are taken off, the person's vision returns to whatever it was previously. Most medications for ADHD currently available last for somewhere between 2 and 12 hours, then they gradually stop being helpful. Some persons who take medications for ADHD find that there is a point where they no longer need to take that medication; they are able to function reasonably well without it. Sometimes this is due to increased development of their brain as they get older; the processes of natural maturation that were a bit slower in them than for their contemporaries eventually kick in. In other cases such an improvement may be due to some change in the situation, a new teacher who is more supportive, a new job that is not as demanding of executive functions as the previous job, or added sources of support. Such improvements without medication may be temporary or quite long-lasting (Chap. 5, pp. 104–113).

19. Most countries outside the U.S. do not have many persons with ADHD; this is primarily a problem in the U.S.

For many years it was assumed that ADHD was a problem unique to the U.S. because the estimated incidence in other countries was much lower. Subsequently it became clear that most of the reported differences were based upon different diagnostic criteria being used in many other countries. More recent studies comparing estimates based on similar diagnostic criteria indicate somewhat lower, but roughly similar prevalence rates in many countries with widely differing cultures and economic strata. A meta-analysis of 102 studies involving 171,000 children from all regions of the world yielded a pooled estimate of 5.29% for children 18 years or younger. Thus far there are few studies outside the U.S. estimating prevalence of ADHD among adults; many countries outside North America do not yet recognize ADHD in adults as a legitimate disorder, but this is gradually changing. Within the U.S., current estimates of ADHD incidence rates based on DSM-IV criteria are about 9% for children and adolescents; for adults estimated incidence is about 4.4% (Chap. 2, pp. 38–43).

20. Stimulant medications used to treat ADHD-related executive functions are highly addictive and carry considerable risk of dangerous cardiovascular problems.

Stimulants are the most widely used medications for treatment of ADHD; some types have been available since the late 1930s, others since the late 1950s. Newer versions tend to be essentially these same active ingredients formulated in more modern delivery systems. There is an extensive body of research on use of these medications for treatment of ADHD. Stimulants are classified as Schedule II medications in the U.S., similar to pain medications. This is because, if taken in excessive quantities or otherwise misused, they can be addictive. However, the incidence of addiction to stimulant medications for ADHD is extremely low, so long as the medications are taken orally, not by injection, and are used as prescribed, even over many years. Large studies of children and adults with ADHD taking stimulants compared with others of similar age have shown that the rate of serious adverse cardiovascular events such as severe hypertension, heart attacks or strokes is no greater among those treated with stimulants than in the general public of the same age without such treatment (Chap. 5, pp. 116–120).

21. The dose and timing of medications used to treat executive function impairment are quite similar for persons of similar age and body mass.

Although some medications can be appropriately prescribed in doses directly related to the patient's age, weight, or severity of symptoms, this is not true for stimulants used to treat ADHD. Fine-tuning of dose and timing of stimulants for ADHD is very important because the most effective dose depends on how sensitive the particular patient's body is to that specific medication. Usually that needs to be determined by trial and error, starting with a very low dose and gradually tapering up until an effective dose is found, significant adverse effects occur, or the maximum recommended dose is reached. Often the dose needs to be higher in the morning and gradually tapered over the course of the day, but sometimes exactly the opposite dosing pattern works better. Some adolescents and adults need smaller doses than what is usually prescribed for young children and some young children need much larger doses than most of their peers. Some of the non-stimulant medications for ADHD are prescribed according to weight because they operate in a different way (Chap. 5, pp. 101–104).

22. There is no evidence that medications for ADHD actually improve executive function impairments or that any improvements last.

There are three different types of evidence that demonstrate the effectiveness of specific medications for ADHD improving impaired executive functions. First, imaging studies have shown that stimulants improve, and may normalize, the ability of individuals with ADHD to get activated for assigned tasks, to minimize distractibility while doing tasks, to improve functional connections between various regions of brain involved in executive functions, to improve working memory performance, to reduce boredom during task performance, and, in some cases, to normalize some structural abnormalities in specific brain regions of those with ADHD (Chap. 5, pp. 104–106).

Second, experiments comparing performance of children with ADHD with matched controls or when on placebo in comparison to prescribed medication have shown that when on appropriate medication, children with ADHD tend to minimize inappropriate classroom behavior and control their behavior more like typical children in their class. Experiments have also shown that medication can help those with ADHD to improve their speed and accuracy in solving arithmetic problems; they increase their willingness to persist in trying to solve frustrating problems; they improve their working memory, and increase their motivation to perform and execute more adequately a wide variety of tasks associated with executive functions. These results do not mean that all children on such medications display these results, but group data demonstrate statistically significant improvements. However, it should be noted that these results are found only during the time the medication is actually active in the person's body (Chap. 5, pp. 106–108).

Third, a very large number of clinical trials comparing the effectiveness of ADHD medications versus placebo for alleviation of ADHD impairments in both children and adults have demonstrated that these medications (both stimulants and some non-stimulants) produce robust improvements in a large percentage of patients with ADHD. Most of these clinical trials have used DSM-IV diagnostic criteria for ADHD, but some have tested medications against the wider range of ADHD symptoms included in the new model described in Chapter 2. Similar effectiveness results have been shown in symptoms from both old and new models (Chap. 5, pp. 108–111, 113).

Despite the fact that the direct effects of medication do not last beyond the duration of the medication's action each day, the improved functioning made possible by the medication has been shown to result in better school classroom and test performance, reduced rates of school dropout, increased rates of graduation and other achievements which can have lasting effects. Medications may also help to support a person's adaptive performance while they await further brain development, enter into employment for which they are better suited, and/or improve their learning of concepts and skills they would otherwise be unlikely to master without the support of medication.

23. It is quite risky to administer medications for ADHD problems to preschool-aged children.

While many children with ADHD do not show significant impairments until they begin elementary school, there are some preschoolers who manifest serious, and sometimes dangerous, behavior problems between the ages of three to six years. Research with children aged three to five and a half years has shown that a majority of children in this age group with moderate to severe ADHD show significant improvement in their ADHD symptoms when treated with stimulant medications. With this younger age group, side effects are slightly more common than is usually seen in older children, though such effects were still minimal. In 2012 the American Academy of Pediatrics recommended that children aged four to five years old with significant ADHD impairments should be treated first with behavior therapy and then, if that is not sufficiently effective within nine months, they should be treated with stimulant medications for ADHD (Chap. 5, pp 110–111).

24. There is no evidence that medication treatment for ADHD executive function impairments improves learning or academic achievement.

Longitudinal studies have shown that children with ADHD tend, as a group, to have lower scores for reading achievement, take fewer advanced classes, have increased rates of absenteeism, more grade retention, are rated by their teachers as having poorer performance, and drop out of school before graduation more than do groups of children without ADHD, even when IQ is not included in the analysis. However, children treated with stimulant medication had higher scores for reading and lower rates of absenteeism when compared to students with ADHD who were not treated with medication. Additional factors such as level of parents' education and presence or absence of comorbid disorders also impacted these outcomes. Another large study in a different country showed that teacher-reported inattention problems in the years from kindergarten through age 12 are associated with the highest rates of dropping out of high school before graduation.

Other studies have shown that duration of treatment with medication also affects outcome. Students with ADHD who receive at least a year of medication achieved better scores on nationally standardized tests of reading, writing and math as well as better report card grades than children with ADHD who did not receive at least that minimal duration of treatment. Another study demonstrated that children with ADHD whose medication starts earlier in their school career tend, on average, to score better on national exams than children whose medication for ADHD is not started until later in their school career (Chap. 2, pp. 37–38; Chap. 3, pp. 47–48; Chap. 5, pp. 111–113).

25. Behavior modification and other psychosocial methods are just as effective for treating executive function impairments of ADHD as are medications.

Studies of the effectiveness of psychosocial methods such as behavior modification and cognitive-behavioral therapy versus medication alone indicate that medication treatment seems to be the critical ingredient for treating most patients with ADHD. Training parents and teachers of young children with ADHD in operant conditioning techniques has been shown to reduce disruptive behavior and to increase attention to tasks. However, psychosocial interventions have not been shown to produce lasting changes in such problematic behaviors any more than medication alleviates symptoms of ADHD after the dose has worn off. Moreover, behavioral interventions have not been shown to improve cognitive impairments such as working memory, sustaining focus, or similar higher cognitive functions at the core of the new model of ADHD impairments (Chap. 5, pp. 120–126).

26. Individuals with ADHD have no more likelihood of having depression, anxiety problems, Obsessive-Compulsive Disorder or other psychiatric problems than anyone else of the same age.

Several epidemiological studies have demonstrated that children and adults with ADHD have a much greater likelihood of having one or more additional psychiatric and/or learning disorders at some time in their life than do those without ADHD. A meta-analysis of 21 studies showed that the likelihood of anxiety disorders, depressive disorders, or conduct/oppositional disorders among children with ADHD was respectively about 3 times, 5.5 times or 10.7 times in prevalence of those disorders among children with ADHD. Among adults with ADHD, the likelihood of their having one or more additional psychiatric disorders by age 44 years was more than six times greater than the likelihood for adults without ADHD. These elevated rates of comorbid disorders among persons with ADHD may be due partially to genetic factors. However, since executive function impairments of ADHD occur in many other learning and psychiatric disorders, it has been proposed that ADHD may be not just one additional psychiatric disorder. It may be a foundational disorder that underlies most other disorders (Chap. 6, pp. 128–135, 162–164).

27. Learning disorders like dyslexia, math disorder and disorder of written expression are quite separate from the executive function impairments of ADHD. They require special education, not medication treatments.

Specific learning disorders such as dyslexia, math disorder, and disorder of written expression have been seen as totally separate from ADHD for decades. More recent research has demonstrated that impairments of executive function associated with the new model of ADHD play an important role in each of the primary learning disorders and that children with ADHD tend to have a greatly increased likelihood of one or more learning disorders relative to students without ADHD. Impairments of ability to focus and sustain attention, to engage with the task, and to utilize working memory are critical elements of being able to read, do math, and give written expression to thoughts. Many students with ADHD have chronic difficulties with one or more of these three basic domains of learning and academic work. For some, their executive function impairments combine with impairments of specific learning abilities to cause difficulties severe enough to warrant diagnosis of a specific learning disorder (Chap. 6, pp. 136–140).

28. Most children with ADHD also have behavior problems of Oppositional Defiant Disorder which usually leads to the more severe delinquent behaviors of Conduct Disorder.

Among children with ADHD, reported incidence of Oppositional Defiant Disorder ranges from 40% to 70%; these higher rates are usually for persons with the combined type of ADHD rather than the inattentive type. This disorder is characterized by chronic problems with negativistic, disobedient, defiant and/or hostile behavior toward authority figures. It tends to involve difficulties with management of frustration and anger and often involves impulsive negative reactions when frustrated. Typically Oppositional Defiant Disorder onsets at about 12 years and persists for approximately 6 years and then gradually remits. More than 70% of children diagnosed with this disorder never go on to meet diagnostic criteria for Conduct Disorder, a diagnosis that reflects much more severe behavior problems and seriously delinquent activities (Chap. 6, pp. 146–148).

29. Obsessive-Compulsive Disorder is rarely associated with ADHD.

Recent research has shifted understanding of Obsessive-Compulsive Disorder from the long-held notion of its being an anxiety disorder toward recognizing this as a disorder which involves primarily impairment of the ability to inhibit or "put the lid on" thoughts or actions that are intrusive, irrational and/or "magical" and cause considerable distress to the affected person. Affected persons tend to get "stuck" in focusing upon specific worries or patterns of action' and have great difficulty in letting go of that preoccupation so they can move on to other concerns; they have considerable difficulty in keeping the broader picture, the context, of the situation in mind. In clinical samples of children and adolescents seeking treatment for Obsessive-Compulsive Disorder, 26% to 59% were found to have ADHD (Chap. 6, pp. 148–152).

30. Recent research has identified a gene that causes executive function problems in persons with ADHD.

Despite extensive exploration of the genome and the high heritability rate of ADHD, no single gene or genes have been identified as a cause of the syndrome of impairments known as ADHD. Recent research has identified two different groupings that together are associated with, though not definitively causal of, ADHD. This combination of some common variant genes and a group of deletions or duplications of multiple rare variants offers some promise of further progress in the search for genetic factors contributing to ADHD. However, at this point, the complexity of the disorder is likely to be associated only with multiple genes, each of which, in itself, has only a small effect upon development of ADHD (Chap. 3, pp. 72–76).

31. If a child or adolescent with ADHD is treated with stimulant medications, they are being put at increased risk of developing a substance use disorder.

There is strong evidence that a child with ADHD, in comparison with peers, has more than double the likelihood of developing a substance use disorder at some point in their adolescent or early adult years. This does not mean that all individuals with ADHD will eventually have a substance use disorder. Rather, it means that those with ADHD are at much greater risk. The substances most commonly abused are cigarettes, marijuana and alcohol. These elevated risks of substance use disorder seem to be related to both genetic vulnerabilities and to chronic frustrations and social pressures resulting from trying to cope with the demands of schooling while struggling with untreated or inadequately treated executive function problems of ADHD. Effective treatment of ADHD with appropriate medication tends to reduce the risk of substance use disorder during adolescence (Chap. 6, pp. 152–157).

32. An individual with an Autistic Spectrum Disorder should not be diagnosed with ADHD and vice versa. These are completely separate disorders which require totally different treatments.

While diagnostic criteria for ADHD in DSM-IV stipulated that a diagnosis of ADHD should not be made for persons diagnosed with Autistic or Pervasive Developmental Disorders, this requirement has been challenged by multiple clinical and some epidemiological studies. Research has demonstrated that many individuals with ADHD also have significant traits related to Autistic

Spectrum Disorders and that many persons diagnosed with disorders on the Autistic Spectrum also meet diagnostic criteria for ADHD. Studies have also shown that ADHD medications can be helpful in alleviating ADHD impairments in individuals on the Autistic Spectrum. Moreover, ADHD medications can also help those on the Autistic Spectrum with ADHD to improve on some of their impairments in social interactions, social perspective taking, and other related problematic characteristics (Chap. 6, pp. 157–162).

33. Problems with lack of adequate sleep often cause impairments of ADHD-related executive functions.

Significant lack of adequate sleep tends to reduce the effective functioning of anyone with or without ADHD. However, the chronic executive function impairments of ADHD are not caused by inadequate sleep. For most affected persons, problems in regulating sleep and awakening are a significant and often impairing aspect of ADHD. Research has shown that a majority of children, adolescents and adults with ADHD tend to have chronic difficulty in getting to sleep at an adequate time, in getting themselves awake and started in morning routines, and in sustaining adequate levels of alertness during the day, especially when they are not physically moving or talking a lot (Chap. 3, pp. 51–52).

34. ADHD impairments sometimes last into early adulthood, but then they usually diminish before middle age.

Impairments of ADHD are determined not solely by the individual's symptoms, but by discrepancies between the demands of daily life facing the individual and their capacity to meet them. A business or professional person with ADHD might function very well in their daily life if they are fortunate enough to have a job that fits their talents, and co-workers, a secretary or others, who are able and willing to take care of functions that are difficult for the person with ADHD. Yet, if that adult is transferred to a different job where there are increased demands and insufficient support, their ADHD impairments may become much more conspicuous and problematic. Likewise, if an adult with ADHD is living with a partner who is able and willing to carry much of the responsibility of planning and preparing meals, managing finances, and attending to household routines, that person with ADHD may live comfortably and contribute to the household in other ways. However, if the help and support of that other person is lost due to illness, separation, divorce or death, the person with ADHD may suddenly be faced with multiple problems that are very difficult to cope with.

While many individuals find their ADHD impairments becoming less problematic as they get older, due to maturation of the brain or changing environmental demands, there are many for whom significant impairment persists well into their adult years. Research has shown that many individuals with ADHD find their functional impairments persist well into middle age and often beyond. In addition, bodily changes may cause late onset of ADHD-like impairments, e.g. for women during and after menopause, and for both men and women as their bodies age. Extension of ADHD impairments into middle and later years of life has not yet been adequately studied (Chap. 2, pp. 43–45; 52–55).

35. ADHD is just one of many psychiatric disorders.

Although ADHD is one of many different disorders listed in the diagnostic manual for psychiatry, it differs from many others in that it cross-cuts many other disorders. The executive function impairments which constitute ADHD as it is conceptualized in the new model described in this book underlie many other disorders as well. Many other learning and psychiatric disorders could be compared to problems with specific computer software packages which, when not working well, interfere just with write text, making slides, or doing book-keeping. In this new model, ADHD might be compared instead to a problem in the operating system of the computer which is likely to interfere with effective operation of a wide variety of different programs and functions (Chap. 6, pp. 162–164).

2

A NEW PARADIGM FOR AN OLD DISORDER

ADHD as Impaired Executive Functions

Old and New Definitions of ADHD

The past two decades have brought a major change in understanding the syndrome currently identified as Attention Deficit Disorder (ADD) or Attention Deficit Hyperactivity Disorder (ADHD). This change is not simply the development of one more new theory about a pattern of behavior. It is a fundamental shift in understanding the nature, the essence, of the disorder—a major shift of paradigm. Research on this syndrome has produced findings that, taken together, render the old model of ADHD as a simple behavior disorder no longer tenable. A totally new paradigm, a new model of ADHD has emerged.

One place to begin understanding this new model of ADHD is to recognize what it is not.

The old exemplar of the person with ADHD was the cartoon character "Dennis the Menace," a little boy who was very restless, impulsive and hyperactive, loveable but always misbehaving and frustrating his parents and teachers. The new paradigm represents the individual with ADHD in a much different and broader way: as a child, adolescent or adult, male or female, who is burdened by a syndrome of chronic difficulties in focusing, getting started on tasks, sustaining effort, utilizing working memory and modulating emotions that chronically impair their ability to manage necessary tasks of daily life. These difficulties are problems experienced by everyone of similar age at some times. What is different for those who warrant diagnosis for ADHD is that these impairments are more persistent and significantly more impairing than those experienced by most others of the same age. For those with ADHD, these impairments are not just occasional, they are chronic.

This book describes and attempts to integrate a wide variety of facts demonstrated by research studies which, when combined, provide a new understanding of the nature of ADHD.

Central concepts of this new paradigm are integrated in the working definition given in the text box below. Elements of this working definition are elaborated in the following pages.

A New Working Definition of ADHD

ADHD =
- a complex syndrome of
- developmental impairments of executive functions,
- the self-management system of the brain,
- a system of mostly unconscious operations.
- These impairments are situationally variable,
- chronic, and significantly interfere with functioning in many aspects of the person's daily life.

This working definition of ADHD has six elements. Each of these elements is elaborated briefly below in a slightly different sequence than is listed above. This full working definition is repeated with each elaboration—to emphasize how the elements of the working definition fit together. A fuller explanation with more details about research support for these concepts is provided in the following chapters.

ADHD =
- **a complex syndrome of**
- developmental impairments of executive functions,
- the self-management system of the brain,
- a system of mostly unconscious operations.
- These impairments are situationally variable,
- chronic, and significantly interfere with functioning in many aspects of the person's daily life.

- ### *ADHD is a Complex Syndrome*

This disorder is complicated—far more complicated than was recognized over the past century when it was known simply as "hyperactivity" or as a disruptive behavior disorder of childhood (American Psychiatric Association, 1980, 1987). In those days this diagnosis was applied only to young children who were chronically restless and impulsive, often misbehaving at home and school. We now know that many individuals with ADHD have never been hyperactive and have never had significant behavior problems. Even for those who have had behavior problems in childhood, those difficulties are generally not as problematic as are the cognitive impairments of ADHD which emerge more fully as the person grows up.

Central to this new understanding of ADHD is the notion that this is not a disorder of behavior, but a developmental impairment of the management system of the brain—its executive functions. Definition of executive function is still evolving, but most researchers agree that the term should be used to refer to the functions of brain circuits that prioritize, integrate and regulate other cognitive functions. Executive functions manage the brain's cognitive functions; they provide the mechanism for "self-regulation" (Vohs & Baumeister, 2004).

In her classic text on neuropsychological assessment, Lezak describes executive functions as: "those capacities that enable a person to engage successfully in independent, self-serving behavior.... Questions about executive functions ask *how or whether* a person goes about doing something (e.g. Will you do it and, if so, how and when?)" (Lezak, et al., 2004, p. 35).

In this description Lezak highlights the importance of executive functions for self-management, for taking care of oneself, as distinguished from simply following directions from others. She also points to the motivational aspect, the role of executive functions in an individual determining what actions he/she will do and when they will do them.

Elaborating on her description, Lezak emphasizes the critical importance of executive functions and notes that these functions are not linked directly to how high one might score on various tests of skills or knowledge. Executive functions are not the same as being smart or skilled.

> So long as the executive functions are intact, a person... can continue to be independent, constructively self-serving and productive. When executive functions are impaired, the individual may no longer be capable of satisfactory self-care, of performing remunerative or useful work independently, or of maintaining normal social relationships... regardless of how high the person scores on tests of skills, knowledge and abilities (p. 35).

She addresses the question of assessment of executive functions by observing that some of the problems of impaired executive functions may be quite noticeable even to casual, untrained observers. More obvious signs of impairment may include:

> defective capacity for self-control... emotional lability or flattening, a heightened tendency to excitability or irritability, impulsivity, erratic carelessness, rigidity, and difficulty in making shifts of attention and in ongoing behavior.... Other defects in executive functions, however, are not so obvious.... Perhaps the most serious of these problems are impaired capacity to initiate activity, decreased or absent motivation... and defects in planning and carrying out the activity sequences that make up goal-directed behavior (p. 36).

ADHD is a syndrome of impairments in these executive functions—not just one or two problematic characteristics, but a cluster of characteristics and related difficulties that tend to appear together in those affected. Individuals with ADHD are not all alike; they may vary widely in specific talents, but most manifest chronic difficulties in several important domains of functioning when compared with others of similar age. The model below describes executive functions needed by everyone; the ADHD syndrome involves chronic impairments of these various functions:

Executive Functions Impaired in ADHD

Executive Functions (work together in various combinations)					
Organizing, prioritizing, and activating to work	Focusing, sustaining and shifting attention to tasks	Regulating alertness, sustaining effort, and processing speed	Managing frustration and modulating emotions	Utilizing working memory and accessing recall	Monitoring and self-regulating action
1. Activation	2. Focus	3. Effort	4. Emotion	5. Memory	6. Action

Figure 2.1 Executive Functions Impaired in ADHD.

The six clusters of the model above do not represent unitary variables like height, weight or blood pressure where it is all one thing and one can have more or less of it. Rather, these six clusters might be considered as baskets of related cognitive functions which interact in a variety of dynamic ways. Paragraphs below elaborate on description of these six clusters:

1   **Activation:** organizing tasks and materials, estimating time, prioritizing tasks, and getting started on work tasks. Patients with ADHD describe chronic difficulty with excessive procrastination. Often they will put off getting started on a task, even a task they recognize as very important to them, until the very last minute. It is as though they cannot get themselves started until the point where they perceive the task as an acute emergency.

2   **Focus:** focusing, sustaining focus, and shifting focus to tasks. Some describe their difficulty in sustaining focus as similar to trying to listen to the car radio when you drive too far away from the station and the signal begins fading in and out: you get some of it and lose some of it. They say they are distracted easily not only by things that are going on around them, but also by thoughts in their own minds. At other times they may find themselves stuck on one focus, unable to shift to another task when they should. In addition, focus on reading poses difficulties for many. Words are generally understood as they are read, but often have to be read over and over again in order for the meaning to be fully grasped and remembered.

3   **Effort:** regulating alertness, sustaining effort, and processing speed. Many with ADHD report they can perform short-term projects well, but have much more difficulty with sustained effort over longer periods of time. They also find it difficult to complete tasks on time, especially when required to do expository writing. Many also experience chronic difficulty regulating sleep and alertness. Often they stay up too late because they cannot shut their head off. Once asleep, they often sleep like dead people and have a big problem getting up in the morning.

4   **Emotion:** managing frustration and modulating emotions. Although DSM-IV does not recognize any symptoms related to the management of emotion as an aspect of ADHD, many with this disorder describe chronic difficulties managing frustration, anger, worry, disappointment, desire, and other emotions. They speak as though these emotions, when experienced, take over their thinking as a computer virus invades a computer, making it impossible for them to give attention to anything else. They find it very difficult to get the emotion into perspective, to put it to the back of their mind, and to get on with what they need to do.

5   **Memory:** utilizing working memory and accessing recall. Very often, people with ADHD will report that they have adequate or exceptional memory for things that happened long ago, but great difficulty in being

able to remember where they just put something, what someone just said to them, or what they were about to say. They may describe difficulty holding one or several things "on line" while attending to other tasks. In addition, persons with ADHD often complain that they cannot pull out of memory information they have learned when they need it.

6   **Action:** monitoring and regulating self-action. Many persons with ADHD, even those without problems of hyperactive behavior, report chronic problems in regulating their actions. They often are too impulsive in what they say or do, and in the way they think, jumping too quickly to inaccurate conclusions. Persons with ADHD also report problems in monitoring the context in which they are interacting. They fail to notice when other people are puzzled, or hurt, or annoyed by what they have just said or done and thus fail to modify their behavior in response to specific circumstances. Often they also report chronic difficulty in regulating the pace of their actions, in slowing self and/or speeding up as needed for specific tasks. Capacity to monitor one's actions and to inhibit impulsive actions is one critical aspect of executive function.

The model above, developed by Brown (1996, 2000b, 2005a, 2009) is one particular model of executive functions. Other models have also been proposed. One of the first descriptions of ADHD as characterized by impaired executive functions was provided by Virginia Douglas (1988) who described three domains of self-regulation impairment in children with this disorder: 1) organization of information processing; 2) mobilization of attention throughout information processing; and 3) inhibition of inappropriate responses. Douglas emphasized that self-regulation influences "the amount of organized, *effortful* attention that is deployed throughout *all* stages of information processing, including stimulus evaluation, response decision, and response execution" (p. 66).

Currently, the most widely recognized model of ADHD as executive function impairment is that proposed by Russell Barkley (1997, 2006). His model is quite similar to Brown's model, shown above, except for three important aspects. First, Barkley describes his model as applying only to the combined type of ADHD, to individuals whose ADHD impairments include hyperactivity and impulsivity, not to those with predominantly inattentive type. Second, Barkley's model highlights the capacity to inhibit as primary among other aspects of ADHD; Brown's model includes the capacity to self-regulate action as one of six clusters of symptoms, none of which holds primacy over the others. Third, Barkley describes executive functions as essentially conscious, effortful actions; he relegates less conscious functions such as alertness, attention, and memory which operate more automatically to a "pre-executive level" which he sees as quite different from executive functions (Barkley, 2012b). In contrast, Brown argues that executive functions operate mostly in automaticity, without deliberation or conscious choice.

More recently, Barkley (2012a) has published a study of adults characterized by symptoms of "sluggish cognitive tempo" (SCT) such as excessive daydreaming, being easily bored, feeling in a fog, being underactive, having difficulty staying alert in boring situations, etc. that significantly impair their executive functioning and adaptation in daily life. On the basis of data obtained by remote self-report on computer, with no clinical evaluation of the participants, he argues that those who suffer from high levels of SCT should be considered as having a distinct disorder and not ADHD. His sample of persons with ADHD used for comparisons consisted of a large majority (two-thirds) of individuals whom he had classified as having ADHD hyperactive-impulsive or combined type; only one-third were classified as predominantly inattentive type. In contrast, Brown's model includes virtually all of the SCT symptoms as aspects of the executive functions impaired in ADHD and would consider those with impairments seen in Barkley's sample as having ADHD.

These various models of ADHD have been developed from different sources. Douglas' (1988) model was developed from laboratory experiments with children diagnosed with ADHD. Barkley's model was derived from a conceptual approach based upon Jacob Bronowski's theory of the unique role of language in human action (Barkley, 1997). Bronowski highlighted the importance of behavioral inhibition so that language and memory can more adequately influence planning and behavior. In his 1997 exposition of his theory, Barkley explained how he utilized Bronowski's model in combination with other theories derived from work of neuroscientists such as Fuster, Goldman-Rakic and Damasio to conceptualize ADHD as impairment of executive functions.

Brown's model, shown in the diagram above, was derived not from laboratory tests or from an overarching conceptual framework, but from clinical studies of child, adolescent and adult patients diagnosed with ADHD as defined by DSM-III/IV criteria (American Psychiatric Association 1980, 1994). It constitutes an expanded phenotype of the ADHD syndrome described by DSM-IV; this model is informed by findings of neuroscience research, but it begins with the phenomenology of the syndrome as seen in clinical interviews and described by child, adolescent and adult patients diagnosed with ADHD, with supporting data from family members or close friends. These observations formed the basis for development of rating scales which have been normed to facilitate comparison with others in comparable age groups who do not have ADHD (Brown, 1996, 2001). The six clusters of the model reflect impairments found in patients with ADHD which tend to appear together, generally operate in integrated, dynamic ways, and often respond together to medication treatment.

ADHD =
- a complex syndrome of
- developmental impairments of executive functions,
- **the self-management system of the brain,**
- a system of mostly unconscious operations.
- These impairments are situationally variable,
- chronic, and significantly interfere with functioning in many aspects of the person's daily life.

- ### *Executive Functions are the Self-management System of the Brain*

Despite the variety of ways executive functions have been defined in relation to ADHD, there is now a sizable body of evidence that these self-management functions are intimately related to the brain. Barkley (2006) has summarized the history of how the syndrome currently known as ADHD has, for decades, in a variety of different ways, been seen as resulting from impairments of brain structure and function.

One of the earliest formulations was after a U.S. epidemic of encephalitis in 1917-1918. Physicians of that time were confronted with many children who, after recovering from encephalitic brain infections, demonstrated impairments in attention, memory and other cognitive functions essential to self-regulation; this led to identification of the syndrome as "postencephalitic behavior disorder."

Later, some children unaffected by encephalitis, but characterized by birth trauma, lead toxicity, or infections such as measles, were found to have similar behavioral profiles. The term "brain-injured child" was used to refer to such children. In the 1950s, since subsequent research had failed to identify any clear evidence of persisting brain damage in such children, the terms "minimal brain damaged" and "minimal brain dysfunction (MBD)" were used to emphasize that these cognitive and behavioral problems were somehow related to impairments of brain that technologies of that time could not delineate. During the 1960s, the term MBD gradually fell out of favor due to lack of evidence to support it. Instead, clinical investigators tended to focus on "hyperactivity" as what was then considered to be the primary characteristic of the disorder.

While researchers sought more evidence of how ADHD might be related to brain functions, several alternative explanations of these difficulties gained popular attention. One popular view was that food additives or excessive consumption of sugar caused hyperactive behavior and related problems. Parent groups organized to promote the Feingold diet which stipulated a regimen devoid of food coloring, preservatives and other additives alleged to cause hyperactivity; others argued that self-control in such children could be improved by eliminating their consumption of refined sugar. Meanwhile, psychoanalytic theorists proposed that inadequate parenting was the cause of such difficulties while behaviorally oriented psychologists emphasized that hyperactivity was the result of poor parental reinforcement of appropriate behavior in their children (Barkley, 2006). None of these theories held up to objective scientific scrutiny.

Over the past two decades, a very substantial body of research, much of it using tools and techniques not available earlier, has provided strong evidence that impairments of ADHD are associated with structural and/or functional impairments in the brain. Bush (2009) has reviewed findings from the exponential expansion of imaging studies of ADHD and the brain. He noted the influential paper by Posner and Petersen (1991) that described the attention system of the brain as comprised of three anatomically distinct, but interacting network subsystems: 1) the orienting system, relying on the parietal cortex, superior colliculus and pulvinar/thalamus; 2) the anterior attention system which includes the anterior cingulate cortex and lateral prefrontal cortex; and 3) the alerting system which consists primarily of the locus coeruleus and related circuits in the right hemisphere.

Dickstein, et al. (2006) reported a meta-analysis of 16 imaging studies that demonstrated ADHD to be associated with hypoactivity of the dorsal-lateral prefrontal cortex (DLPFC), ventral-lateral prefrontal cortex (VLPFC), the superior parietal cortex, the caudate, and the thalamus. Bush (2009) described findings from diffusion tensor imaging studies that have demonstrated white matter abnormalities in brains of persons with ADHD; these abnormalities are associated with problems in interactive communications between various regions of the brain. He also reviewed findings that demonstrated fronto-temporal abnormalities in ADHD patients during a working memory task. He noted multiple studies showing hypoactivity in another area of the brain shown repeatedly in various studies to be hypoactive in persons diagnosed with ADHD: the daMCC, a segment of the dorsal anterior cingulate on the medial surface of the frontal lobe that plays a critical role in attention, motivation, and feedback-based decision making.

Bush (2009) has also described other areas of brain implicated in impairments associated with ADHD. One such area is the cerebellum which contributes not only to motor coordination, but also to language, verbal working memory, processing of emotions, and other executive functions. Structural abnormalities have been found in cerebella of persons with ADHD.

Imaging studies have not only demonstrated impairments of brain functioning in individuals with ADHD; they have also demonstrated that such impaired functioning can often, though not always, be improved with medication treatment that impacts brain functioning. Epstein, et al. (2007) used fMRI to show that, in both children and adults with ADD, methylphenidate can significantly improve insufficient activation of the caudate and the cerebellum. Pliszka and colleagues (2007) have shown with event-related potentials that stimulant medication increases ACC activity in ADHD. In a long-term study using fMRI Konrad, et al. (2007) demonstrated long-term methylphenidate-induced changes in the insula, putamen and cingulate cortex of children with ADHD. These and many other studies provide strong evidence not only that persons with ADHD show impairments in many areas of brain associated with executive function; imaging studies also have demonstrated that specific medications that act upon brain processes and can significantly alleviate many of those impairments for patients with ADHD.

ADHD =
- a complex syndrome of
- **developmental impairments of executive functions,**
- the self-management system of the brain,
- a system of mostly unconscious operations.
- These impairments are situationally variable,
- chronic, and significantly interfere with functioning in many aspects of the person's daily life.

- *ADHD is a Developmental Impairment of these Executive Functions*

There are many ways in which executive functions can become impaired. If an individual hits his head hard enough against the dashboard in a motor vehicle accident, depending on the location and extent of the swelling, there may be

28

impairment of executive functions. In Alzheimer's dementia where many critical circuits of the brain are encrusted and deteriorated by tangles of plaque, one of the first signs is often impairment of executive functions. Unlike traumatic brain injury or Alzheimer's dementia, where the patient usually has had adequate executive functions and then lost them secondary to tissue damage to the brain, impairments of ADHD are *developmental*—they have not unfolded and "come on line" for the individual in the way that occurs for most others of the same age. Contrary to Barkley's formulation that executive functions and ADHD "are two views or names for the same common single construct" (2011a, p. 85), this model stipulates that executive function impairments of ADHD are *developmental* impairments.

Executive functions are developmental in the sense that they emerge incrementally over the course of development. They are not fully developed in early childhood. From the descriptions of executive functions in the model shown above, it is clear that many of these functions do not appear, except in very rudimentary ways, in young children. They emerge only gradually, starting from primordial forms that emerge at first in the rudimentary effortful control that develops in preschoolers; these functions progressively become more elaborated and refined throughout childhood and adolescence. Usually these executive functions are not fully developed until the late teens or early twenties.

Most governments will not allow children under the age of 16 or 18 years to drive a motor vehicle. This is not because their legs are too short to reach the pedals. That would be an easy problem to fix in the design of the car. Young children are not allowed to drive motor vehicles because they lack sufficiently developed executive functions to be able to manage the complexities and risks of driving a motor vehicle safely on the street. Research described in Chapter 3 of this book has demonstrated that for most individuals with ADHD, certain areas of brain critical as infrastructure for executive functions tend to mature three to five years later than in most of their age mates.

One implication of the developmental nature of ADHD is that its signs and symptoms are manifest in different ways at various points in the developmental process. Executive functions are required for very young children to learn to dress themselves, to cross streets safely, to play cooperatively with others, and to manage frustration in social situations. Many, but not all, youngsters with ADHD tend to struggle with developing these basic self-management skills.

For adolescents, executive functions are needed for organizing and prioritizing their work for school, for keeping track of assignments and getting their homework done; for sustaining attention for longer reading and writing tasks. Adolescents with ADHD complain that they often drift off and lose focus during school classes, that they are disorganized in trying to manage their schoolwork, and that they need to re-read text passages multiple times in order adequately to comprehend their meaning.

During adult years, demands on executive functions multiply to deal with demands of higher education, getting and working effectively in employment, managing money and one's household, driving a motor vehicle, managing dating and family relationships, and, for many, parenting and/or mentoring. Adults with ADHD tend to have excessive difficulty in prioritizing tasks and managing their time and money; often they are late to work or forget appointments they intended to keep. Frequently they struggle with multiple demands of work, household, social relationships and family responsibilities.

The old model of ADHD assumed that any person with this disorder would show some signs of ADHD impairments early in their development, at least before age seven years (American Psychiatric Association, 1994, 2000). Clinicians and researchers have challenged that assumption as they found that many persons who qualify for ADHD diagnosis do not manifest any noticeable symptoms of ADHD until adolescence or beyond. Persons with ADHD who have high IQ often get very high grades in elementary school where they have most of their classwork with one teacher who can provide support for their deficits in executive function. But, if untreated, these students tend to have significantly lower grades in secondary school and often have major struggles in college or university studies where they are required to function independent of adult support (Brown, 2005a; Brown, et al., 2011c).

Faraone and colleagues (2006d) reported on a sample of adults who fully met all DSM-IV diagnostic criteria for ADHD except for the stipulation of some symptoms manifest by age seven years. They compared that group with a sample of adults who fully met all DSM-IV criteria including the seven-year age of onset stipulation. Results indicated that those groups did not differ in number of ADHD symptoms met, in severity of impairment, in comorbidities or in family genetics. While some individuals are clearly recognizable as having ADHD during early childhood, there are many with this disorder whose impairments are not apparent until they confront the challenges of adolescence or adulthood when they are required to manage more of life for themselves.

The fact that impairments of ADHD are often not apparent until the individual encounters challenges that do not emerge until adolescence or beyond can be compared to another area of medicine. An electrocardiogram (EKG) administered to a person lying still on a table may be quite clean with no indications of cardiovascular problems. Yet if that person is given the same test after shoveling a heavy load of snow or running on a treadmill, EKG results may reveal cardiovascular problems not observed until the greater challenges to the cardiovascular system were encountered. ADHD is a developmental impairment of executive functions which may not become apparent until more advanced and consistent executive functions are required in challenges not encountered in childhood.

For individuals with ADHD, this disorder may also be developmental in another sense; it can be a developmental delay that tends to remit as the affected individual matures. Shaw and colleagues (2007) used longitudinal imaging methods to compare brain development of a large sample of children with ADHD to an age-matched sample of children without the disorder. Results, described in more detail in the next chapter of this book, indicate that for some persons with ADHD, a few specific areas of brain that provide essential infrastructure for executive functioning reach maturity about three years later than in their peers. This may be at least part of the reason that some individuals with ADHD do poorly in high school and early college, then, a few years later demonstrate significant and consistent improvement in their ability to do academic work that previously overwhelmed them.

An early prospective study of children diagnosed with hyperactivity in childhood and followed into adulthood found that about one-third of those with ADHD functioned fairly well in adulthood, quite similar to typically developing controls (Weiss & Hechtman, 1993). In contrast, most young adult hyperactives, about 50% to 60%, were functional, but continued to have significant problems with concentration, impulsivity and social interaction in adulthood. A much smaller percentage, about 10% of that sample, continued to have significant psychiatric or antisocial problems, or both, which caused very significant continuing difficulties in adulthood.

ADHD =
- a complex syndrome of
- developmental impairments of executive functions,
- the self-management system of the brain,
- a system of mostly unconscious operations.
- These **impairments are situationally variable,**
- chronic, and significantly interfere with functioning in many aspects of the person's daily life.

- **ADHD Impairments of Executive Functions are Situationally Variable**

One of the most puzzling features of this disorder is that, across the lifespan, executive function impairments of ADHD tend to be situationally variable. Every child, adolescent and adult with ADHD tends to have some situations or activities in which they are able to exercise very well those same executive functions on which they tend to be quite impaired in most other situations.

The early model developed by Douglas (1988) emphasized that basic information processing capabilities of children with ADHD are intact, that sometimes they perform such tasks quite adequately with minimal effort. She observed that impairments of ADHD are most likely to be seen when children with the disorder are faced with tasks that make heavy demands on self-regulation while offering minimal external control, support or motivation. She also noted studies demonstrating converging evidence that for children with ADHD, stimulant medications tend to "produce improvement on a wide range of academic and cognitive measures... improving both motivation and processing efficiency" (p. 78).

Pennington (1991) extended this view of ADHD symptoms as situationally variable. He observed that those with ADHD tend to vary in their task performance depending on task conditions. He emphasized that "this dependence of deficits on task conditions reinforces the hypothesis that the underlying deficit [in ADHD] is not in a particular information processing domain, like verbal memory, but in executive functions that regulate all of information processing" (p.94).

Brown (2005a) has elaborated on situational variability of ADHD symptoms with multiple case examples over all age levels. From extensive clinical observations he has found that virtually all persons diagnosed with ADHD have a few domains of activity in which they demonstrate none of the executive function impairments that they suffer in most other situations. Usually this occurs in situations where they have strong personal interest in the task or where they are faced with an imminent deadline and they expect something quite unpleasant to occur very quickly if they do not manage this task right here and right now. Research that helps to explain this paradox of situational variability is described in the next chapter of this book.

Some with ADHD function very well in athletic pursuits. While playing a favored sport, they are alert and strongly motivated, able to sustain focus and shift attention readily from one aspect of the action to another as needed. In this activity they sustain vigorous effort, ignoring fatigue and discomfort. While engaged, they are able to keep clearly in mind multiple facets of planned plays and contingent alternatives. Even in the midst of frustration and, sometimes, repeated provocation, they can modulate their strong emotions appropriately to sustain their efforts to play well and try to win the game. Yet these same individuals may have enormous difficulty in mobilizing similar motivation, effort and self-control in many other tasks that they themselves consider important and where they want to be successful.

It is not always athletics that activates more effective executive functioning for those with ADHD. For some it is playing video games, for others it is making art or music; in others more effective executive functioning is activated during childhood only by doing Lego constructions or, during adolescence or adulthood, by cooking meals or taking auto engines apart and rebuilding them. Typically these individuals report that they have no difficulty in focusing and working effectively on tasks that interest them. They tend to be unable to mobilize such interest voluntarily or upon direction from others. It is activated spontaneously or not at all.

One adult patient described this problem in this way:

> Having ADHD is like having erectile dysfunction of the mind. If the task you are faced with really interests you and turns you on, you're "up" for it and you can perform. But if the task is not something that really interests you, you can't get it up and you can't perform. In that situation it doesn't matter how much you may say to yourself, "I need to, I ought to, I want to, I should." You can't make it happen because it's just not a willpower kind of thing.

Often this "you can do it here, why don't you do it there?" problem leads parents, teachers and those who suffer from ADHD to assume that this disorder is simply a matter of insufficient willpower when, in fact, it is a problem of the dynamics of the chemistry of the brain. Research supporting and explaining situational variability of ADHD symptoms is described in the next chapter of this book.

ADHD =
- a complex syndrome of
- developmental impairments of executive functions,
- the self-management system of the brain,
- a system of **mostly unconscious operations.**
- These impairments are situationally variable,
- chronic, and significantly interfere with functioning in many aspects of the person's daily life.

- *Self-management Functions Impaired in ADHD Mostly Operate Unconsciously*

Executive functions are not only situationally variable and dependent upon dynamics of the chemistry of the brain; they operate mostly in unconscious ways, without conscious deliberation. Moreover, as is implied in the example of "erectile dysfunction of the mind" above, mostly they do not operate under conscious control. In this context, the term "unconscious" does not refer to the psychoanalytic concept of repression. Here "unconscious" refers to "automaticity," the capacity of humans to initiate, execute and modify complex behaviors instantaneously, without having to deliberate consciously about what to do.

This view of "unconscious" is similar to what Nobel prize-winning psychologist, Daniel Kahneman (2011) described as the fast-thinking, unconscious "System 1" of the brain which "is the origin of... most of what we do. Our thoughts and actions are routinely guided by System 1 and generally are on the mark" (2011, p. 416). Kahneman explains that System 1 draws upon the individual's personal memory stores of learning and experiences to quickly and automatically produce adequate responses to countless demands of daily life, pulling in learned skills and impressions from past experiences to cope with current situations in a wide variety of contexts. For example, this system guides most of our conversations and routine driving of motor vehicles and most other human activities when we do not perceive a need for or do not have opportunity to make deliberate decisions.

Kahneman contrasts the rapid and automatic System 1 to the slower, more deliberate and more conscious and effortful operations of System 2 which takes over in situations perceived as more puzzling or complicated: circumstances where more thoughtful attention is required. This is the system called into play when there is an unexpected turn in a conversation or a need to navigate a motor vehicle through rapidly moving, congested traffic.

Kahneman emphasized that "System 1" and "System 2" of his model are just modes of thinking that do not correspond to any specific structures of the brain. Those terms are simply a shorthand to refer to two types of cognitive operations. He argues that "control of attention is shared by the two systems" (2011, p. 22). He also asserts that System 1 *effortlessly* originates impressions and feelings that are the main source of the explicit beliefs and deliberate choices of System 2 (italics added). System 1 is the source of automaticity. "System 1 operates automatically and quickly, with little or no effort and no sense of voluntary control" (2011, p. 20).

The main difference between Kahneman's model and the processes described in the new model of ADHD presented here is that research on the new paradigm for ADHD does demonstrate linkages between executive functions and dynamic interactions of brain regions. At this point, however, research has only partially explained the complex linkages that serve as the infrastructure for executive functions and their automaticity.

An example of automaticity might be a basketball player dribbling in toward the backboard to make a layup shot. That player does not move deliberately while saying to self "now I move my right foot forward, now I move my left foot forward, now I drop my left shoulder, now I raise my right arm and look toward the basket" etc. The player is certainly conscious of his intention to make a layup shot, but his moves to implement those intentions are executed automatically in seamless sequences so rapid that there is not time for conscious deliberation. There is a steady flow of moves and shifts of speed, position and direction not only in conformity with templates from past experiences, but also in response to the specific, rapidly shifting movements of defenders and teammates as they act moment by moment to facilitate or block the scoring of a goal. Most of these moves are determined and executed without much conscious thought. This is but one of many activities in which increased conscious attention and deliberate control is likely to be problematic. DeCaro and Beilock have written about both the benefits and perils of conscious efforts at attentional control, a topic currently receiving increased attention in the neuroscience literature (2010).

Other common examples of automatized behavior include driving a car, typing a letter or essay, moving through a crowded hallway, and interacting with others in social conversation, a class discussion or a business meeting. Automatized behaviors in these and many other situations are not simple reflexes, they are complex assessments of an ongoing situation in which each individual's shifting assessment of the current situation, in combination with learning from past experiences, provides the basis for acting or refraining from acting in particular ways. When one is first encountering such tasks, actions are typically slower, more conscious and more deliberative. As the skill is practiced and repeatedly encountered, most individuals learn how to move more quickly, with minimal reflection, to adapt their stock scripts of perception and action and modify them to operate in the current circumstances.

"Automaticity", as used in this context, refers not only to automatic execution of well-practiced skills. The term also applies to environmental activation of a specific goal that, in turn, activates relevant actions to pursue or avoid aims associated with that goal, even without any conscious recognition of the impact the situation has had in shaping the relevant behaviors being performed. Bargh and Barndollar (1995) have described this "auto-motive" model which posits that "goals and motives can become automatically associated with mental representations of environmental features in the same way that perceptual representations do—through frequent and consistent coactivation" (p. 462).

Bargh (2005) extended this model to argue that:

> Goals and motivations can be triggered by the environment without conscious choice or intention, then operate and run to completion entirely unconsciously, guiding behavior in interaction with a changing and unpredictable environment, and producing outcomes identical to those that occur when the person is aware of having that goal (p. 52).

Executive functions described in this book tend mostly to operate effortlessly, unconsciously, with automaticity, though there are certainly many situations in which each of us needs to call upon the slower and more deliberate thought processes described in Kahneman's System 2. Sometimes this works quite well as a check upon inappropriate plans and actions, though, as Kahneman noted,

> System 2 is not a paragon of rationality. Its abilities are limited and so is the knowledge to which it has access. We do not always think straight when we reason, and the errors are not always due to intrusive and incorrect intuitions (2011, p. 415).

The model of ADHD presented in this book conceptualizes executive functions as operating primarily with automaticity; this differs from the view of executive functioning proposed by Barkley's model. He describes most aspects of executive function included in the model described here as "Pre-executive."

> Included at the Pre-executive level of the model are many of the routine neuropsychological functions such as attention, alertness, visual-spatial performance, autonomic-emotional actions, memory, sensory-perceptual functions, language and motor abilities.... This level can be fruitfully regarded as the "automatic" level of human activity often described in models of self-regulation.... They are not in and of themselves forms of self-regulation and are therefore not components of EF (2012b, pp. 76-77).

In contrast to Barkley's model which seems to limit the notion of "self-regulation" to conscious functions, the model of ADHD proposed here conceptualizes executive functions as mostly carried on with automaticity, effortlessly, without much conscious effort or thought. This is an important element of this model and a major reason for the persistence of ADHD impairments, despite the often strong wishes of persons with ADHD to change their problematic patterns of behavior.

ADHD =
- a complex syndrome of
- developmental impairments of executive functions,
- the self-management system of the brain,
- a system of mostly unconscious operations.
- These impairments are situationally variable,
- **chronic, and significantly interfere with functioning in many aspects of the person's daily life.**

- *ADHD Symptoms are Chronic and Significantly Interfere with Functioning in Many Aspects of the Person's Daily Life*

Research studies of children and adults with ADHD have identified a wide variety of significant impairments in their functioning in many aspects of daily life. Most of these are described in the next chapter, but some examples are provided here.

Much research on ADHD impairments has focused on behavioral and academic achievement problems of children with ADHD; some studies have followed children over years to learn about how ADHD identified in childhood impacts subsequent functioning in school. Massetti, et al. (2008) followed a cohort of 125 children diagnosed with ADHD at age four to six years and 130 matched comparison children without ADHD. These children were assessed seven times over a period of eight years. Results demonstrated that a diagnosis of ADHD in childhood predicted significantly lower scores for reading, spelling and math on standardized achievement tests in adolescence than scores from matched controls, even after IQ had been controlled for. Interestingly, children diagnosed with predominantly inattentive type ADHD had lower scores on those academic achievement tests than did those with a diagnosis of combined type ADHD.

A study by Kent and colleagues (2011) investigated 326 adolescents who had been diagnosed with ADHD in childhood whom they followed with annual assessments at the end of ninth, tenth, eleventh and twelfth grade. They compared these students with 213 peers who were matched for demographic characteristics, but did not have ADHD. These comparisons were done using data from parents, teachers and schools. Comparisons of the two groups indicated that students diagnosed with ADHD: 1) received lower grades; 2) took fewer advanced level courses; 3) failed significantly more advanced level courses; 4) were rated by teachers as performing more poorly; 5) had poorer school attendance; and 6) were more likely to drop out of high school before graduation (p. 458).

These weaker academic outcomes were not accounted for by the severity of ADHD symptoms at the start of the study or by baseline characteristics such as students' IQ or the educational level of their parents. Despite controlling for IQ, high school students with ADHD earned, on average, C grades, while the comparison students without ADHD carried grades that averaged B–/C+. In the ninth grade there was almost a full letter grade difference between the two groups (2011, p. 458).

Students with ADHD, on average, missed 9.7% of school days while comparison students missed 5.8%. Students with ADHD were also rated by teachers as completing less work and working below their potential. In all academic courses, rates of failure were higher for adolescents with ADHD. They failed 7.5% of their courses while comparison students failed 1.7% (2011, p. 459).

As persistence of ADHD impairments into adulthood has become more recognized, researchers have studied the impact of ADHD impairments over the longer term on adults.

De Graaf, et al. (2008) did a study that estimated prevalence of ADHD among employed adults in ten countries including Belgium, Colombia, France, Germany, Italy, Lebanon, Mexico, the Netherlands, Spain, and the U.S. Findings indicated that an average of 3.5% of adult workers met current diagnostic criteria for ADHD; among unemployed adults the prevalence of ADHD was higher, at 5.5%. Data from that study also found that workers with ADHD tended to have a higher average of sick days and excess numbers of missed work days associated with reduced quantity and quality of work. These data suggest that ADHD, even under current diagnostic criteria, is a disorder that causes significant impairment in many adults as well as children. More information about such impairments at various points throughout the life cycle of individuals with ADHD is provided in the next chapter.

Similarities and Differences between the
Old and New Models of ADHD

The working definition of ADHD offered at the outset of this chapter and described thus far in this chapter constitutes a considerable expansion of the range, complexity and duration of the previous phenotype of this disorder. This new model applies not just to children, but also to adolescents and adults. It focuses on a wide range of self-management functions that are not limited to readily observable behaviors; functions included in the model are primarily cognitive and often operate without conscious deliberation. Functions included are linked to complex operations of brain, some of which can be studied with various imaging methods recently developed, though currently the most effective assessment methods, to be described in later chapters, depend heavily on data from clinical interviews and self-report, sometimes supplemented by data from other observers or standardized cognitive assessments. Unlike diagnostic criteria for ADHD in the DSM-IV (American Psychiatric Association, 1994, 2000), this new model includes problems with modulation of emotions, motivations, sleep and alertness, and multiple aspects of working memory. One study by Brown and colleagues (2011a) comparing adult patients diagnosed with ADHD by both DSM-IV diagnostic criteria and the executive function impairments of ADHD assessed by the Brown ADHD Scale for Adults found just a 20% overlap between those two specific measures. However, the two models are not altogether different conceptually.

Despite the many differences between the old model of ADHD provided by the DSM-III and IV versus our more recent formulation, there are substantial and important points of overlap. Most individuals who are assessed with measures of ADHD symptoms built on the new model of ADHD as comprised of developmentally impaired executive functions will also meet current DSM-IV diagnostic criteria for ADHD with its description of nine symptoms of inattention and nine symptoms of hyperactivity/impulsivity and its requirement of impairment from these symptoms.

Rating scales for ADHD-related executive function impairments in adolescents and adults published by Brown (1996) were all based on normative samples of individuals who had been clinically diagnosed with ADHD using DSM-III diagnostic criteria; Brown's rating scales for ADHD-related executive function impairments in children (2001) used a normative sample of children all of whom had been diagnosed with ADHD by DSM-IV criteria. In 2011 Barkley published the Barkley Deficits in Executive Functioning Scale which was demonstrated to detect 94% of adults who met DSM-IV diagnostic criteria for ADHD. Thus, each of these published scales that assess for executive function impairments associated with ADHD incorporates existing DSM diagnostic criteria for ADHD while they also elicit data on a much wider range of related executive function impairments.

The old model of ADHD is no longer tenable not because it identifies individuals with a totally different disorder; the old model is no longer tenable because it does not adequately capture the wide breadth, complexity and persistence of this syndrome. It describes just the tip of the proverbial iceberg; it does not capture the much wider and more subtle dimensions of the syndrome as it is found across the lifespan in patients diagnosed with ADHD.

Prevalence of ADHD According to Old and New Models

There are not yet data on the percentage of children or adults in the general population who suffer from ADHD as understood in the new model described in this book. Since, as described above, most individuals diagnosed with ADHD using current diagnostic criteria are likely also to meet criteria for the broader phenotype of ADHD described here, prevalence data based on current DSM-IV criteria for ADHD may provide a conservative estimate that is likely to be a serious underestimate. New research is needed to assess the prevalence of children and adults who suffer from ADHD as described in this broader phenotype.

The most recent study of the prevalence of ADHD among children in the U.S., a household survey by the U.S. Centers for Disease Control, estimated that about 9% of 6- to 17-year-old children have been diagnosed with ADHD (Centers for Disease Control and Prevention, 2010). There are a number of methodological limitations to this survey study, but it might be taken as the upper end of the range of reasonably derived estimates. A slightly earlier national study of U.S. children aged 8 to 15 years was done by Froehlich and colleagues (2007) and yielded a very similar estimate of 8.7% for this somewhat narrower age range.

A more conservative estimate was provided in a meta-analysis by Polanczyk and colleagues (2007). They reviewed studies done in many countries with widely differing cultures and socioeconomic strata; they found rather consistent estimates of the prevalence of ADHD in their meta-analysis of 102 studies involving 171,000 children from all regions of the world. The pooled estimate of prevalence of ADHD across these various samples of individuals 18 years or younger was 5.29%. There were many methodological differences among the studies included in this study, e.g. specific diagnostic criteria used, source of information about each individual included in the study, and the presence or absence of a requirement for impairment. No significant differences in estimated prevalence were found in comparisons of studies done in Europe versus North America.

Few studies of the prevalence of ADHD have included the full age range of adolescents. The most substantial study of adolescents thus far is the National Comorbidity Replication Study-Adolescent Supplement reported by Merikangas and colleagues (2010). This nationally representative face-to-face survey of 10,123 U.S. adolescents aged 13 to 18 years collected data on lifetime prevalence of a wide range of mental disorders among this age group. ADHD was one of many disorders assessed for in the study. Findings indicated that approximately 8.7% of adolescents meet DSM-IV diagnostic criteria for ADHD and that about half of these adolescents are severely impaired by it. In this sample ADHD was three times as prevalent among males as females.

The Merikangas, et al. study (2010) collected data not only on prevalence of ADHD, but also on prevalence of mood disorders, anxiety disorders, behavior disorders, substance use disorders, and eating disorders among adolescents in the U.S. Overlap of those other disorders with ADHD is discussed in Chapter 6 of this book.

For many individuals who suffer from ADHD in childhood and adolescence, impairments of this disorder tend to persist into adulthood. A national community survey by Kessler and colleagues (2010) found that almost half of respondents who had childhood ADHD continued to meet full DSM-IV diagnostic criteria for current adult ADHD. Data indicated that persistence was much greater for inattention symptoms than for hyperactivity symptoms. That study also found that executive function impairments were more specific and consistently important predictors of DSM-IV adult ADHD, despite executive function (EF) symptoms not being included in the DSM-IV. This finding led those authors to urge that DSM diagnostic criteria for ADHD in adults should be broadened to include more symptoms associated with EF impairments.

From their epidemiological study of adults in the U.S. with ADHD, Kessler and colleagues (2006) found an estimated rate of 4.4% of adults aged 18 to 44 in the general population currently met diagnostic criteria for ADHD. Within that sample, the incidence of adult ADHD in males was 5.4% while the incidence for females was 3.2%. This yields an odds ratio of 1.6, a smaller discrepancy than the 3.0 odds ratio between males and females as reported by the Merikangas study of adolescents.

Discrepancies in prevalence of ADHD among males versus females have been questioned because most studies of ADHD have utilized few if any females among their participants. An early meta-analysis found few significant differences between boys and girls in clinical samples of children with ADHD, though gender differences were reported in the few non-clinical samples. Authors of that meta-analysis suggested that the elevated rates of boys among children diagnosed with ADHD might be related to higher rates of externalizing behavior problems that are more common among boys than girls, resulting in referral bias in estimates of prevalence of ADHD. That study also suggested that then-current diagnostic criteria for ADHD might be insufficiently sensitive to ADHD impairments experienced by girls (Gaub & Carlson, 1997).

Two large clinical samples of girls with ADHD versus controls were followed prospectively to clarify patterns of impairment among girls with ADHD versus girls without ADHD. One study began with girls aged 6 to 18 years (mean = 11.2 years) and followed them prospectively over 11 years; the other study started with girls aged 6 to 12 years (mean = 9.6 years) who were followed prospectively for 10 years. Findings indicated that girls diagnosed with ADHD showed significant and persisting impairments associated with ADHD in patterns that did not differ substantially from those reported for samples of boys with ADHD (Biederman, et al., 1999, 2010, 2011; Hinshaw, 2002; Hinshaw, et al., 2002; 2007, 2012; Miller, et al. 2012a).

Comparison of a large number of adult males and females who sought evaluation for ADHD in a clinic setting versus matched controls found no evidence of significant differences between genders in the symptoms of ADHD experienced, prevalence of lifetime or current comorbid disorders, or patterns of cognitive and psychosocial functioning. These results were fully consistent with characteristics reported in multiple studies of children with ADHD. This study also noted that, despite the higher prevalence of ADHD found in males versus females in child and adolescent populations, adult samples tend to be more balanced between males and females (Biederman, et al., 2004). It may be that many females with ADHD do not make sufficient trouble for parents and teachers to trigger referral and assessment, but they are more likely to refer themselves for ADHD assessment as they become aware of their impairments in this domain during adult life.

In many countries around the world, the diagnosis of ADHD is still reserved for just children and younger adolescents. Gradually, recognition that older adolescents and adults also suffer from ADHD is increasing, but, at this point, many countries do not officially recognize persistence of ADHD into late adolescence and adulthood.

De Graaf, et al. (2008) commented that prevalence studies of ADHD in adults using current diagnostic criteria are likely to be underestimates because:

DSM-IV criteria for ADHD were developed with children in mind and offer only limited guidance regarding adult diagnosis. Clinical studies make it clear that symptoms of ADHD are more heterogeneous and subtle in adults, leading some researchers to suggest that assessment of adult ADHD might require an increase in the variety of symptoms assessed, a reduction in the severity threshold, or a reduction in the DSM-IV six-of-nine requirement. To the extent that such changes would lead to a more valid assessment, our estimates of prevalence and related impairment would be conservative.

It seems likely that these comments could also apply to estimates of prevalence of ADHD in children and adolescents using DSM-IV criteria rather than this more recent conceptualization of the disorder. Nevertheless, despite limitations of the DSM criteria, available data on prevalence of ADHD by current criteria can provide at least a minimal estimate of how many individuals are directly impacted by this disorder.

Executive Function Impairments Arising in Later Adult Years

At the outset of this chapter, the working definition offered describes ADHD as developmental impairment of the brain's management system, its executive functions. Virtually all of the literature on ADHD published thus far continues to focus on the earlier stages of development, the years from birth to the early twenties; a smaller number of studies extend into middle adulthood, e.g. Kessler's study of the incidence of ADHD in adults included only persons between the ages of 18 and 44 years. One small pilot study by Manor, et al. (2011) was entitled "When does it end? Attention-Deficit/ Hyperactivity Disorder in the middle aged and older populations." That study of just 11 adults who were aged 55 to 70 years at the time of first diagnosis found ADHD impairments very similar to those seen in younger individuals and noted that those older adults responded well to treatment with methylphenidate. Yet there are very few studies that extend into the middle and beyond age groups.

One exception is an Australian population-based study by Das, et al. (2012) which administered the World Health Organization's ASRS rating scale for ADHD to all members of a cohort sample of over 2,000 Australian men and women aged between 47 and 54 years. Using validated cutoffs for the ASRS, these researchers identified 6.2% of the cohort as having reported scores suggestive of ADHD. They found no differences between men and women in the percentages who met cutoffs for ADHD. Those participants were then queried with multiple measures of mental and physical health, employment and relationship status, financial problems, and overall health and wellbeing.

Results indicated that ADHD symptoms were negatively associated with full-time employment and positively associated with financial problems. ADHD symptoms were also negatively associated with reported quality of relationships, social life, health and wellbeing; these associations remained significant even after controlling for anxiety and depression. Researchers concluded that ADHD symptoms continue to be associated with ill-health and functional impairment in mid-life and are likely to be a major source of late-life morbidity which has not yet been adequately acknowledged or studied (Das, et al., 2012).

There is a substantial body of research on executive function impairments arising in the elderly (e.g. Lowe & Rabbitt, 1997; Robbins, et al., 1997), but that literature is rarely linked to the syndrome of ADHD, probably because of persistence of the earlier notion that ADHD is a disorder of childhood onset.

If ADHD is truly going to be considered a developmental disorder, it would seem reasonable to consider the course of this syndrome across the full range of development from early childhood to old age. Some might object that cognitive impairments are frequent, if not inevitable, among those in the fifth or sixth decade of life and beyond. Yet it may be useful to try to distinguish between those cognitive impairments that seem to occur naturally in virtually all individuals in their later years and those cognitive impairments that are the result of disease processes such as cardiovascular disease, Parkinson's disease or Alzheimer's dementia.

Imaging studies have demonstrated age-related decline in various elements of brain that provide the infrastructure for executive functioning. Volkow and colleagues (1996) demonstrated a 6.6% decrease per decade of life in availability of striatal dopamine transporters of healthy volunteers. Wang and others (1995) demonstrated with healthy adults that serotonin $5HT_2$ receptor availability also tends to decrease significantly with age. Volkow's group (2000) also reported age-related decline in brain dopamine activity associated with reduced metabolism in frontal and anterior cingulate regions in healthy adults. This reduction was coupled with decline in the number of dopamine D_2 receptors in the frontal cortex, anterior cingulate gyrus, temporal cortex, and caudate; this decline was associated with disrupted executive functions as well as with motor impairments. Backman and colleagues (2000) found a gradual, age-related deterioration for multiple cognitive tasks involving processing speed and episodic memory in healthy volunteers, but they demonstrated that D_2 receptor binding tends to be more important than just chronological age in this association.

It is not only the neurotransmitter systems that decline in their functioning with age. Marner and colleagues (2003) have demonstrated that white matter is the structure of brain that declines most with age. Males were found to have a total myelinated white matter fiber length of 176,000 km at age 20; this reduced to 97,200 km at age 80. Total length of myelinated white matter fibers in the female brain was 149,000 km at age 20; by age 80 this had reduced to 82,000 km. This amounts to a 10% decrease per decade or a total decrease of 45% from the age of 20 to 80 years, with a sex difference of 16%.

Another decline in brain function associated with age and difference between the sexes is found in the menopausal process that affects most women sometime in the fourth or fifth decade of life. Concurrent with the protracted cessation of their menstrual periods, many women complain not only of hot flashes and difficulties in sleeping, but also unexpected impairments of working memory and the capacity to organize and complete many tasks of daily life that were never problematic for them earlier in adulthood. Brown (2005a) has reviewed some of the evidence that such cognitive changes might be related to reduced levels of estrogen, a primary modulator of the release of dopamine in the female brain, during and after the peri-menopausal period. This too could be considered a developmental process related to executive functions. A small pilot study by Epperson and colleagues (2011) has demonstrated that some women reporting peri-menopausal onset of cognitive impairments similar to executive function impairments of ADHD find some improvement in those impairments when treated with medication used for treatment of ADD. More research is needed to determine how much decline in executive functioning during the latter decades of life is due to developmental processes of decline which affect most individuals as they grow older, and how much is due to disease processes.

3

WHAT RESEARCH REVEALS ABOUT THE CAUSES AND UNFOLDING NATURE OF ADHD

Varieties of Impairment in ADHD

ADHD is a disorder, a syndrome of symptoms and related impairments that tend to occur together. Impairments associated with the disorder can be considered in terms of role performance, i.e. impaired ability to do adequately what is expected or required of a person in one or more significant roles or functions of daily life. Such expectations and requirements vary considerably according to the age and situation of the individual. More is expected of older children than younger children, more of adolescents, and still more is expected of adults.

Children are expected to function as students, and to participate appropriately in social interactions with peers and adults within and outside their family. During teen years, most individuals continue to function as students and in various social interactions while they also may take on additional roles as dating partners, as part-time employees, as drivers of motor vehicles, and as managers of their own time and money. During adult years, demands continue to include previous roles and expand to include earning a living, managing one's household and finances, possibly developing and sustaining intimate relationships, and perhaps parenting.

Impairments can also be considered in terms of cognitive impairments which underlie and play an essential role in various aspects of these role performances. These include ability to regulate alertness and focus, ability to organize and prioritize tasks, ability to sustain effort, ability to respond to and regulate emotions, ability to inhibit impulsive behavior, and ability to utilize working memory for keeping several items in mind simultaneously and for retrieving needed information efficiently from the files of memory. These capacities, aspects of executive functions, develop, come on line and are refined quite slowly over the first two decades of life. Information about development and impairments of brain infrastructure that underlie these functions is discussed later in this chapter.

When considering impairments in children, a primary concern is their ability to function effectively in school so they can develop concepts and skills that will allow them to meet developmental demands and eventually to support themselves and their families. A review of 16 prospective studies has demonstrated that students with inattention and hyperactivity problems tend to suffer significantly more from academic problems such as lower achievement test scores, more need for special education services, and having to repeat a grade than do students without such difficulties (Polderman, et al., 2010).

A meta-analysis of 72 studies assessed the magnitude of academic achievement problems associated with ADHD. This meta-analysis found a moderate to large discrepancy in academic achievement between individuals with ADHD and typical controls. Students with ADHD were found to perform considerably lower on achievement measures (weighted effect size was d = 0.71). The largest discrepancies found were on standardized achievement test scores, particularly reading measures (Frazier, et al., 2007). ADHD tends to have a negative effect on reading performance specifically as well as on grade point averages in other academic subjects.

These and other prospective efforts to assess the impact of ADHD on academic performance of affected children have generally lumped together hyperactivity symptoms and inattention symptoms as though the disorder always included both elements. Pingault and colleagues (2011) took a different approach. They studied a population-based sample of 2000 children in Canada starting at age 6 years and followed them until age 12 years, obtaining teacher evaluations each year with separated ratings for inattention and hyperactivity. They used yearly reports to map the separate trajectory of each child's teacher ratings for inattention problems and for hyperactivity problems over each year. Subsequently they obtained public records indicating which children in their sample had obtained a diploma for high school graduation by age 23 years. Comparison of these data sets allowed these researchers to determine how teacher ratings of inattention and hyperactivity separately predicted the outcome of high school graduation by early adulthood.

Four different trajectory patterns were found for inattention ratings from ages 6 to 12 years:

1   minimal problems with inattention (46.3% of study sample);

2   significant problems with inattention (16.8%);

3   increasing problems with inattention as the child got older (17.6%);

4   gradually reduced problems with inattention as the child got older (19.3%).

Four different trajectories were also found for hyperactivity problems:

1   minimal problems with hyperactivity (59.4%);

2   initially high hyperactivity level that gradually declined to a more moderate level (10.3%);

3   high level of hyperactivity that sharply declined and stabilized at the level of minimal (16.0%);

4   initially low level of hyperactivity that gradually increased to a moderate level over time, then declined slightly (14.3%).

Overall, findings of this large, prospective study indicated that inattention problems during elementary school were strong predictors of the likelihood of high school graduation by early adulthood. Those children who were reported by teachers to have the highest levels of inattention symptoms between kindergarten and age 12 years had the highest risk of not having obtained a high school diploma by age 23 years; 70.8% of those children had not graduated from high school by early adulthood. In contrast, those children with the lowest reported rates of inattention problems had the lowest risk of failing to graduate by age 23 years (11.5%). These data clearly indicate that chronic inattention, in itself, is conducive to later educational underachievement, with or without being accompanied by hyperactivity symptoms (Pingault, et al., 2011). It should be noted that inattention problems in this study included not only weak capacity for sustaining concentration, but also excessive distractibility, absentmindedness and tendency to give up easily; all of these are aspects of the broader notion of EF in the new paradigm described in Chapter 1.

In addition to functioning adequately as students, children and adolescents are also expected to develop social skills to get along with peers and adults. Many studies have demonstrated that not all, but many children with ADHD tend to have significant impairments in their interactions with peers. Hoza, et al. (2005) assessed peer ratings on 165 children diagnosed with combined type ADHD at ages seven to nine years and followed them for six years. When rated by peers, 52% of those children with ADHD fell in the rejected range while just 1% were seen by peers as having popular status. Pelham and Bender (1982) reported that 82% of children with ADHD have peer rejection scores one standard deviation or more above the mean and 60% are two standard deviations or more above the group mean. These impairments are most clearly seen in peer rankings of ADHD children rather than in ratings by adult observers. Peer-reported variables have been shown to be better predictors of later adjustment than assessments by adults (Cowen, et al., 1973).

Hoza (2007) has emphasized that peer relationships are extremely important for all children because they provide the context in which children learn cooperation, negotiation, and conflict resolution, skills that are critical for effective social functioning throughout life. She argued that peer interaction impairments of ADHD children tend to be manifest not only in excessive negative behaviors and deficits in social skills, but also in problems with monitoring their own social behavior to see how others are reacting to them, and problems in flexibly shifting roles when needed in social situations. Hoza suggested that these various problems in peer interaction may be related to impairments in social information processing.

Other researchers have noted that such difficulties of children with ADHD often appear early in social groups and are quite resistant to change because they tend to create self-fulfilling prophecies, vicious cycles and cascades of negative effects over time (Murray-Close, et al., 2010).

Executive functions tend to play a significant role in peer relationship problems of children with ADHD, just as they do in their academic problems. Miller and Hinshaw (2010) and Miller, et al. (2011) followed an ethnically and socioeconomically diverse U.S. sample of 140 preadolescent girls with ADHD and a matched comparison group from middle childhood until late adolescence/young adulthood. They used several neuropsychological tests of executive function with rating scale data to test the ability of such measures of EF to predict academic achievement, social skills and peer acceptance in their participants at five and subsequently ten years post-baseline. They found that better performance on childhood measures of EF predicted better academic achievement and social functioning in all the girls in their sample. For girls with ADHD, EF scores also predicted global level of functioning, independent of IQ. They found that poorer EF scores predicted lower academic achievement, especially in math, in all girls, not just in those with ADHD. These authors noted that their findings highlight the non-specificity of EF deficits because most of the associations between baseline EF measures and follow-up outcome measures of academic achievement and social functioning abilities were found across the entire sample and not solely in the ADHD group.

Academic, social, and other adaptive impairments found in children and younger adolescents with ADHD often, but not always, tend to persist into later adolescent and adult years. In a study of university students Heiligenstein, et al. (1999) found that students with ADHD had lower mean grade point averages, were more likely to have been on academic probation, and had more academic problems than students without ADHD.

A study of adaptive functioning in 105 young adults and matched controls (mean age 24 years) found that young adults with ADHD tended to have fewer years of education, were less likely to be attending full-time university (32% versus 16%), had lower grade point averages (3.21 versus 2.71), and had lower personal incomes ($29,400 versus $21,300), despite having comparable IQ and similar socioeconomic backgrounds. Adaptive impairments in their sample were accounted for by inattention-disorganization symptoms of ADHD, but not by hyperactivity-impulsivity ADHD symptoms (Stavro, et al., 2007).

Another domain of daily life in which adults with ADHD tend to demonstrate impairment is driving motor vehicles. Barkley, et al. (2002) have shown that adults with ADHD tend to get more traffic violation citations, have more vehicular crashes and have their driving licenses suspended significantly more than a non-ADHD comparison group. Weafer, et al. (2008) found that in a driving simulator test, a sample of adults with ADHD, when sober, tended to resemble intoxicated drivers with significantly more deviation of lane position, more abrupt steering maneuvers, and more speed variability than was shown by controls. The complexity of consistently operating a motor vehicle in a safe and appropriate manner is a significant challenge for many, but not all individuals with ADHD.

Biederman and colleagues (2006) used telephone interviews with adults to compare reported impairments in a wide range of activities of daily life. They compared 500 non-referred individuals who had been diagnosed with ADHD as adults with 501 age and gender-matched community adults without any ADHD diagnosis. In that sample adults with an ADHD diagnosis were more likely to have left high school without earning a diploma (17% versus 7% of controls); were less likely to have obtained a college degree (19% versus 26%); were less likely to be currently employed (52% versus 72%); were less likely to have a good current relationship with their parents (47% versus 70%); were less likely to report getting along with co-workers (47% versus 66%); were less likely to report stability in love relationships and had higher rates of divorce (28% versus 15%).

Barkley, Murphy and Fischer (2008) reported an interview study of 146 adults diagnosed with ADHD, 97 adults with clinical problems not identified as ADHD, and 109 community controls. These interviews queried participants about impairments in major domains of adult life: education, home responsibilities, occupation, dating or marriage, social activities and community activities. The vast majority of participants with ADHD, more than 70%, reported themselves to be "often impaired" in the first three domains cited above; significantly lower percentages of the other two groups made similar reports. These findings provide considerable evidence that functional impairments in adults with ADHD are manifest in multiple aspects of daily life and in underlying impairments of executive functioning.

Another domain of impairment for many children and adults with ADHD is regulation of sleep and alertness. The model of ADHD-related executive functions described in Chapter 2 of this book includes problems with regulating sleep and alertness. Cortese and colleagues (2009) reported a meta-analysis of 16 studies of sleep in a pooled sample of 722 children with ADHD versus controls. Some of these studies utilized subjective measures such as self-report and parental reports; others utilized objective measures such as polysomnography or actigraphy. Results from subjective measures indicated that children with ADHD had significantly more resistance to going to bed, more difficulties with getting to sleep, more awakenings during the night, more difficulty with getting up in the morning, more sleep-disordered breathing, and more drowsiness during the day when compared to controls.

The Cortese meta-analysis found that laboratory studies using polysomnography or actigraphy indicated that in children with ADHD, sleep latency, number of sleep stage shifts per hour of sleep, and the index of apnea/hypopnea were all significantly higher versus controls. On laboratory measures children with ADHD also had less true sleep time, less efficient sleep and more evidence of drowsiness during the day than did children without ADHD. Together these studies provide considerable evidence of impairment in children with ADHD in most of the subjective and some of the objective measures of sleep.

Children with ADHD also tend to be more sleepy during the day and have longer reaction times. This was shown by Lecendreux and colleagues (2000) who used the Multiple Sleep Latency Test to test daytime alertness in 30 children aged five to ten years and 22 matched controls. They showed that this daytime sleepiness was not the result of alteration in the quality of their sleep. This suggests that children with ADHD tend to have impairment not only in their sleep, but also in their daytime alertness, independent of the quality or duration of their sleep. A study by Golan, et al. (2004) of children with ADHD and matched controls yielded similar findings indicating that children with ADHD tended to demonstrate more objectively measured daytime somnolence than did matched controls.

Gau and Chiang (2009) demonstrated similar sleep problems in adolescents with ADHD. They studied self-reported sleep problems and disorders in a sample of 281 adolescents (aged 11 to 17 years) with ADHD versus controls. They found that adolescents with ADHD were more likely to report current and lifetime sleep problems such as insomnia, sleep terrors and nightmares than matched controls.

Research on sleep problems in adults with ADHD is, thus far, more limited (Philipsen, et al., 2006). Many adults with ADHD report chronic difficulties with falling asleep, getting awake and started on morning routines, and/or maintaining daytime alertness (Brown & McMullen, 2001). Rybak, et al. (2007) have studied seasonal mood changes and circadian preferences of adults with ADHD; they found that a delay in circadian phase may contribute significantly to core pathology in many adults with ADHD.

Many adults with ADHD report that they have great difficulty in "turning off" their thinking when it is time to go to sleep. Van Veen, et al. (2010) used sleep logs and actigraphy to study sleep onset in 40 adults with ADHD. They found that, in comparison to controls, adults with ADHD had significantly more delay in falling asleep and lower sleep efficiency. They also found those with ADHD to have delayed onset of melatonin and attenuated amplitude in their rest-activity pattern. Baird and colleagues (2011) studied circadian rhythms of adults with ADHD and matched controls. They measured alterations of circadian rhythms using actigraphy and monitoring of salivary cortisol and melatonin. They found that ADHD in adults is often accompanied by significant changes in the circadian system which regulates sleep and alertness; these changes tend to lead to decreased sleep duration and reduced quality of sleep. There is need for more research on these issues, but present research clearly supports the notion that problems with managing sleep and alertness are typical of many adults with ADHD.

Duration of Impairment in ADHD

Taken together, the various studies mentioned above and many others have documented that children, adolescents and adults diagnosed with ADHD tend to suffer from a wide range of impairments in their daily functioning. However, the duration of impairment is not the same for all who receive this diagnosis. While some individuals diagnosed with ADHD as young children continue to suffer ADHD-related impairments throughout their lifetime, there are others whose ADHD impairments tend to remit or significantly improve during childhood or adolescence. For these children, ADHD symptoms may be manifestations of developmental lag. It is also true that in some individuals,

ADHD impairments are not noticeable in early childhood, but do become more apparent as the individual encounters challenges to executive functions encountered during adolescence or early adulthood.

Longitudinal studies have demonstrated that hyperactivity-impulsivity symptoms of ADHD often follow different developmental trajectories than do inattention symptoms. This was demonstrated in the study by Pingault and colleagues (2011) described earlier in this chapter which followed teacher reports on inattention and hyperactivity from age 6 to 12 years.

Among children with ADHD, not all follow the same patterns as they grow older. Larsson, et al. (2011) reported a study of 1,450 twin pairs in Sweden followed from age 8 to 17 years. These researchers found two trajectory patterns for parent-reported hyperactivity-impulsivity and two different trajectory patterns for parent-reported inattention. Parents of 91% of the sample reported that their children demonstrated low levels of hyperactivity-impulsivity over the nine-year reporting period; parents of the remaining 9% reported initially high, but decreasing levels of hyperactivity-impulsivity in their children over those years. Persisting low levels of inattention were seen by parents of 86% of participants over this age range; parents of 14% of participants reported high/increasing levels of inattention in their children over the years from 8 to 17.

The Larsson (2011) report is consistent with other studies in noting that ADHD subtypes are often not persistent over time. It cites additional support for the most commonly reported finding which is that hyperactive-impulsive symptoms of ADHD tend to decline over time while inattentive symptoms tend to have a later onset and/or a progressive increase in level of impairment over the years of childhood and adolescence. The Larsson (2011) findings also found strong genetic influences on the high and then gradually decreasing trajectory pattern for hyperactivity-impulsivity and on the high/increasing trajectory for inattention. More information about genetic factors in ADHD is provided in a later section of this chapter.

When considering the duration of ADHD, there are several different ways in which persistence of the disorder can be defined. Faraone, Biederman and Mick (2006b) published a meta-analysis of 31 controlled follow-up studies to summarize findings on persistence of ADHD into adulthood. They noted that rate of persistence of ADHD depends upon what definition of persistence is utilized. When their pooled analysis defined persistent ADHD as including only individuals who continued to meet full DSM diagnostic criteria for ADHD, the persistence rate was low, about 15% at age 25 years. When they included cases that met DSM-IV criteria for ADHD "in partial remission," the rate of persistence was much higher, approximately 40% to 60%. However, it should be noted that these estimates were based upon DSM diagnostic criteria, all of which are based upon field trials of children and none of which have been based upon field test studies of adults.

Most, but not all individuals diagnosed with ADHD in childhood continue to have significant impairment for ADHD symptoms as they get older. Biederman and colleagues (2010a) reported a ten-year follow-up study of 110 boys with ADHD and 105 non-ADHD controls. The mean age of these participants at follow-up was 22 years with a range from 15 years to 31 years. They classified participants into four categories of persistence based upon their current status at follow-up: a) "syndromatic persistence": met full DSM-IV criteria for ADHD; b) "symptomatic persistence": more than half of symptoms required for full diagnosis of ADHD; c) "functional impairment": functionally impaired with a Global Assessment of Functioning (GAF) score of ≤ 60; d) "not meeting criteria a, b or c, but currently being medicated for ADHD".

Using these categories of persistence, Biederman and colleagues (2010a) found that 35% had syndromatic persistence; 22% had symptomatic persistence; 15% had functional impairment; and 6% did not meet the other categories of persistence, but were currently being medicated for ADHD. This left 22% of the sample as fully remitted while a total of 78% showed persistence of ADHD impairments under one of the four definitions utilized. Among participants who were 18 years or older 76% met one of the definitions of persistence utilized.

Girls with ADHD tend to suffer from persisting ADHD symptoms beyond their childhood years just as do most affected boys. The Biederman group (2010b, 2011) also reported an 11-year controlled follow-up of 96 girls diagnosed with ADHD during childhood and 91 matched controls. Among the 96 girls diagnosed with ADHD, at follow-up, 33.3% met full diagnostic criteria for ADHD while 29.2% met subthreshold diagnostic criteria for ADHD. By the mean age of 22 years, 77.1% of girls with ADHD continued to manifest impairing ADHD symptoms. Predictors of persistence included psychiatric comorbidity, family history of psychopathology, and their level of functioning at baseline when they first entered the study.

Taken together, available research clearly demonstrates that ADHD tends to persist with impairment into adulthood in a substantial majority of cases, though it is also true that there are some individuals with an ADHD diagnosis in childhood and/or adolescence who do not remain significantly impaired by ADHD in their adult years. In considering ADHD persistence, however, it is important to keep in mind that an individual's level of persisting functional impairment is dependent upon multiple factors, many of which are environmentally based.

Clinical experience indicates that some individuals find their ADHD impairments to be much less problematic as they reach later years of university study where they are allowed to specialize in areas of greater personal interest and are not required to continue study in academic domains in which they have little or no interest. For some, ADHD symptoms become much less problematic when they have completed school and find employment which allows them to specialize in work that fits their interests, where other employees manage tasks that would present a greater challenge to their ADHD impairments, and where there are more immediate financial consequences for success or failure. An effective business or professional person with ADHD may be much less impaired if they have a good secretary or administrative assistant to monitor their paperwork, schedule their appointments and assist in preparing their reports. Just as some children and adolescents function well with the supportive "scaffolding" provided by their parents, so some adults with ADHD find or create for themselves scaffolding to help them compensate for many of their ADHD impairments. Adaptive functioning of any individual depends not only on their own strengths and difficulties, but also on what demands are placed upon them and what supports and resources they have, at any given time, to meet those demands.

Emotional and Motivational Aspects of ADHD

Official diagnostic criteria for the disorder currently known as ADHD do not include any recognition of problems with emotional regulation or motivation. Yet such problems are included in one of the earliest descriptions of this syndrome in the medical literature. In 1902 George Still, a pediatrician in London, published descriptions of 43 children in his practice who demonstrated significant problems with self-control. He noted that many of these children showed "a quite abnormal incapacity for sustained attention" and "a morbid exaggeration of emotional excitability" as well as a strong tendency to seek "immediate gratification of the self" (cited in Barkley, 2010, p. 7). All three of these characteristics, including problems with emotion and impatience with delay of gratification, are often reported by contemporary clinicians in their descriptions of patients with ADHD (Brown, 2005a).

Sobanski, et al. (2010) studied 1,186 children in Europe aged 6 to 18 years diagnosed with ADHD combined type, and compared them with 1,827 siblings without ADHD to investigate "emotional lability" in children with ADHD.

Their study defined "emotional lability" as symptoms such as irritability, hot temper, low frustration tolerance, and sudden, unpredictable shifts toward anger, dysphoria or sadness. They predicted that these characteristics would occur with greater intensity or frequency than would be expected from most children of comparable age in similar contexts.

Rating scale data indicated that about 25% of the ADHD probands demonstrated low levels of emotional lability, approximately 50% manifested mild-to-moderate emotional lability, and another 25% were found to have severe emotional lability. In many cases, siblings of probands were reported to have levels of emotional lability similar to their ADHD brother or sister. Thus the Sobanski, et al. (2010) study found that a clinically significant degree of emotional lability occurs in many, though not all, children and adolescents with the combined type of ADHD.

Additional evidence of problems with emotional regulation in children with ADHD was provided by Biederman and colleagues (2012). They compared a sample of 111 children aged 6 to 18 years with ADHD and 224 matched controls without ADHD in which they assessed for two levels of severity in impairments of emotional regulation. They combined data from three subscales of the well-normed Child Behavior Checklist (CBCL): aggression/anxiety-depression, and attention to create a measure of deficient emotional self-regulation (DESR). While just 2% of controls showed a comparable level of impairment, 36% of the children with ADHD scored above their established cutoff score for emotional dysregulation. They also identified a higher threshold for severe dysregulation; 19% of their ADHD sample met that higher cutoff while none of the controls were impaired at that level.

Results indicated that not all children diagnosed with ADHD suffer from problems with emotional dysregulation, but that the percentage of the ADHD sample scoring as impaired on that measure was substantially higher than controls. Data also indicated significant differences between those children who scored at the deficient level and at the more severely impaired level. Those who scored at the severely impaired level had higher rates of mood disorders, oppositional defiant and conduct disorders, psychiatric hospitalizations, and an elevated rate of severe emotional dysregulation in siblings. Those less severely impaired, but who met the deficient level had more comorbid disruptive behavior, anxiety disorders and impaired social functioning compared with other children with ADHD.

One limitation of the studies by Sobanski, et al. (2010) and Biederman, et al. (2012) is their exclusive emphasis on management of negative emotions in individuals with ADHD. A broader view of the role of emotion in ADHD is included in two current models of ADHD as developmentally impaired executive function. Models proposed by Barkley (1997, 2006, 2012b) and Brown (1996, 2001, 2005a) both include management of emotion as one of five or six central components of executive function impaired in ADHD. Barkley's model emphasizes the capacity to inhibit; he notes the critical importance of self-regulation of emotion/motivation/arousal, but he explicitly notes that "it is the inhibition of frustration, impatience, anger, hostility, and even reactive social aggression that are more closely involved in the emotional self-regulation problems associated with ADHD (Barkley, 2010, p. 15).

The UMass interview study of adults with ADHD reported by Barkley, Murphy and Fischer (2008, pp.176–179) demonstrated the elevated percentages of adults with ADHD who reported difficulty in managing negative emotions. They compared them with adults who had sought treatment for various psychiatric problems other than ADHD and with community controls. Percentages shown reflect those in each group who reported the problem as occurring "often" or more over the preceding six months.

Item	ADHD %	Clinical %	Community %
Finds it difficult to tolerate waiting; impatient	75	63	5
Quick to get angry or become upset	63	46	7
Easily frustrated	86	70	8
Overreacts emotionally	68	49	6
Easily excited	70	48	15

A different view of emotional problems associated with ADHD is provided in Brown's model which emphasizes that ADHD involves difficulty in modulating a wider variety of emotions. He notes that "Irritability and anger are not the only emotions that are problematic for persons with ADHD syndrome. Many individuals with ADHD have equal or greater difficulty modulating other emotions, such as hurt or sadness, worry or anxiety" (Brown, 2005a, p. 43). Brown's model also notes problems with being sufficiently sensitive to emotions such as anxiety: sometimes being excessively sensitive to anxiety and, at other times, being relatively insensitive, not worrying enough when there is good reason to get anxious and activate.

Some evidence for problems with managing anxiety has been provided by Levy (2004). She has reviewed research supporting the notion that individuals with ADHD may be impaired in their ability to modulate excessive intensity of anxiety due to a lack of sufficient "synaptic gating" between the prefrontal cortex, hippocampus and amygdala. Yet for others with ADHD there is a problematic "fearless" attitude toward anxiety which is based on impaired reinforcement gradients.

Brown's clinically-based model of ADHD also includes impairments in motivational functions such as activating to work and sustaining effort. "Many individuals with ADHD syndrome chronically delay starting tasks until they are face-to-face with the immediate pressure of an imminent deadline. They have chronic problems with cognitive activation" (Brown, 2005a, p. 24). The same model also notes difficulty in sustaining effort for work tasks. "Though they may have a virtually inexhaustible reservoir of energy for tasks intrinsically interesting to them, they tend quickly to run out of steam when engaged in jobs that require sustained effort with little immediate reward" (Brown, 2005a, p. 37). Problems with insufficient anticipatory anxiety emotional/motivational difficulties were queried by the Barkley, et al., (2008) study; five relevant items below actually yielded scores higher than the five items above related to negative emotions:

Item	ADHD %	Clinical %	Community %
Can't seem to get things done unless there is an imminent deadline	89	82	6
Has trouble motivating self to start work	80	72	6
Not motivated to prepare in advance	80	62	4
Has difficulty resisting urge to do something more interesting when working	87	74	5
Has difficulty doing work by its priority	84	63	4

(Barkley, et al., 2008, pp. 176–179)

These data suggest that individuals with ADHD often suffer significant problems from being insufficiently worried soon enough about tasks which need to be done. Insufficient anxiety and lack of sufficient interest can be even more problematic than difficulties in managing negative emotions, especially when one is trying to perform adequately in school or employment.

Motivation problems in children with ADHD were described by Diamond (2005) who reviewed studies of laboratory tests of executive functioning in children to argue that ADHD without significant hyperactivity/impulsivity should be considered as a different disorder from ADHD that includes hyperactivity. She proposed that children with ADHD are not so much easily distracted as they are easily bored.

> Their problem lies more in motivation than it does in inhibition. ...
> It is not so much that external distraction derails them as that they are
> looking for external (or internal) distraction because their interest in
> what they are supposed to be doing, or had started, has dwindled. ...
> Under the right circumstances, when sufficiently motivated, children
> with ADHD... can perform well, but it is hard for them to sustain that
> level of performance (p. 819).

Because of the high rates of crossover from combined type to predominantly
inattentive type found in several studies cited earlier in this chapter, it is
difficult to sustain Diamond's argument that ADHD with and without
hyperactivity are two totally different disorders, but her emphasis on the role
of motivation in cognitive impairments of ADHD is appropriate not only for
children with both types of ADHD, but also for adults. It is also consistent with
the view of situational specificity described in Chapter 2 and later in this
chapter.

A different approach to study of impairments in motivation in ADHD is
provided in a study by Torrente, et al. (2010) which assessed apathy symptoms
in adolescents and adults with predominantly inattentive or combined type
ADHD compared to healthy controls. Torrente and colleagues (2010)
conceptualized apathy as "a behavioral dimension expressing pervasive and
sustained motivation failures ranging from total lack of intrinsic motivation to
varied degrees of reduced motivation, including troubles in taking initiatives,
acting without immediate reward, or completing tasks without external
support" (p. 3). On laboratory measures of executive functions, self-report
rating scales, and observer reports, participants in both groups of ADHD
patients demonstrated significantly higher levels of apathy than did controls.
This is consistent with work by Sergeant (2005) whose cognitive-energetic
model emphasizes the critical importance of impaired effort, arousal and
activation in ADHD.

Motivational problems in ADHD include not only lack of initiative and
difficulty in sustaining effort, but also chronic difficulties in dealing with
short-term frustrations or delays in order to obtain longer term rewards.
Luman, et al. (2005) reviewed 22 studies involving 1,181 children and found
that children with ADHD, when required to make a choice between an
immediate and a delayed reward, chose more often for an immediate reward
than did controls, even though the delayed reward was larger. This is
consistent with the work of Sonuga-Barke (2005) and Sonuga-Barke, et al.
(2010a, 2010b) who demonstrated that motivational impairments of ADHD

children are often due to delay aversion, a reluctance/unwillingness to wait for delayed rewards.

This preference for immediate rewards and reluctance to wait for gratification was also demonstrated in a study of preschoolers by Campbell and von Stauffenberg (2009). In a sample of over 1,000 children participating in a longitudinal study, they tested each at age 36 months on a measure of resistance to temptation; at age 54 months they administered a test on delay of gratification; and at 54 months they tested each with a Continuous Performance Test. When children reached third grade, researchers assessed which children, according to parent and teacher report, had symptoms of ADHD, either the combined type with hyperactivity-impulsivity symptoms or the predominantly inattentive symptoms without significant hyperactivity-impulsivity.

Analysis of data showed significant differences in third grade between children who, at age three years, had been unable to resist touching the attractive toy when asked to and those who were able to keep their hands off the toy for 2.5 minutes as requested. Likewise, there were significant differences between those who at age 54 months were unable to delay gratification of eating a small reward of candy rather than waiting seven minutes to get a larger reward of candy and those who were able to wait in order to get the bigger candy reward.

Children in the groups that had greater difficulty in tolerating those brief delays at 36 months or 54 months had much greater likelihood of meeting diagnostic criteria for ADHD by the time they reached third grade than did those who were better able to tolerate the delay of gratification. Similar results were found for those children who, at age 54 months, made more errors of omission or commission on a computerized Continuous Performance Test and those who, while in first grade, did more poorly on a test of efficiency in planning how to solve the Tower of Hanoi puzzle (Campbell & von Stauffenberg, 2009).

These data suggest that impairment shown at ages three to six years on measures of delay capacity, impulse control, attention, and planning tend to predict which children are more likely to be suffering from ADHD impairments by age nine years. Follow-up from other studies of preschoolers doing various delay-of-gratification tasks have shown that the seconds of time preschool children were willing to delay for a preferred outcome predicted their cognitive and social competence and coping as adolescents and even showed correlation with their scores on SAT tests (Shoda, et al., 1990) as well as with their performance on laboratory tests of inhibition taken a decade later (Eigsti, et al., 2006).

This very early onset of such difficulties suggests that there may be some structural or functional differences in the brains of children diagnosed with ADHD during the elementary school years. A recent functional imaging study of adults in their 40s who, as preschoolers, participated in delay-of-gratification studies has shown that there are relatively stable differences between those more able and those less able to delay gratification in preschool years that tend to persist over decades. Those differences are in fronto-striatal circuitries that regulate motivational and control processes in the brain (Casey, et al., 2011).

Another possible cause of such motivational impairments may be found in the brain mechanisms that signal potential pleasure or satisfaction. Volkow and colleagues (2010) used PET to argue that a deficit in motivation is an important aspect of ADHD. Using radioactive ligands with a sample of adults with ADHD and controls without ADHD, they demonstrated disruption in the dopamine neural pathways that constitute primary components of the brain system for activating reward-seeking behavior and the brain system for gaining pleasure from rewards sufficient to sustain reward-generating behavior. For participants with ADHD, their scores on a rating scale of achievement motivation were negatively correlated with their levels of inattention symptoms.

In a related study Volkow and colleagues (2009) assessed biological factors that underlie the demonstrated deficits of individuals with ADHD in their responses to rewards, e.g. their difficulty in sustaining effort to obtain desired outcomes and their difficulty in tolerating delay which leads them often to settle for smaller rewards immediately rather than obtaining bigger rewards by waiting or working a bit longer. Their PET study of 53 non-medicated adults with ADHD versus 44 controls demonstrated a significantly lower number of dopamine transporters in the nucleus accumbens, midbrain and left caudate regions of those with ADHD; they also found significantly fewer D_2/D_3 receptors in the same regions as well as in the hypothalamic region.

These biological markers in the brain reward system were correlated negatively with participants' scores on a rating scale of achievement motivation. Taken together, these data indicate reduced efficiency in the dopamine reward pathways of participants with ADHD that is correlated with relatively weaker or more inconsistent reward-seeking behavior. This reward mechanism is a key component of what causes an individual to anticipate any action or task as potentially bringing pleasure or satisfaction; it is also the brain mechanism that registers how much pleasure or satisfaction is coming from an activity in which one is currently engaged.

Anticipation of potential reward is often impaired in adolescents with ADHD as well as in adults. Scheres, et al. (2007) used fMRI to study brain activity in adolescents with ADHD versus controls. They were particularly focused on "reward anticipation," i.e. on brain activity in individuals with ADHD compared to controls when both were anticipating winning or losing various amounts of cash. They found that adolescents with ADHD showed significantly reduced activation in the brain area most directly registering potential reward, the ventral striatal area, when anticipating reward than did the control group, but not when they were anticipating loss of payoff. This suggests that anticipated rewards do not "turn on" ADHD adolescents with ADHD as much as they do those of similar age without ADHD. These researchers interpreted their findings to indicate that ADHD abnormalities occur in neural pathways critical to motivation as well as in neural pathways previously recognized as underlying executive functions. These findings are consistent with arguments by Tripp and Wickens (2008) who reviewed studies that support the theory that individuals with ADHD tend to suffer from diminished anticipatory dopamine cell firing which makes it more difficult for them to sustain motivation for activities that do not provide immediate and continuing reinforcement.

Intra-Individual Variability of ADHD Impairments

In a 2002 paper, Castellanos and Tannock noted that "the most striking clinical characteristics of ADHD include the transient, but frequent lapses of intention and attention, and the moment-to-moment variability and inconsistency in performance" (p. 624). Three years later Castellanos and colleagues suggested that temporal and contextual variability in symptom expression might be considered the essence of ADHD (2005). Yet most studies of ADHD have focused on differences in task performance between groups of individuals with ADHD and those without ADHD. Until recently, there has been very little interest in studying variability of performance within individuals with ADHD over time. Castellanos and colleagues (2005) have suggested that variability within the task performance of a given individual, intra-individual variability, may be at least as important in ADHD impairments as is inter-individual variability between those with ADHD and those without ADHD.

Variability in individual task performance was demonstrated by West, et al. (2002) who compared younger adults with older adults on tasks requiring relatively little executive function (EF) control and tasks which required greater EF control. They found that aging is normally associated with greater intra-individual variation in performance on tasks that require more executive control, but found no significant differences between age groups for tasks that did not require much use of executive functions. These data suggest that insofar as impairments of individuals with ADHD are developmental impairments of executive functions, those affected with ADHD are likely to vary considerably on tasks requiring relatively high levels of EF, but are likely to be not significantly different from those without ADHD on tasks not requiring EF control. One example of such impairment is provided by Sheridan, et al. (2007) who used fMRI to show the relative inefficiency of prefrontal cortex (PFC) function in girls with ADHD versus controls during a working memory task, but not during a task that involved the primary motor cortex.

Stuss and colleagues (2003) have demonstrated that intra-individual variability in performance is found as a consequence of two different types of damage to the prefrontal cortex: focal damage which is associated with a specific and discrete cognitive process, or, alternatively, intra-individual variability may result from a more general deficit in regulation of attention to any task, without association to any one distinct cognitive domain. These researchers noted that this latter type of generalized intra-individual variability is most consistently described in patients with impairments of executive functions, such as those with ADHD, with or without any overt finding of focal frontal lesions. They also noted the importance of intra-individual variability: "because success in real-life tasks may depend as much on predictability and consistency as on average performance" (p. 2377).

Thus far, most research addressing intra-individual variability of performance in ADHD is limited to laboratory tasks where relatively simple cognitive tasks are given repeatedly to determine the degree to which the participant performs with relatively consistent speed and accuracy, e.g. reaction times. Less controlled, but striking examples of intra-individual variability are readily found in reports of clinical evaluation and treatment of children, adolescents and adults with ADHD, e.g. Brown (2005a).

Brain Development, Structure and Functioning in ADHD

Recent research has demonstrated significant differences in structure, development and functioning of brain in individuals with ADHD compared with controls without ADHD. An important study by Shaw, et al. (2007) compared repeated MRI brain scans of 223 children with ADHD and 223 typically developing controls to assess for differences in the rate of brain development between the ages of 10 and 18 years. The usual pattern of brain maturation during these years involves a massive proliferation of cortical cells that usually peaks shortly before puberty. This is generally followed by a protracted period of pruning that allows the brain to develop more efficient circuits.

Results of their study showed that timing of this developmental sequence was similar in the two groups for most areas of brain. However, there were a few specific areas of brain where development of ADHD participants was significantly slower; this delay was most prominent in the prefrontal regions of the brain, particularly the lateral prefrontal cortex, a region particularly important for controlling attention and motor planning. Among participants with ADHD the median age for reaching maximum cortical thickness in these regions was three years later than the median for the typically developing children (Shaw, et al., 2007). Since full maturation of that brain region was eventually attained by most ADHD participants, albeit several years later, this study indicated that ADHD is often characterized by delay in development of certain brain regions, not usually by permanent failure to develop. However, this delay in attaining maximum cortical thickness is not insignificant; it is likely to cause delay in the pruning process which plays an important role in increasing efficiency of cognitive functioning during adolescence (Shaw, et al., 2007). Moreover, an earlier study by Shaw and colleagues (2006) found that normalization of cortical thickness tended to occur eventually only in those persons with ADHD who demonstrated a better outcome. Those in their sample with a worse outcome had cortical thinning in the left medial prefrontal cortex which tended not to normalize over the longer term.

Ducharme and colleagues (2012) demonstrated in healthy children the relationship between cortical thickness and capacity to pay attention. These researchers administered the Attention Problems (AP) segment of the Child Behavior Checklist to a representative sample of 357 healthy children aged 6 to 18 years on whom they did repeated MRI scans. Findings indicated a negative correlation between scores on the AP rating scale and cortical thickness in these healthy children during the ages of six to ten years. Participants who scored higher on AP during those early years tended to be more delayed in developing the increased cortical thickening commonly seen in children in that age range. This is quite similar to data of the Shaw (2007) study of children diagnosed with ADHD. Healthy children with relatively high scores on the AP scale, like those in the ADHD sample, tended to have a longer period of thinner cortical tissue and greater delay in brain maturation. This difference from normal controls without the elevated AP scores gradually disappeared as they developed the thickening of cortex and subsequent pruning for more efficient circuits, several years later than other healthy controls.

Another study that demonstrated differences of brain development in individuals with ADHD versus normal controls was reported by Proal and colleagues (2011). These researchers did a long-term follow-up of a group of boys carefully assessed and diagnosed with ADHD at a mean age of 8.3 years and a matched group of boys free of ADHD at a comparable age. They obtained MRI scans of 59 probands with ADHD and 80 comparison participants about 33 years after the initial ADHD diagnosis of the ADHD probands had been made; the mean age of the participants at that follow-up was 41.2 years.

In comparisons with adults of comparable age who had not been diagnosed with ADHD in childhood, Proal, et al., (2011) found that brain gray matter was significantly thinner globally in adults who had been diagnosed in childhood with ADHD regardless of whether they continued to meet diagnostic criteria for ADHD in adulthood. Thinner cortex was not found in the prefrontal cortex, but it was found in regions of the dorsal attentional network (including bilateral parietal and precentral regions), an area that mediates top-down executive control processes and helps to facilitate shifting of attention. Thinner cortex was also found in multiple limbic regions including the temporal pole, insula, parahippocampus, and subgenual ACC which are involved in regulation of emotional and motivational processes often impaired in ADHD. Interestingly, comparisons of probands who continued to meet diagnostic criteria for ADHD at follow-up did not differ from probands whose ADHD symptoms had remitted sufficiently that they no longer met diagnostic criteria. However, probands who had remitted tended to show fuller development of prefrontal, cerebellar and thalamic circuitry; the authors suggested that remission from ADHD may involve compensation for ADHD impairments by fuller development of these alternative circuits in later adolescence.

A meta-analysis of studies of gray matter volume abnormalities in ADHD has been provided by Nakao and colleagues (2011). Fourteen data sets comprising 378 patients and 344 controls met inclusion criteria for their meta-analysis. The most robust finding across these studies was that the ADHD participants had global reductions of gray matter volumes, most of which were located within the region of the basal ganglia. Data from these multiple studies also indicated that ADHD patients may gradually catch up with their developmental delay of brain structure as they get older. This is consistent with findings of the Shaw (2007) study. Nakao and colleagues (2011) also found that patients with ADHD who have been treated with stimulant medication may be more likely to achieve normalization of their earlier structural abnormalities.

Another step in identifying structural differences in brain development of individuals with ADHD was provided by Shaw and colleagues (2012) subsequent to the meta-analysis described above. Doing further analysis of their longitudinal series of MRI scans of children with ADHD and controls followed into and through adolescence, these researchers found that those with ADHD were delayed not only in the thickness of their cortical tissue, but also in the total surface area of the cortex. For example, the mean age by which participants with ADHD had developed peak area surface of the right prefrontal cortex was 14.6 years, considerably later than the sample of typically developing controls where the mean age for peak surface area was 12.7 years. These findings suggest that children and adolescents with ADHD tend to have fairly widespread disruptions and resulting delays in the maturation of the mechanisms that guide cortical maturation.

Differences between those diagnosed with ADHD and more typically developing individuals are not limited to differences in area, volume or thickness of brain tissue. Another important dimension of difference is in functional connectivity between various regions of brain, connections carried primarily by white matter tracts. These differences are currently measured with fractional anisotropy (FA) and mean diffusivity (MD) rates; these are assessed with diffusion tensor imaging, a relatively new MRI technique which assesses the integrity of white matter by measuring the non-random diffusion of water within axons. Bush (2009) reviewed a variety of studies which had demonstrated that children with ADHD tended to have decreased FA in a variety of brain areas closely associated with attention and executive functions.

White matter plays a critical role in maintaining effective communication between various regions of the brain. Some white matter pathways are largely developed by late childhood, but others, particularly those which sustain association and projections to and from the prefrontal cortex typically continue development well into adolescence. In 2011 Nagel and colleagues presented data from their study of children with ADHD and matched controls to show that the distributed microstructure of white matter is atypical in children with ADHD aged seven to nine years compared to healthy controls. These differences were found to be widely distributed in the fronto-parietal, fronto-limbic, cerebellar, corona radiate, and temporal-occipital regions. This study indicates that even before adolescence, individuals with ADHD are likely to have widespread abnormalities in white matter pathways that play a critical role in facilitating efficient communication between various regions of brain.

Similar findings have been obtained in studies of adults with ADHD. Konrad and colleagues (2010) used diffusion tensor imaging to assess white matter integrity in adults with ADHD compared to healthy controls. In adult patients with ADHD they found reduced FA as well as higher MD bilaterally in orbitomedial prefrontal white matter and in the right anterior cingulate bundle; they also found elevated FA present bilaterally in temporal white matter structures. Direct correlations between integrity of white matter and measures of attention and impulsivity were found in these adults with ADHD. These data suggest that problems with inadequate white matter connectivity may underlie and partially explain problems of inattention and impulsivity in persons with ADHD.

A meta-analysis of 15 studies of white matter integrity in children, adolescents and adults with ADHD compared to controls found that those with ADHD had decreased integrity of white matter, probably due to damaged, decreased or delayed myelination. These identified areas of disturbed white matter were located primarily in tracts serving fronto-striatal-cerebellar neurocircuitry (van Ewijk, et al., 2012).

A review article published in 2010 by Konrad and Eickhoff summarized the recent major shift in research on ADHD brain functioning from focus on abnormalities in specific isolated regions of brain to abnormalities in distributed network organization and functioning that integrate the complex inter-regional interactions of the brain. The title of the Konrad and Eickhoff paper asks the question: "Is the ADHD brain wired differently?" Research involving both children and adults summarized in their review suggests that the answer to this question seems to be in the affirmative, particularly with reference to functional connectivity in the resting state default mode.

Functional connectivity refers to the process by which low voltage electrical oscillations in regions of brain that are spatially separated become correlated with one another in coherent patterns. This occurs primarily where these separated regions are not immediately engaged in specific tasks. Studies using fMRI administered when the brain is not being perturbed by any external stimuli have identified a default-mode network (DMN), a resting state of brain regions that oscillate in coordinated rhythm when the mind is not occupied with anything else, when it is occupying itself with tasks irrelevant to current stimuli, and/or when the mind is simply wandering and/or monitoring the environment, body state, or current emotional status (Fassbender, et al., 2009).

The human brain is never completely static, even in sleep; within the brain there are constant oscillations which occur at different frequency rates. Zuo, et al. (2010) have summarized information about how the human brain generates a hierarchical organization of ten frequency bands extending from 0.02 hz to 600 hz, each of these levels of oscillation is associated with a variety of neural processes. They studied amplitude, spatial distribution and test-retest reliability of low frequency oscillation patterns (≤ 0.1 Hz) which are particularly important in default-mode functioning of the brain.

There is evidence indicating that the brain exchanges information between regions of the DMN when it is not activated by environmental stimuli (Konrad

& Eickhoff, 2010: Buzaki, 2006). There is also evidence that when the brain is called upon to focus upon any specific task, its attention to that task is proportional to the degree to which the DMN can be shut down or suppressed. Persistence of DMN activity during task performance is associated with increased errors, longer reaction times, and impaired task performance (Konrad & Eickhoff, 2010). This persistence of DMN activity when trying to focus on a task resembles what many individuals with ADHD identify as their "losing focus," and "spacing out" when trying to listen, read, or work on a project.

Fassbender, et al. (2009) have demonstrated that children with ADHD between the ages of 8 and 14 years show increased intra-individual variability and increased task errors in a variety of cognitive tasks when compared with healthy controls of the same age. They described their results as generally consistent with the default-mode interference hypothesis of Sonuga-Barke and Castellanos (2007) which stipulates that the increased reaction time variability in ADHD may be due to intrusions by the default attention network into goal-directed activity.

More recent research has demonstrated two abnormal characteristics of functional connectivity density in brains of children with ADHD when compared to controls: enhanced connectivity within reward-motivation regions and decreased connectivity in dorsal attention and default-mode networks and in functional connectivity to the cerebellum. Tomasi and Volkow (2012) offered these findings from a large sample of children as evidence that ADHD is characterized not only by inattention and hyperactivity/impulsivity problems, but also by deficits in motivation.

Problems with brain connectivity in ADHD are also linked to emotional regulation. Using fMRI with a sample of adolescents with and without ADHD, Posner, et al. (2011) assessed connectivity between two brain regions associated with emotional reactivity: the amygdala and the lateral prefrontal cortex (LPFC). Dynamic causal modeling of data from the two groups indicated that adolescents with ADHD became hyperactivated in amygdala response to subliminally presented fearful stimuli and that they showed significantly greater bi-directional connectivity between the amygdala and LPFC, an aspect of the neural substrate of emotional reactivity. These researchers suggest that the functional connections and response patterns revealed in their study may be the basis for the excessive emotional reactivity often present in youth with ADHD. They also demonstrated that stimulant medication can have a normalizing effect upon emotional processing in adolescents with ADHD.

Effects of medications for ADHD are discussed in Chapter 5. However, it should be noted here that effectiveness of medications for ADHD in improving brain functions underlying executive function impairments of the disorder has been demonstrated in multiple brain imaging studies. In addition to the findings of Posner, et al. (2011) regarding improvement of brain functions involved in emotional processing, stimulant medications have also been reported as normalizing dysfunctional connectivity between brain regions for other tasks. In 7- to 18-year-old children and adolescents with ADHD, Peterson and colleagues (2009) demonstrated that stimulant medications improved suppression of default-mode activity and normalized activity within the ventral anterior cingulate and posterior cingulate cortices, improving their performance on the Stroop task.

One therapeutic effect of stimulant medication in individuals with ADHD is to improve the brain's capacity to suppress the mind-wanderings of DMN at times when the brain needs to be paying attention to something specific. Liddle, et al. (2011) used fMRI with a sample of children aged 9 to 15 years, all of whom had been diagnosed with ADHD and compared them to a matched sample of controls on performance of a Go/NoGo task both on and off methylphenidate. They found that when children with ADHD were off medication and did not have a strong incentive to put forth careful effort on the task, their DMN suppression was significantly lower than that of controls. When those children were on medication, their brains showed suppression of DMN mind-wandering that was fully comparable to that of healthy controls.

Using fMRI, Rubia, et al. (2009) demonstrated that methylphenidate (MPH) normalized attention differences between children with ADHD and controls by up-regulation of dysfunctional fronto-striato-thalamo-cerebellar and parieto-temporal attention networks. Their study also demonstrated that MPH provided down-regulation of hypersensitive orbitofrontal activation for reward processing. Thus MPH was shown to provide context-dependent dissociative modulation of both motivational and attentional neuro-functional networks detectable in brain imaging studies of children with ADHD.

In a follow-up study Rubia and colleagues (2011) used fMRI to demonstrate that in medication-naïve boys with ADHD, MPH significantly normalized the fronto-striatal under-functioning seen relative to controls during interference inhibition on placebo, but did not affect medial frontal or temporal dysfunction. Those researchers concluded that MPH has a regionally-specific up-regulation effect on frontal-striatal activation.

Most of the fMRI studies cited above involve fairly small numbers of participants. However, the much larger pooled samples assessed in the meta-analysis done by Nakao and colleagues (2011) demonstrated that treatment with stimulant medications may be associated with normalization of atypical brain structure in ADHD patients and function as measured by brain imaging studies, particularly in the striatum region. Longitudinal studies are needed to confirm such findings, but the wide variety of studies reporting similar findings, coupled with clinical observations described in the next chapter of this book certainly provide substantial preliminary evidence of the benefits of stimulant medications for alleviating brain dysfunctions associated with ADHD.

Intelligence and ADHD

Executive function impairments that comprise ADHD as understood in the new paradigm described in this book are not equivalent to intelligence as measured by conventional IQ tests. Delis and colleagues (2007) did a large scale correlational study between measures of EF and measures of IQ using data from 470 normal functioning children and adolescents. Their data demonstrated that IQ and EF skills are divergent cognitive domains and that IQ tests do not provide a sufficient or comprehensive assessment of higher-level executive functions. IQ measures accounted for only 0% to 18% of the variance on various measures of EF administered in that study. Similar conclusions about the inadequacies of IQ tests for assessing EF were reported by Ardila, et al. (2000) in their study of 50 students aged 13 to 16 years.

This view of IQ and EF as independent of one another is also supported by data from Rommelse, et al. (2008) whose large study of children with ADHD versus controls found that group differences on EF were not explained by group differences on IQ and vice versa. In principal components analysis that study also demonstrated that EF and IQ are relatively independent of each other in the same child. This is consistent with the argument of Schuck and Crinella (2005) that children with ADHD do not necessarily have low IQ; they demonstrated that correlations between EF measures and IQ scores account for less than 5% of the variance.

While there are some data showing that groups of children diagnosed with ADHD tend to have lower full-scale IQ scores than children without ADHD (Frazier, et al., 2004), these studies tend to suffer from bias in sample selection and do not take into account that most measures of full-scale IQ include measures of some aspects of executive function. Although there are currently only very limited data estimating incidence of ADHD among various levels of IQ, several studies demonstrate that high IQ individuals can suffer from this disorder.

Katusic and colleagues (2011) compared children with ADHD who had various levels of IQ. They reported data from 331 children in a population-based birth cohort study, all of whom had been diagnosed with ADHD. They found core symptoms and age of onset of ADHD, rates of comorbid learning and psychiatric disorders, rates of substance abuse, and rates of treatment to be similar across 34 children with high IQ, 276 with normal IQ and 21 with low IQ who fully met diagnostic criteria for ADHD. ADHD impairments were similar across the different levels of IQ.

A sample of 49 high IQ (≥ 120) children who fully met DSM-IV diagnostic criteria for ADHD showed a pattern of cognitive, psychiatric and behavioral features typical of children with average IQ diagnosed with ADHD. These very bright children with ADHD tended to have significant difficulty with schoolwork; 22% had repeated a grade at least once, while only 3% of matched controls had ever been retained. These very bright children also had more comorbid psychopathology and were more impaired in multiple domains, relative to similarly bright children without ADHD. Moreover, incidence of ADHD among first degree relatives of these bright children with ADHD was much higher (22.9%) than among such relatives of matched controls (5.6%). Those researchers concluded that the diagnosis of ADHD can be valid in high IQ children (Antshel, et al., 2007).

In a follow-up study, Antshel and colleagues (2008) demonstrated that over a 4.5 year period high IQ children with ADHD, in comparison to high IQ controls without ADHD, continued to have higher rates of mood, anxiety and disruptive behavior disorders. Participants with ADHD also continued to demonstrate elevated rates of impairment relative to controls across most social, academic and family function domains. The high IQ scores of both groups persisted without significant change over the 4.5 year follow-up period.

In a study of 117 children and adolescents with high IQ and ADHD, Brown, Reichel and Quinlan (2011c) identified several specific cognitive functions which tend to be areas of relative cognitive weakness. In addition to the wide range of cognitive impairments identified by the Brown ADD Scales for Children and Adolescents (Brown, 1996, 2001), high IQ youths in that sample demonstrated significant impairments in their working memory, processing speed and auditory verbal memory, relative to their own strengths in verbal comprehension and/or visual-perceptual reasoning. These same patterns of relative cognitive weaknesses versus cognitive strengths were found in a sample of 157 adults with high IQ studied by the same team of researchers (Brown, et al., 2009).

Taken together, available data support the notion that ADHD impairments may be found across the full spectrum of IQ. However, clinical data (Brown, et al., 2009, 2011c) suggest that individuals with high IQ who suffer from ADHD may not be recognized as having this disorder until quite late in their educational career, due to the assumption widespread among parents, teachers and clinicians that ADHD impairments do not appear among individuals with high IQ.

Heritability and Genetics of ADHD

ADHD tends to run in families. Four primary sources of information about the genetics of ADHD provide evidence for this fact. One source is familiality (the likelihood that close relatives of an individual with ADHD will also have the disorder). Another source is adoption studies (the likelihood that a child with ADHD who has been adopted will have more relatives with ADHD in the family of biological origin than among relatives in the adoptive family. A third source is twin studies (the likelihood that both of a pair of twins who share 100% of their genes with one another will have ADHD as compared to the likelihood of ADHD in fraternal twins who share only 50% of their genes). The other source of information about the role of genetics in ADHD is molecular studies which involve efforts to identify specific genes that occur with significantly greater frequency in individuals with ADHD than in persons without ADHD.

An early, but large and well-controlled study by Faraone, et al. (1992) compared rates of ADHD in families of 140 boys aged 6 to 17 years old carefully diagnosed with ADHD versus a matched control group of 120. When they examined first degree relatives (parents or siblings) of boys diagnosed ADHD versus boys in the control sample, the following percentages of first degree relatives qualified for the diagnosis of ADHD.

Relationship to Proband	Boys Diagnosed with ADHD %	Boys in Control Sample %
Father	17	3
Mother	11	2
Brother	17	5
Sister	13	1

In a similar controlled family study of girls diagnosed with ADHD, Faraone, et al. (2000) found that the rate of ADHD among relatives of girls with ADHD was significantly higher than for the comparison sample (24% versus

7%). That study also confirmed that heritability of ADHD is not specific to subtype. Whether a parent has predominantly inattentive or combined subtype of ADHD, their offspring has a significantly elevated risk of having ADHD, but the child will not necessarily have the same subtype of ADHD as the parent.

Biederman and colleagues (1995) also did a pilot study of 84 adults diagnosed with ADHD to ascertain the rate of ADHD of their offspring. Of those adults with ADHD who had children, 84% had at least one child with ADHD and 52% had at least two children with ADHD while the average number of children was 2.7 children per parent with ADHD. The overall rate of ADHD among this sample of children of adults with ADHD was 57%, considerably higher than the 15% risk for ADHD among siblings of children diagnosed with ADHD. Those researchers also found that rates of school failure among this sample of children with ADHD who had parents with ADHD was quite similar to the rate of school failure found in other samples of children with ADHD.

Additional data on heritability of ADHD from parents was provided by Smalley and colleagues (2000). They assessed parents in 256 families where two or more children had been diagnosed with ADHD. Researchers found that 55% of those families with two or more children with ADHD had at least one parent with ADHD of lifetime duration. Similar to findings of the Biederman, et al. (2000) study, Smalley's group found no evidence that parents with one particular subtype of ADHD were more likely to have offspring with the same subtype.

Studies of adopted children also provide evidence for a high rate of heritability of ADHD (Sprich, et al. (2000). Faraone, et al. (2000) compared the rates of ADHD in adoptive parents and siblings of 25 adopted children or adolescents diagnosed with ADHD and compared them with the rates of ADHD among biological parents and siblings of those adopted individuals; they also compared these rates of ADHD with the rates among non-ADHD controls. Results indicated that 6% of adoptive parents of adopted children with ADHD had ADHD while 18% of the biological parents of adopted children with ADHD had ADHD; among biological parents of children without ADHD (controls) the rate of ADHD was just 3%. Among adoptive siblings of those adopted children the rate of ADHD was 8% while among siblings in the control group the rate of ADHD was 6%. In contrast, the rate of ADHD among biological siblings of the adopted children with ADHD was 31%. These data strongly suggest that the ADHD impairments in adopted children are primarily due to genetic rather than family environmental factors.

Twin studies provide additional important evidence regarding the genetic influences on ADHD. In 2005 Faraone and colleagues reported a review of 20 twin studies from the United States, Australia, Scandinavia, and the European Union. Those studies compared ADHD rates in identical twins who share 100% of their genes versus fraternal twins who share just 50% of their genetic heritage. The mean heritability estimate from that review of multiple studies was 0.76. Scores on this index run from 0, which indicates no apparent genetic influence of the variability, to 1, which suggests that genetic factors substantially determine whether a person has ADHD or not. This very high rate of heritability makes ADHD one of the most heritable of psychiatric disorders (Faraone, et al., 2005).

Despite the high rate of heritability of ADHD, intensive searches using a variety of molecular methods, have not identified any specific genes that in themselves or in combination cause ADHD. Mick and Faraone (2008) noted that:

> molecular genetic studies suggest that the genetic architecture of ADHD is complex. The handful of genome-wide scans that have been conducted thus far show divergent findings... candidate gene studies of ADHD have produced substantial evidence implicating several genes in the etiology of the disorder... yet even these associations are small and consistent with the idea that the genetic vulnerability to ADHD is mediated by many genes of small effects (pp. 275-276).

A meta-analysis of genome-wide association studies of ADHD (Neale, et al., 2010) echoed a similar finding: "No genome-wide significant associations were found.... Given that ADHD is a highly heritable disorder, our negative results suggest that the effects of common ADHD risk variants must, individually be very small" (p. 884). Yet a more recent review by Poelmans, et al. (2011) suggests that 85 specific candidate genes for ADHD considered together may be seen in a more illuminating way if they are considered as aspects of a protein signaling network. These researchers propose a signaling network involved in neurite outgrowth which includes 45 of those 85 top-ranked genes identified in genome-wide studies. Interestingly,

> several proteins from that network appear to be under control of the stimulants methylphenidate and amphetamine that are used to treat ADHD symptoms. Both stimulants have been shown to stimulate neurite outgrowth and directly or indirectly regulate the expression

and/or function of several genes/proteins involved in neurite outgrowth (p. 369).

Current research has extended this view by combining use of standard single-nucleotide polymorphism (SNP) data on common variant genes with data on a group of deletions or duplications of multiple rare variants. This combined approach seems to offer a more promising route to understanding the genetic complexity of ADHD (Stergiakouli, et al., 2012; Williams, et al., 2012; Rucker & McGuffin, 2012).

In addition to the direct influences of genetic factors on development of ADHD, a number of other pre-natal, perinatal and other environmental factors have been investigated as possible contributing factors. Controlled studies of dietary factors and television watching have not been found to increase the risk for ADHD, but exposure to toxic substances such as lead, maternal cigarette smoking, maternal alcohol abuse or dependence, and chemical PCBs have been shown to increase risk of ADHD. Children whose mothers abused alcohol during pregnancy have double the risk of developing ADHD; those whose mothers were alcohol dependent during pregnancy were three times more likely to have ADHD (Banerjee, et al., 2007).

Some pregnancy-related complications such as toxemia or eclampsia, poor maternal health, long duration of labor, and low birth weight ($\leq$ 2500 grams) have also been identified as increasing risk for ADHD. Examination of individuals born prematurely with very low birth weight has shown that the critical variable is not simply low birth weight, but intrauterine growth retardation which is usually associated with very low birth weight and small gestational age. There are limited data on how long impairments associated with these factors are likely to persist, but in a study of young adults with low birth weight, Strang-Karlsson, et al. (2008) showed that intrauterine growth retardation, as reflected by small for gestational age status in very low birth weight individuals, confers increased risk for impairments of executive function, emotional instability and ADHD. A population-based study of adults with ADHD showed that low birth weight, preterm birth and low Apgar scores increase the risk of ADHD, persisting up to 40 years after birth (Halmoy, et al., 2012)

Psychosocial adversity is another factor which may increase risk of ADHD or increased severity of ADHD symptoms. The classic study by Rutter, et al. (1975) demonstrated that six risk factors within a family correlated significantly with psychiatric disability in children: a) severe marital discord; b) low social class; c) large family size; d) paternal criminality; e) maternal mental disorder;

and f) foster placement. In Rutter's analysis, no one of these variables specifically impaired development, but each one added increased substantially the net negative effect on the children. Neglect, abuse and emotional trauma also have been shown significantly to increase likelihood of ADHD, Oppositional Defiant Disorder, and post-traumatic stress disorder (Famularo, et al., 1992).

An integrative perspective has been offered by Nigg, et al. (2010). They proposed that a more adequate understanding of the etiology of ADHD might be found in study of gene-by-environment interactions. They note that "environment" may refer to any biological or psychosocial experience that impinges on the child, many of which represent an aggregation of multiple processes and mechanisms, and most of which have not been systematically studied in ADHD. These authors also note that a developmental view of ADHD requires assessment of how environmental factors may impact the ADHD symptoms over time, sometimes conferring protection and in other instances increasing vulnerability and impairment. Such developmental influences are likely to be mediated by complex interactions between children and caregivers as well as by the unfolding and consolidation of neural networks that develop gradually under direction of genetic programming and response to expected or unusual environments.

Expanding Directions of Neuroscience Research in ADHD

This chapter reflects the rapid expansion of research on ADHD from exclusive focus on problems with neural transmission in the prefrontal cortex and very basic cognitive operations to studies of multiple neuronal systems throughout the brain which support more complex and integrative higher-cortical functions. Cortese and colleagues (2012) reviewed 55 fMRI studies which provide a foundation for a systems neuroscience approach to ADHD. This expanding research perspective offers promise for much greater understanding of the neural processes which underlie the complex cognitive impairments described in the new model of ADHD described in this book.

4

HOW THE NEW MODEL CHANGES
ASSESSMENT OF ADHD IN
CHILDREN AND ADULTS

The new paradigm for ADHD described in this book has significant implications for how this disorder should be assessed, diagnosed and treated. This broader phenotype is comprised of a wider range of cognitive impairments than is encompassed by current DSM diagnostic criteria. As was mentioned in Chapter 2, most individuals assessed with measures of ADHD impairments built on the new model of the disorder will also meet DSM-IV diagnostic criteria for ADHD. For them, the proposed model recognizes the wider range of their existing impairments beyond those listed among current criteria. However, there are some who suffer significant impairments from this syndrome who would not qualify for an ADHD diagnosis under current DSM-IV diagnostic criteria.

Age of Onset

One possible impediment to diagnosis of ADHD under current criteria is the assumption that a diagnosis of ADHD requires that the individual manifested some symptoms of this disorder in early childhood. This assumption is based upon the old model of ADHD and the stipulation of DSM-IV that at least some symptoms of ADHD must have been noticeable in the individual by age seven years. As noted in Chapter 1, within the new model it is understood that some individuals suffering from this disorder do not manifest their ADHD symptoms until they meet the challenges of adolescence or adulthood. This has important implications for assessment.

Barkley (2010) has described how that stipulation for early age of onset was included in the DSM-IV criteria for ADHD without any basis in empirical data. In fact, the stipulation was contradicted by data from the field study on which the DSM-IV diagnostic criteria were based. Members of the research team that designed and completed that field study (Applegate, et al., 1997) themselves questioned the validity of the stipulation and noted that while 82%

of children diagnosed with the combined subtype of ADHD met that early onset criterion, 43% of the children diagnosed with predominantly inattentive subtype did not meet the criterion for onset of some symptoms before the age of seven years. In 1997 Barkley and Biederman reviewed research on this matter and urged that either the age of onset criterion should be abandoned altogether or interpreted as occurring sometime in childhood, broadly construed.

The newest version of the Diagnostic and Statistical Manual for Psychiatric Disorders, the DSM-V, reflects a compromise in establishing 12 years as the age of onset.

To assess the possible impact of using an age of onset of 12 years rather than 7 years as a criterion for ADHD, Polanczyk, et al. (2010) assessed a birth cohort of over 2,000 British children prospectively at age 7 years and again at age 12 years. They found that children identified at age 12 years but not at 7 years as having ADHD symptoms did not differ significantly from children recognized as having ADHD symptoms noticeable before age 7 years.

The inadequacy of the seven-year age of onset criterion has also been demonstrated in adults. Faraone, et al. (2006d) compared 127 adults who met full DSM-IV diagnostic criteria for ADHD, including the seven-year age of onset criterion, with a sample of 79 adults who met all of the DSM-IV diagnostic criteria for ADHD except for that age of onset criterion. They found that those identified as having late onset ADHD did not differ significantly in patterns of functional impairment, number of blood relatives having ADHD or levels of comorbid psychiatric disorder. A subsequent report from the same research team (Faraone, et al., 2006a) added the finding that similar neuropsychological impairments were found in both early and late onset groups.

Taken together, available data suggest that lack of evidence of ADHD symptoms during childhood should not be taken as an impediment to ADHD diagnosis for individuals whose symptoms of ADHD do not become apparent until adolescence. Conceptually, given the new model, it would seem that requiring any specific age of onset for ADHD makes little sense.

Specific Symptoms and Cutoffs for Diagnosis

In 2004 McGough and Barkley pointed out that there had been little discussion about the validity of diagnostic criteria for ADHD in adults. They noted that the DSM-IV criteria for ADHD were developed for assessment of children and were based upon a field trial of 380 clinically referred children aged 4 to 17 years. Those DSM-IV criteria were written to describe problems found in children, were never tested on adults, and include a number of items like "runs and climbs excessively" and "has difficulty playing quietly" that are simply not appropriate for adults. Despite these limitations, as mentioned earlier, those DSM-IV criteria, especially the inattention criteria, remain useful, though not sufficient, for assessing ADHD in adults, except for the DSM-IV requirement that at least six of the nine symptoms of inattention and/or hyperactivity-impulsivity be present.

The "at least six of nine" rule may be useful in assessing children in the 4 to 17 year age range, but it has been shown to be excessively stringent for assessing adults. This is a critical shortcoming of the DSM-IV. Murphy and Barkley (1996) demonstrated that use of the six of nine rule with adults sets the cutoff for diagnosis at the ninety-ninth percentile, 2.5 to 3 standard deviations above the mean, so that only the most impaired 1% of adults would be found to qualify for an ADHD diagnosis. This is in contrast to the usual method used for the cutoff in children, i.e. setting the cutoff at the ninety-third percentile so that the most impaired 7% are considered eligible for diagnosis. Murphy and Barkley reported that setting the cutoff at four inattentive or five hyperactive-impulsive symptoms would identify the most impaired 7% of individuals in the 17 to 29 year age group. Corresponding cutoffs for those in the 30 to 49 year age group would be three and four symptoms while the cutoff could be dropped to two and three symptoms for identification of those 50 years or older whose symptoms meet or exceed the ninety-third percentile. In the DSM-V the cutoff for adults is four symptoms and six symptoms for those 17 years and under.

Alternative Ratings of ADHD Symptoms

More recently, studies of possible alternative diagnostic criteria for ADHD in adults have been tested and reported by Barkley, Murphy and Fischer (2008), by Biederman, et al. (2008c), by Faraone, Biederman and Spencer (2010) and by Kessler, et al. (2010). Each of these studies utilized some symptoms from the DSM-IV diagnostic criteria for ADHD, but added additional symptoms related to other impairments of EF, most of which were taken from various versions of a 89 to 100-item Current Behavior Scale (CBS), a rating scale developed by Barkley. This rating scale includes a wide variety of behaviorally defined EF impairments. A more refined version of Barkley's scale, along with the history and statistics of its development was published in 2011.

In 2008 Barkley, Murphy and Fischer summarized their research from several studies to report a list of nine symptoms which best differentiated adults with ADHD from adults in a community control sample and a clinical control sample. Those items marked as (DSM) are from the DSM-IV and those marked (EF) were derived from Barkley's scale:

- Is often easily distracted by extraneous stimuli (DSM-IV) or irrelevant thoughts (EF)
- Often makes decisions impulsively (EF)
- Often has difficulty stopping his or her activities or behavior when he or she should do so (EF)
- Often starts a project or task without reading or listening to directions carefully (EF)
- Often shows poor follow-through on promises or commitments he or she may make to others (EF)
- Often has trouble doing things in their proper order or sequence (EF)
- Often more likely to drive a motor vehicle much faster than others (excessive speeding) [or, alternatively for those without driving experience, often has difficulty engaging in leisure activities or doing fun things quietly] (EF)
- Often has difficulty sustaining attention in tasks or play activities (DSM)
- Often has difficulty organizing tasks and activities (DSM) (p. 188).

Based on data from their studies, Barkley, Murphy and Fischer (2008) reported that if these nine symptoms were to be used for assessing adults with ADHD and six of the nine were taken as the cutoff, only 1% of the community control group would be falsely identified as having ADHD. They found that almost 47% of their clinical control group would meet the same cutoff, but this might be taken to suggest that many of their clinical control group might be considered to have ADHD in addition to other psychiatric problems that had brought them to the clinic (p. 191).

A similar abbreviated list of ADHD symptoms was identified by Biederman, et al. (2008c) after they administered Barkley's 99-item CBS of behaviorally defined executive function deficits to a different sample of 200 adults diagnosed with ADHD. Utilizing factor analysis, these researchers identified eight items, (each with a factor loading of over 0.70) that together explained 31% of the variance. These items included:

- Have trouble planning ahead or preparing for upcoming events
- Can't seem to accomplish goals I set for myself
- Can't seem to hold in mind things I need to remember to do
- Easily frustrated

- Have difficulty motivating myself to stick with my work and get it done
- Have trouble doing what I tell myself I ought to do
- Lack self-discipline
- Have trouble organizing my thoughts.

Analysis of results from this study indicated that these 8 items derived from the CBS were highly correlated with the 99 items of the total scale and were equally as predictive of impaired functional outcomes as the longer form of the CBS. Comparison of the short symptom lists developed by Biederman and Barkley indicates that the Biederman list includes items related to planning and starting tasks, utilizing working memory, regulating emotion, and self-motivating that fit closely to the model described in Chapter 1 of this book; the Barkley short-list covers some, but not as many of the affected domains of executive functioning.

Faraone, Biederman and Spencer (2010) tested the set of nine symptoms proposed by the Barkley group, as shown above, against two alternative diagnostic algorithms based on symptoms from the CBS self-report measure developed by Barkley. Their sample included 206 adults carefully diagnosed with ADHD and 164 adults who did not meet DSM-IV diagnostic criteria. They tested each of three diagnostic algorithms with their sample: the Barkley 9-item algorithm, the best 9-item algorithm derived from their sample using the CBS, and the best 18-item algorithm derived from their CBS data. Their statistical analysis of the data from the CBS administered to their sample identified the following 18 items as having the best odds ratio for predicting current ADHD:

- Prone to daydreaming
- Lacks self-discipline
- Trouble doing what I tell myself
- Can't defer gratifying things
- Trouble thinking clearly
- Can't hold things in memory
- Difficulty persisting in uninteresting tasks
- Makes decisions impulsively
- Trouble organizing thoughts
- Difficulty explaining things
- Forgets point while talking
- Can't get to the point
- Difficulty doing things in order

- Can't remember things read/heard
- Difficulty staying with tasks
- Trouble planning ahead
- Starts project without directions
- Takes shortcuts with work.

Results from a receiver operating analysis showed that their best 9-item and best 18-item algorithms, despite some differences, were no more efficient at distinguishing adults with ADHD from adults without ADHD than was Barkley's 9-item algorithm. This similarity in diagnostic efficiency does not establish superior utility of any of these three algorithms for clinical diagnosis. Each may be equally efficient in differentiating individuals with ADHD from controls, but there are additional criteria that should be considered in assessing diagnostic utility. For example, some items on one of the scales may make it sensitive to a range of impairments not picked up by another equally efficient scale for making the diagnosis.

Kessler, et al. (2010) extended the work of Barkley, et al. (2008) and Faraone, et al. (2010) by assessing two national community samples of adults screened for ADHD; this national sample included 345 adults. That study confirmed earlier findings that attention symptoms of ADHD in childhood were significantly more persistent into adulthood than were childhood hyperactivity symptoms. However, its most important finding was that "EF problems are consistently important predictors of adult clinical diagnoses of ADHD" and that:

> none of the adult EF symptoms had significant comorbidity with other classes of DSM-IV disorders after controlling for the general gradient of adult ADHD... [which] suggests that EF symptoms are those most specifically differentiating adult ADHD from other adult DSM disorders" (p. 1175).

Kessler, et al. (2010) noted that their results are consistent with those of Barkley and Faraone in finding that a variety of symptoms of EF impairment not included in the DSM are more effective in distinguishing adults with ADHD from controls than are ADHD symptoms in the DSM-IV. They also noted that their results were consistent with other evidence that "EF problems are evident in virtually all adults with ADHD" (p. 1175).

Taken together, lists of symptoms of ADHD shown in these studies by Barkley, by Biederman, and by Kessler with their colleagues to be most effective in differentiating adults with ADHD from controls map very well onto the six clusters of the new model of ADHD described in Chapter 2.

Normed Symptom Rating Scales for ADHD-Related Impairments of Executive Functions

Currently three normed rating scales have been published for assessing in adults executive function impairments such as are included in the model described in Chapter 1: one by Brown (1996), one by Roth, Isquith and Gioia (2005), and another by Barkley (2011a).

The Brown ADD Rating Scale for Adults (BADDS) (Brown, 1996) queries 40 items related to five of the six clusters of the new model of ADHD presented in Chapter 2: organizing, prioritizing and activating to work; focusing, sustaining and shifting attention to tasks; regulating alertness, sustaining effort and processing speed; managing frustration and modulating emotions; and utilizing working memory and accessing recall. This scale was normed on 142 adults diagnosed in clinical interviews using DSM diagnostic criteria for ADHD compared with 143 controls matched for age and socioeconomic status. This scale demonstrated significant differences between adults diagnosed with ADHD and matched controls and is designed to indicate probability that the individual will meet diagnostic criteria for ADHD while also profiling relative strengths and weaknesses in each cluster of executive functions assessed.

The Behavior Rating Inventory of Executive Function: Adult Version (Roth, et al., 2005), was developed as an extension of the Behavior Rating Inventory of Executive Function (BRIEF) parent and teacher rating scales for use with children; these are discussed below. It is a 75-item self-report form and an informant report form designed for use with adults aged 18 to 90 years. This scale elicits data to assess for nine clusters of executive functions: inhibit, shift, emotional control, self-monitor, initiate, working memory, plan/organize, task monitor, and organization of materials.

The Behavior Rating Inventory of Executive Function: Adult Version (BRIEF-A) was standardized on a sample of 1050 adults with various impairments and was then administered to a wide variety of diagnostic groups including patients diagnosed with Alzheimer's Disease and Mild Cognitive Impairment, Multiple Sclerosis, Traumatic Brain Injury, Epilepsy, and ADHD. However, the manual for the BRIEF-A stipulates that:

> Although the BRIEF-A profiles offer a view of executive function in context, the BRIEF-A is not intended as a tool for independently diagnosing specific disorders such as ADHD... the executive function

profiles are not sufficiently specific for a diagnosis of these disorders (Roth, et al., 2005, p. 87).

This caution is appropriate since the norming sample included only 43 adults with ADHD, some of whom were medicated while others were not.

The Barkley Deficits in Executive Functioning Scale (BDEFS) is a revised version of the 99-item Barkley Scale referred to earlier in this section (Barkley, 2011a, BDEFS). This 89-item rating scale for adults aged 18 to 70+ elicits data to assess for impairments in the following executive functions: self-management to time; self-organization; self-restraint; self-motivation; and self-regulation of emotion. It offers both long and short forms for self-report and for other-report. The BDEFS was standardized on more than 1,200 individuals in six age groups representative of the U.S. population. Administration of this scale to adults diagnosed with ADHD in the UMass study by Barkley and Murphy indicated that 89% to 98% of the adults with ADHD placed in the clinically significant range on the BDEFS compared to 8% to 11% of their community control sample. Barkley argued that the extremely high scores obtained on the BDEFS by adults diagnosed clinically with ADHD support the notion that "EF and ADHD are two views or names for the same common single construct" (2011a, p. 85). This view is discussed in Chapter 2.

Four currently published rating scales are designed for specific and detailed assessment of executive function impairments associated with the new model in children and adolescents: the Brown ADD Scales (BADDS), the Behavior Rating Inventory of Executive Function (BRIEF), the Barkley Deficits in Executive Functioning Scale: Children and Adolescents (BDEFS-CA), and the Comprehensive Inventory of Executive Functions (CEFI). All four of these instruments assess for a wider range of executive function impairments than is included in the DSM diagnostic criteria. All four also include items related to most of the clusters of the new model of ADHD described in Chapter 2. Each rating scale has its own strengths and limitations in style, format of reports, specific items queried, size of normative and clinical samples, and cost.

The Brown ADD Scales for Children aged three to seven years and eight to twelve years (Brown, 2001) assess symptoms of impairment in each of the six clusters of EF impairments described in Chapter 2; the Brown ADD Scales for Adolescents (Brown, 1996) assess for the first five clusters of those executive functions. The Brown Scales were developed from clinical studies of children and adolescents who fully met DSM diagnostic criteria for ADHD.

The Brown Scales were normed on a clinical sample of 208 children aged 3 to 12 years who had been diagnosed with ADHD by experienced psychologists using clinical interviews with children and parents, teacher reports and standardized psychoeducational testing. These were compared with a matched national standardization sample of 210 children representative of the U.S. population stratified for race, ethnicity and parent education level within each of four age group bands. These scales measure ADHD-related executive function impairments in the following six domains described with the diagram in Chapter 1:

1   Organizing, prioritizing and activating to work

2   Focusing, sustaining and shifting attention to tasks

3   Regulating alertness, sustaining effort and processing speed

4   Managing frustration and modulating emotions

5   Utilizing working memory and accessing recall

6   Monitoring and self-regulating action.

Data from the standardization of the Brown ADD Rating Scales for Children indicated that these rating scales discriminate effectively between children diagnosed with ADHD by DSM-IV criteria and matched controls when assessed by the parent report, teacher report or self-report versions.

The Brown ADD Scales for Adolescents offer a 40-item format for self-report by 12- to 18-year-olds and by their parents. (Brown, 1996, 2001). Those rating scales assess impairments in Clusters 1 through 5 of the model of ADHD presented in Chapter 2. The adolescent scales were normed on a sample of 191 students diagnosed with ADHD in three age groups between ages 12 and 18 years compared to 190 students without ADHD matched for age, gender and socioeconomic status. These scales differentiated significantly between those with ADHD and the matched controls.

The Behavior Rating Inventory of Executive Function (Gioia, et al., 2000) offers parent and teacher forms to assess symptoms of executive function impairment in children aged 2.5 to 5.11 years and 5 to 18 years; the BRIEF also offers a self-report version for adolescents 11 to 18 years. Items of the BRIEF are organized around two indexes: Behavioral Regulation and Metacognition. These indexes are based on subscales to assess the child's perceived ability to:

1   Inhibit: control impulses, appropriately stop behavior at the proper time

2   Shift: move freely from one situation or activity as the situation demands

3   Emotional Control: modulate emotional responses appropriately

4   Initiate: begin a task or activity; independently generate ideas

5   Working Memory: hold information in mind to complete a task or stick with an activity

6   Plan/Organize: anticipate future events, set goals, carry out tasks in systematic manner

7   Organization of Materials: keep workspace and materials in an orderly manner

8   Monitor: check work, assess performance during or after finishing a task.

Norms are provided to compare the child being evaluated with others of comparable age and gender. The BRIEF was based on data from samples of children and adolescents from a wide mix of diagnostic groups including ADHD, autism spectrum disorders, anxiety and depressive disorders, and insulin-dependent diabetes. The BRIEF parent form was normed on 53 children with ADHD versus 77 matched controls; the BRIEF teacher form was normed on 120 children with ADHD versus 101 matched controls. The Adolescent Self-Report Form of the BRIEF was normed on 127 adolescents with ADHD versus 127 matched controls. The manual for the BRIEF version for children indicates that two subscales on both parent and teacher forms exhibit adequate predictive validity, sensitivity and specificity to differentiate between children with ADHD of the combined or predominantly inattentive types and those with no clinical diagnosis. In contrast, the manual for the BRIEF-SR form for adolescent self-report indicates that this rating scale "is not intended as a tool for independently diagnosing specific disorders such as ADHD" (Guy, et al., 2004, p. 77).

The Barkley Deficits in Executive Functioning Scale for Children and Adolescents (BDEFS-CA) (Barkley, 2012b) is a downward extension of the Barkley Deficits in Executive Functioning Scale for Adults discussed above. Its 70 items were designed to assess for executive function impairments in children and adolescents aged 6 to 17 years. Categories assessed include:

•   Self-management to time
•   Self-organization

- Self-restraint
- Self-motivation
- Self-regulation of emotion.

The BDEFS-CA was normed on a nationally representative sample of more than 1,900 parents in the U.S. who had children between the ages of 6 and 17 years. This is a very large and well-designed sample of parents for collection of normative data, but the scale has several important limitations. Its ADHD-EF index score was based solely on analysis of parents' responses to a computerized version of the BDEFS-CA and of the versions of the DSM-IV diagnostic criteria for ADHD. There were no face-to-face clinical assessments of the actual children or adolescents being rated and no opportunity to meet face-to-face with parents to assess and clarify their understanding of the questions they were being asked and the specific basis for their ratings. Moreover, this scale does not have additional versions for teacher report or for self-report, even for older children and adolescents. These are significant limitations for a scale intended for clinical use.

The Comprehensive Executive Function Inventory (CEFI) (Naglieri & Goldstein, 2013) is a 100-item rating scale designed to assess executive functions in children and adolescents aged 5 to 18 years. Categories assessed include:

- Attention
- Emotion Regulation
- Flexibility
- Inhibitory Control
- Initiation
- Organization
- Planning
- Self-Monitoring
- Working Memory.

The CEFI offers parent, teacher and self-report formats that have been normed on three clinical groups evaluated face-to-face by a licensed clinician: 172 diagnosed with ADHD; 51 diagnosed with Autistic Spectrum Disorder; 37 diagnosed with mood disorders; and 48 diagnosed with a specific learning disorder. These data were compared with data from a representative sample from the general population of children and adolescents in the U.S. utilizing parent, teacher and, for those 12 years and over, self-report. The CEFI offers several types of reports which indicate specific areas of strengths or weaknesses in executive functions when compared with a nationally standardized comparison group. It is not specifically set up to identify children with ADHD impairments. The recommended mode of administration for the CEFI is for the individual rater to complete the form independently with minimal involvement from the examiner. This mode may be problematic because it does not provide ample opportunity for the evaluator to be certain that the rater understands the questions being asked.

Despite differences between these three rating scales for adults and the four rating scales for children and adolescents, these normed measures provide considerable evidence that a wide range of EF impairments similar to those included in the new model described in this book can be identified in individuals with ADHD across a wide range of age groups. These studies also demonstrate that significantly higher levels of impairments related to the new model of ADHD as impaired executive function are found in individuals with ADHD of all ages, when compared with matched controls from the general population.

While no rating scale should be considered to be, in itself, an adequate basis for making or withholding a diagnosis of ADHD, these scales do provide a systematic and efficient way to screen and assess for the wide range of executive function impairments that characterize the new model of ADHD described in this book. When combined with data from a careful clinical assessment interview and collaborative data, these scales can be quite useful in helping to determine whether a given individual suffers from ADHD and which specific executive functions are most impaired.

Rating Scales versus Neuropsychological Tests

There has been conflict in the field as to how executive function impairments of ADHD should be assessed in individuals to determine whether that diagnosis is appropriate. In 2006 Brown described two conflicting views of how executive function impairments are related to ADHD. One of these views argues that some, but not all individuals who meet DSM-IV diagnostic criteria for ADHD suffer from significant impairments of executive function. The alternative view asserts that all individuals with ADHD suffer from significant impairments of executive function, and that ADHD essentially is a developmental impairment of executive functions. Each of these conflicting viewpoints rests upon a very different understanding of the nature of executive functions and how these functions should be assessed.

In one of these conflicting views, executive functions are defined as cognitive functions measured by neuropsychological tests identified in the neuropsychological literature as "tests of executive function." Most of these neuropsychological tests were originally developed by neuropsychologists to evaluate for frontal lobe impairments from stroke, schizophrenia, or traumatic brain injury. Examples include the Wisconsin Card Sort (Heaton, 1981), the Rey–Osterreith (Waber & Holmes, 1985), the Tower of Hanoi/London (Shallice, 1982) and others. One involves sorting cards with differing patterns into categories; another requires copying a complex figure drawing and then drawing it again depending on recall. The third asks the participant to rearrange colored beads on pegs in as few moves as possible to match a target design. These measures are presumed to test for memory, planning, holding and shifting set, etc., but their applicability to complex activities of daily life is highly questionable.

Efforts to assess these executive functions in individuals with ADHD using these instruments have produced mixed results. Willcutt, et al. (2005) reported a meta-analysis of 83 studies that administered neuropsychological "tests of executive function" to groups of children and adolescents with (N=3,734) and without (2,969) ADHD. Their analysis indicated that individuals with ADHD exhibited significant impairment on measures of response inhibition, vigilance, working memory, and planning. Effect sizes from the meta-analysis of these studies were generally in the medium range (0.46–0.69). Willcutt's group concluded that while their results "clearly indicate that EF weaknesses are associated with ADHD, they do not support the hypothesis that EF deficits are the single necessary and sufficient cause of ADHD in all individuals with the disorder" (Willcutt, et al. p. 1342).

Neuropsychological "tests of EF" are no more effective for assessing ADHD in adults than in children. Hervey, Epstein and Curry (2004) reported a meta-analysis of 33 studies of neuropsychological "tests of executive function" administered to adults with ADHD; results were more consistent with the notion of "impairment in brain functioning as a whole, where deficits in processing speed and the ability to contend with more complex processing are revealed" (p. 497).

Data from both children and adults point to one fact: If executive function impairment is defined as getting very low scores on such neuropsychological tests, many, but not even a majority of those with ADHD show significant impairment. If such "tests of EF" are taken as a valid measure of who is impaired in executive functioning, only about 30% of those diagnosed with ADHD appear to have significant executive function impairments. A review of neuropsychological function in adults with ADHD by Seidman, et al. (2004) noted that most neuropsychological tests of executive function lack negative predictive power, i.e. normal scores on such tests cannot rule out an ADHD diagnosis. This is because "a substantial proportion of children and adults with ADHD do not show abnormalities on neuropsychological tests" (p. 275).

Barkley (1997, 2006) and Brown (2000a, 2005a) have proposed slightly differing versions of an alternative view of how ADHD and executive function impairments are related. They argue that 100% of those diagnosed with ADHD suffer from executive function impairments and that the essence of ADHD is developmental impairment of executive functions.

The difference between the point of view presented by Barkley and Brown and that of Willcutt and others rests on conflicting understandings of how impairments of executive functions are to be measured. Barkley and Brown have proposed views similar to those of Rabbitt (1997) and Burgess (1997) who argue that neuropsychological tests cannot adequately measure an individual's impairments in executive functions because "an essential property of all 'executive function' is that, by its very nature, it involves the simultaneous management of a variety of different functional processes" (Rabbitt, 1997, p. 14).

The usual "isolate the variable and test it" approach that underlies neuropsychological tests simply cannot encompass the complex, interactive, situationally-variable nature of executive functions. Put another way, if seeking a new conductor for a symphony orchestra, one could not adequately evaluate candidates simply by having them rhythmically wave their arms or hum bars of a specific instrument's part in a section of a particular symphony. The ability to integrate and guide a large group of musicians through the performance of diverse musical pieces simply cannot be assessed in detachment from the actual orchestra. One would need to evaluate the candidate's ability to interact dynamically with the whole group of musicians as they play a variety of complex and challenging pieces. A person's ability to perform the complex self-managed tasks of daily life, such as are identified in the symptom lists in the preceding section of this chapter, can be assessed much more adequately by eliciting systematic self-report about daily functioning in managing various tasks than by neuropsychological "tests of EF."

Barkley (2011) has provided a thoughtful description of executive function and the relative usefulness of neuropsychological "tests of EF" versus self-report rating scales that raise queries about patterns of EF in daily life. He argues that "tests of EF" assess only very brief samples of behavior, typically over time frames of just 5 to 30 minutes and presume to extrapolate to assess longer term patterns of functioning. Barkley points out that rating scales can raise queries over patterns of behavior across weeks or months, thus eliciting data regarding longer term patterns of functioning. He also notes that EF tests simply do not assess important aspects of EF such as self-motivation, awareness of context, ability to sustain effort over time, etc.

Essentially, Barkley argues that neuropsychological tests of EF lack ecological validity; they do not adequately predict patterns of self-management in the realities of daily life: "they are very poor at capturing the higher adaptive, tactical and strategic levels of EF as they are deployed in daily adaptive functioning, human interactions, and social cooperative and reciprocal activities that play out over much longer spans of time (days, weeks, months and years)" (2011, p. 19).

An illustration of this discrepancy between neuropsychological "tests of EF" and self-management tasks of everyday life was provided by Shallice and Burgess (1991) whose study demonstrated that patients with frontal lobe damage were unable to perform adequately everyday shopping errands that require planning and multi-tasking, even though they achieved average or well above average scores on traditional neuropsychological tests of language, memory, perception and "executive functions".

Barkley's argument (2011, 2012b) that EF rating scales are far superior to neuropsychological tests of EF for assessment of impairments in major domains of daily life is supported by findings of a study in which Barkley and Murphy (2010) compared neuropsychological tests of EF versus self-reported rating scale data for predicting occupational impairments in a sample of adults with ADHD versus clinical and community controls. Results indicated that self-report rating scales were significantly more effectively predictive of impairment in 11 measures of occupational adjustment.

A study by Biederman and colleagues (2008b) provides additional support for the superiority of self-report rating scale data for assessing impairments of EF such as are included in the model described in Chapter 2. In a sample of 194 adults diagnosed with ADHD, Biederman's study compared self-report ratings of EF with data from assessments using a battery of neuropsychological tests of EF. Results showed just modest overlap between the two measures. Neuropsychological tests identified primarily participants with lower IQ and achievement test scores. Self-report measures of EF impairment identified individuals with higher levels of ADHD symptoms, psychiatric comorbidity and interpersonal deficits.

Consideration of the theoretical arguments and the data described above, leads to the conclusion that self-report rating scales of EF impairment associated with ADHD should be included routinely in assessment of patients for impairments of ADHD as described in our new model. Neuropsychological tests of executive functions are not ecologically valid, not readily accessible to many patients, are quite expensive, and are generally not useful in assessment for ADHD. They may, however, be useful for assessing brain damage associated with stroke, dementia, traumatic brain injuries, etc.

The Clinical Interview

The most sensitive instrument for assessment of ADHD is a semi-structured clinical interview conducted by a skilled clinician familiar with the characteristics and developmental course of ADHD who is also able to differentiate ADHD from other psychiatric disorders. In this interview the clinician follows a semi-structured format to inquire about the history and nature of the patient's current functioning and life situation as well as his or her earlier life experiences, noting the presence or absence of patterns of impairment in school, work, family life and social relationships.

An adequate initial interview to assess for ADHD usually requires at least two hours. During this session the clinician asks the patient and any accompanying family members about what brought them to seek evaluation for ADHD and what they see as their current adaptive strengths and weaknesses, what they do for fun, and what they struggle with in daily life. The clinician inquires about the patient's current work and living situation, asks for brief descriptions of members of the patient's family and others important in the patient's life. History of school achievement and any struggles with particular subjects is important, as is inquiry about relationships with peers, family members, teachers, employers and friends.

It can be useful to inquire about any blood relatives, living or dead, who have struggled with similar or related learning, emotional or behavioral problems. This may yield clues about possible comorbid problems for which the patient may be at elevated risk. It is also important to query sleep and eating habits and well as health history, focusing on any medical or developmental problems and any medications or procedures used to treat them. Inquiry should also include current mood patterns, and any significant problems with anxiety, depression, or behavior as well as any previous mental health evaluations or treatment.

Screening for Possible Comorbid Disorders

Given the high rate of co-existing disorders found among persons with ADHD, an initial evaluation interview should also include screening for possible comorbid disorders. The clinician should ask about the individual's history of problems with mood, anxiety, substance abuse, learning problems, behavioral difficulties, etc. Outlines for inquiry about possible comorbid disorders are included in the Brown ADHD diagnostic forms for adults (1996) and for children and adolescents (2001). More information about comorbidity of other disorders with ADHD is provided in Chapter 6.

After the clinician has taken an adequate initial history, an age-appropriate rating scale for executive function impairments associated with ADHD should be administered to elicit self-report from the patient and, if possible, at least one other person who knows that person well and is willing and able to offer impressions of the patient in response to specific items read from the rating scale, after the identified patient has first given their own response.

Following administration of the self-report rating scale, the patient and collateral should be queried on each of the current diagnostic criteria for ADHD in the canonical diagnostic manual, e.g. DSM-IV or DSM-V.

Additional Measures for the Clinical Interview

Upon completion of the patient history, rating scale and formal diagnostic criteria, it can be useful for the clinician to administer two brief measures of auditory working memory. Although these measures are not essential to making a diagnosis of ADHD, they can elicit a brief sample of the patient's working memory function that can be compared with standardized norms and the patient's general cognitive ability. Two inexpensive standardized measures that can be administered by any clinician in less than ten minutes are often helpful in assessment for ADHD. The digit span assesses working memory for numbers; the story memory test helps to measure working memory for auditory verbal narrative. Many individuals with ADHD demonstrate significant weakness in one or both of these measures relative to their general verbal intelligence.

In the digit span test the individual is asked to listen to a string of numbers spoken by the examiner and then repeat those numbers back to the evaluator in the same order. After a series of increasingly long digit strings, the person is once again started on short strings of digits and asked to repeat each string back to the examiner in reverse order. Many, but not all individuals with ADHD demonstrate weakness on the digit span test relative to their overall cognitive abilities (Wechsler, 1997a, 2003).

Also useful is the story memory subtest included in the Children's Memory Scale (Cohen, 1997) for children aged 5 to 16 years or the Logical Memory Subtest of the Wechsler Memory Scale (Wechsler, 1997b) for individuals aged 16 years or more. These tests offer two brief, developmentally appropriate stories, each about one paragraph in length, for each age group. One story is read by the evaluator to the participant who is then asked to repeat it back to the evaluator in words as close as possible to the words just read. A second story is then read and repeated back in the same way. After a delay during which a different activity is done, the participant is asked to repeat each of the stories once again.

In a large study of adolescents and adults diagnosed with ADHD, Quinlan and Brown (2003) showed that over two-thirds of participants demonstrated significant weakness of working memory, relative to their verbal comprehension ability, for two simple stories each containing just 25 word units. Such a difference is found in less than 16% of the general population.

Brown (2001) reported similar findings for children aged 8 to 12 years and for adolescents aged 13 to 19 years using stories from the Children's Memory Scale and/or the WMS-III. Additional evidence of impairments of most individuals with ADHD on these simple auditory verbal memory measures was reported in a study of high IQ adults by Brown, Reichel and Quinlan (2009) and a study of high IQ children and adolescents by the same research team (Brown, et al., 2011c).

Limitations of "Objective" Measures

Often clinicians, patients and their families seek more "objective" measures to assess for ADHD. These include computerized measures which typically ask the patient to respond to intermittent visual stimuli presented on a computer screen or to auditory stimuli presented intermittently via a recording. From patterns of speed and accuracy in responding, the computer estimates the likelihood of an ADHD diagnosis for the patient. Such tests may appear to be more "objective" because they are administered by a computer, but these measures suffer from the same limitations as the neuropsychological "tests of EF" discussed above.

Other procedures sometimes used for assessment of ADHD include electroencephalograms, and SPECT scans. Research on assessment of ADHD over the past 15 years has provided little basis on which to challenge the statement on these matters in the treatment guidelines for ADHD published by the American Academy of Child and Adolescent Psychiatry in 1997:

> There are insufficient data to support the usefulness of computerized EEG measures (neurometrics or brain mapping), event-related potentials, or neuroimaging as clinical tools, though they have promise in research. Computerized tests of attention and vigilance (CPTs) generally are not useful in diagnosis because they suffer

from low specificity and sensitivity. They are useful, however, as research tools (p. 87S).

Huang-Pollock, et al. (2012) did a meta-analysis of 47 studies of CPT performance. Their results indicated that, when corrected for sampling bias, estimates were moderately sized ranging from 0.37 for reaction times to 0.62 for omissions. When additional correction was made for publication bias, reaction time dropped to 0.29. They concluded "our meta-analytic results provide clear evidence that measurement unreliability accounts for a significant proportion of the variability in effect sizes (ranging from 32% to 100% in the current review)" (p. 6). They recommend that CPTs should not be used in a clinical manner to assist in the diagnosis or treatment monitoring of ADHD.

Imaging studies, at present, are also limited in their usefulness for assessment of ADHD. In a review addressing the question of whether neuroimaging of the brain can be useful in clinical assessment of ADHD, neuroimaging researcher Bush (2008) wrote:

> Currently there are no accepted uses for imaging in diagnosing ADHD.... Using brain imaging to study the pathophysiology of ADHD is intrinsically important, but it is another matter to try to translate that type of research (which can be done with group-averaged brain data) into the development of a clinically useful diagnostic imaging test for ADHD [with] the capability to reliably identify unique imaging biomarkers of ADHD in single subjects.... It must be remembered that colorful brain images can be dramatic, and this fact (when combined with brain imaging's highly technical nature) can unfortunately lead to a situation with potential for misinterpretation or worse—outright misuse and deliberate exploitation (pp. 386–387, 400).

Education about ADHD as an Aspect of Assessment

At this point in understanding ADHD it appears that the most useful and efficient tools for assessment of ADHD are: the clinical interview including screening for possible comorbid disorders, ADHD/EF rating scales, DSM-IV/DSM-V diagnostic criteria and the two tests of working memory described above. After these data have been collected, the clinician should take time to describe cluster by cluster the modern model of ADHD presented in Chapter 2. A few brief examples of each from day to day life should be included. After each cluster has been briefly illustrated and described, the clinician should pause briefly to inquire how much the symptoms described fit or do not fit this particular patient. This didactic/clinical conversation is very important. It can enrich the evaluation by providing more detailed information about the patient's symptoms in a systematic way. It also helps to educate the patient and those accompanying him/her about the nature of the disorder, increasing the likelihood that they will be informed and cooperative in treatment.

At the conclusion of the initial evaluation, it is important for the clinician to provide a summary impression and recommendations to the patient and any family members present. One format for such a summary is the "Circles Inside Squares" graphic organizer described by Brown (2005b). First, the clinician draws a simple square within which are noted several specific strengths of the patient, e.g. "very bright," "good at fixing things," "hard worker," "supportive of family," "great soccer player," "excellent guitar player." It is important to begin with recognition of the patient's strengths to counteract the tendency of patient and family during an initial consultation to focus solely on the patient's weaknesses and failures. The sample below describes a sixth grade student who suffered from ADHD and specific learning problems with reading and written expression. He had become quite depressed near the end of his sixth grade year because he feared losing the support of a specific teacher who helped him to avoid embarrassment in class by not forcing him to read aloud in front of his peers.

After mentioning and writing important strengths in the "patient square," several overlapping circles can be drawn within that square to represent each appropriate diagnosis, perhaps one circle for ADHD overlapped with others to represent other diagnoses that currently fit the patient's condition: for anxiety, dysthymia, reading disorder, etc. These circles can comprise a Venn diagram in which the largest circle represents the most important diagnosis while other diagnoses are represented in sizes proportional to their apparent importance in the patient's current life situation.

If the clinician is uncertain about how to conceptualize and label a specific problem with a diagnostic label, or in order to make the observations more understandable to the patient and family, the problem can simply be described at the observational level, e.g. "social problems with other kids" for a child who may have Asperger's Disorder, or "smoking too much marijuana" for an adolescent who may be addicted to THC.

In the process of summarizing findings from an evaluation, it is often helpful to elicit responses from the patient and family as to what strengths could be added and/or how big each circle representing a diagnosis or problem ought to be if it is going to represent how much difficulty that problem is, at present, for the patient's daily life.

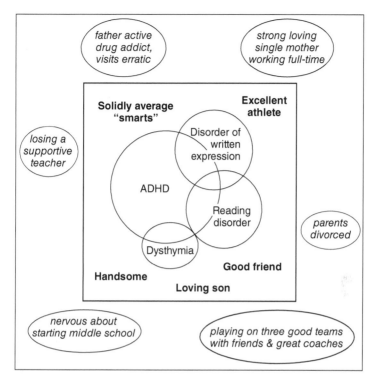

Figure 4.1   (Brown, 2005)

After the patient square and the overlapping circles within it are drawn and discussed, another larger square can be drawn around the first square to represent the environment in which the person lives and works or goes to school. In this square, important environmental supports and stressors are noted. This could include supports like "lots of friends at school," "playing on a little league team with a great coach," or "brother who helps a lot with homework." In the same space, environmental stressors can be noted: "Grandma is very sick," "picked on by two kids on the school bus," "company is planning a lot of layoffs," "older sister gets drunk a lot," etc.

Once this drawing is completed, the clinician can elicit reactions from the patient and family so they can express agreement or disagreement with the formulation, and can suggest important strengths or stressors that have been omitted. This can become a focus for recognizing differences of opinion in the family and can also provide a basis for discussion of what options are available for trying to improve the current situation of the patient and family.

5

HOW TREATMENTS FOR ADHD AFFECT THE BRAIN AND IMPROVE EXECUTIVE FUNCTIONS

Medical and psychological treatment usually has two goals: 1) to minimize suffering and alleviate impairment; and 2) to improve functioning. Treatment also has two primary constraints: 1) availability of knowledgeable persons and resources necessary for adequate treatment; and, 2) willingness of the patient to engage in the necessary procedures.

Education about ADHD: A Critical Component of Treatment

For ADHD, adequate education of the patient and family about the nature and treatment of ADHD is an essential aspect of minimizing suffering and damage; it is also a critical factor in eliciting willingness of the patient to engage adequately in the treatment process. When not adequately treated, ADHD can produce considerable psychological damage. It can cause a person to feel stupid and lazy when they are neither. Children and adults significantly impaired by ADHD often suffer years of frustration, demoralization and humiliation from their inability to do what most of their peers are able to do and what they themselves and those around them expect them to do. Repeatedly they are confronted with reminders of their failure to fulfill hopes and expectations held by themselves and those around them.

Often these difficulties are exacerbated by the persisting inconsistency that is typical of those with ADHD. When parents, teachers, co-workers and friends observe repeatedly that an individual with ADHD is able to focus very well and exercise excellent executive functioning for playing a sport or video game or some other favored activity while not demonstrating even adequate EF for many other tasks that may be more important, they understandably respond with "If you can do it for this, why don't you do it for that?" They tend to assume that the problem is a simple lack of willpower, an unwillingness to do here and now what this person has clearly been able to do in another task or setting.

Most patients seeking an initial consultation for ADHD and many of those significant in their life are likely to be operating with an implicit, if not explicit assumption that the person with ADHD is stubbornly refusing to do what they clearly seem able to do when they are motivated to do so. And it is assumed that the needed motivation can be generated by the individual if only they were willing to try harder more often or were more frequently and forcefully reminded to do so.

The educational aspect of treatment provides opportunity to explicitly recognize and challenge such erroneous assumptions by providing the patient and family a clear and understandable factual description of the nature of ADHD, the wide scope of the syndrome, its developmental aspects and its situational specificity. Education of patient and family about ADHD should also include honest description of the nature, uses and limitations of treatment. It is important that such education be provided not only for the patient, but also for others with whom the patient is currently involved, parents and teachers for children, spouses and/or others for adults—anyone whose support is needed and who may be likely to exacerbate the patient's demoralization or to undermine their motivation for sustaining appropriate treatment. Effective education about ADHD can help to reduce the patient's suffering from demoralization; it may also help to increase their willingness to engage in the process of treatment.

ADHD is essentially a problem in the chemical dynamics of the brain. Changes in the environment of the affected individual sometimes can make a positive difference: increased opportunities to earn positive recognition for appropriate performance, reduced exposure to unnecessary frustration, introduction of more effective strategies for work and learning, more adequate support, removal from toxic social environments, etc. However, though environmental changes may be quite helpful, in themselves, they are rarely sufficient to alleviate the syndrome of executive function impairments characteristic of our new model of ADHD.

Mechanism of Action in Medication Treatment for ADHD

The most effective treatment for ADHD impairments is usually a regimen of medication to facilitate more effective functioning of the brain's self-management system. A regimen of appropriate medication, well-tailored to the specific individual, cannot cure ADHD, but for about 80% of those affected it may provide significant reduction of impairment and substantial improvement of functioning. Such benefits from medication treatment are achieved by transient modifications of the dynamics of the chemistry of the brain.

Often people speak of ADHD as caused by "a chemical imbalance in the brain." This makes it sound as though the problem were a lack or excess of sufficient salt in the soup of the cerebral spinal fluid which continually flows around the brain. That is simply wrong. The impairments of ADHD are not due to a global excess or lack of a specific chemical within or around the brain. The problem is at the level of synapses, the infinitesimal junctions between certain networks of the 100 billion neurons that manage activities within the brain.

When an electrical impulse (action potential) travels along neural networks, it encounters numerous junctions between neurons over which the electrical impulse must travel with an action somewhat like a spark plug. To continue traveling down the network, this action potential must jump across each synapse from one neuron to another. This jump requires the release of micro-dots of the neurotransmitter chemical made in each neuron and released when the electrical impulse arrives at the edge of the synapse for each neuron.

Volkow and colleagues (2002a, 2002b) and Swanson, et al. (2011) have described the mechanisms by which stimulant medications improve this communication between neurons to alleviate impairments of ADHD. Using PET scans they have shown that stimulant medications such as methylphenidate operate in multiple synapses of the brain where they bind to dopamine transporter proteins (DAT) which "suck up" dopamine released from the presynaptic neuron, thus terminating its connective action. This binding onto the transporters, when sufficient, (usually 50 to 70% occupancy is required) slows reuptake of the dopamine, leaving more of it in position to make and briefly sustain a better connection; this results in more effective communication between that presynaptic neuron and the post-synaptic neuron with which it is attempting to communicate. A similar mechanism is involved in the actions of medications for ADHD that target neuronal communication between neurons utilizing norepinephrine, the other primary neurotransmitter involved in ADHD impairments.

This mechanism of slowing reuptake of dopamine is the same for both methylphenidate and amphetamine medications for ADHD; however amphetamines have a secondary mechanism. They also stimulate some additional release of dopamine as well as slowing its reuptake. For many with ADHD, methylphenidate and amphetamine medications work equally well, though one type may cause adverse effects while the other may not. However, if neurons of an individual are chronically releasing an insufficient quantity of dopamine into the synapse, slowing reuptake is not likely to produce significant improvement in synaptic communication because the insufficient quantity of dopamine constitutes a rate-limiting effect which may not allow adequate correction of the inter-neuron communication problem. In such cases, amphetamine may be more effective than methylphenidate.

Arnsten and Li (2005) have reviewed the influence of both dopamine and norepinephrine on executive functions. Citing relevant studies of both animals and humans, they highlight the sensitivity of the PFC to its neurochemical environment within the brain. They noted that small changes in the catecholamine modulation of PFC cells can have profound effects on the capacity of the PFC to guide behavior utilizing working memory. They argue that low doses of D1 agonists improve working memory and attention regulation while excessively high levels of dopamine release impair PFC function. Similarly, low to moderate levels of norepinephrine have important beneficial effects on the functioning of the PFC while excessively high levels, such as may be released in stress, contribute to impaired PFC function. Another review of the separate and interactive roles of dopamine and noradrenaline in the pathophysiology and treatment of ADHD has been provided by Del Campo, et al. (2011).

Most of the research done on medications approved by the U.S. Food and Drug Administration (FDA) thus far for treatment of ADHD has been focused on stimulants (methylphenidate and amphetamines) which act to increase levels of both dopamine and norepinephrine in neuronal networks. One non-stimulant medication, atomoxetine, which functions as a selective norepinephrine reuptake inhibitor acting specifically upon the norepinephrine and not on the dopamine, has also been the focus of considerable research. Long-acting formulations of two alpha-2 agonists, guanfacine, and clonidine, have more recently been approved for treatment of ADHD, either as monotherapy or as adjunctive treatment with stimulant medications. These more recent additions to the approved medications for treatment of ADHD have not yet been systematically tested on the broader range of ADHD-related executive functions which is the primary focus of this book.

Individual Variability in Response to Medication Treatment for ADHD

The amount of stimulant needed to produce a therapeutic effect in persons with ADHD is not determined by how old the individual is, how much he/she weighs, or by the severity of their ADHD symptoms. It is a function of how sensitive that individual's body is to the particular medication administered. Volkow, et al. (2002a, 2002b) reported that in some of their participants a single 60 mg dose of MPH had little impact, while in others it changed the dopamine level between 3% and 27%. Individual differences in the amount of

MPH needed to improve attentional functioning are also influenced by the individual's baseline dopaminergic tone as well as by receptor blockade. PET images from Volkow, et al. demonstrate that when methylphenidate is effective, it tends to enhance ability to distinguish signal from noise and increases the salience of available stimuli so individuals feel stronger interest in the task.

The dynamic complexity of dopamine distribution in the brain has been highlighted by Cools and D'Esposito (2011) in a review of multiple studies. They note that optimal levels of dopamine (DA) in the PFC and in the striatum are quite variable depending upon specific cognitive tasks being undertaken and the baseline levels of this neurotransmitter in the individual at the time. These differences exist not only across persons, but also within any specific individual across different tasks and times. Cools and D'Esposito emphasize that dopamine plays a critical role in cognitive control, a multifactorial phenomenon which requires a dynamically shifting balance between maintaining stability and allowing flexible updating of information in working memory. They argue that:

> Understanding the precise effects of dopamine on these subcomponent processes is not straightforward, partly because the relationship between DA and performance is nonlinear and inverted U-shaped, with both excessive as well as insufficient levels impairing performance. In addition, effects of DA depend on the brain region that is targeted with modulation of one and the same brain region having paradoxical consequences for different subcomponent processes (p. 120).

Their view suggests that some of this complexity may be linked to interactions between baseline levels of dopamine in the PFC versus the striatum. They also suggest that presynaptic autoreceptors may play a significant role as they may cause paradoxical inhibition of firing, synthesis and/or release of dopamine. An additional complicating factor, not yet adequately understood, is the possible interaction of DA with other neurotransmitters as well as neurohormonal systems, e.g. estrogen, which has been shown to have a significant influence on the synthesis, release and turnover of DA.

In a review article Arnsten (2011) emphasizes that both dopamine and norepinephrine modulate functioning of the prefrontal cortex. She cites studies to show that norepinephrine strengthens PFC connectivity and maintains persistent firing during working memory tasks by actions on α_{2A} adrenoceptors on PFC neurons. Arnsten describes how dopamine narrows tuning within brain networks to sculpt network inputs so "noise" is decreased and relevant focus is stabilized. She notes that while stimulant medications and atomoxetine increase catecholamine actions by blocking transporter proteins to allow better connections with receptors, guanfacine, a medication more recently approved for treatment of ADHD strengthens network connectivity by acting on post-synaptic α_{2A} receptors.

An expanded view of the complexity of these cognitive operations central to effective information processing has been provided by Arnsten and colleagues (2010) who have proposed that working memory functions which are central to executive functions involve a rapidly adjusting form of neuroplasticity within pyramidal cell networks that interconnect on dendritic spines. They suggest that rapid and reversible molecular signaling events within these long, slender spines produce cascades of interaction among networks that can connect or disconnect at any given moment in ways that provide immense cognitive flexibility, but also are vulnerable to genetic or environmental insults which can "dysregulate network connections and erode higher cognitive abilities, leading to symptoms such as forgetfulness, susceptibility to interference, and disorganized thought and behavior" (p. 1).

The clinical implication of these various research findings is that use of medications, particularly stimulant medications, for treatment of ADHD needs to be quite sensitive to individual differences across persons and in performance of different cognitive tasks by the same person. For example, some individuals need higher levels of dopamine release for reading comprehension and recall than they do for driving their car.

These neurobiological complexities explain why effective prescription of medications for ADHD requires not just laboratory-based science, but also individualized tailoring that is dependent upon clinical arts to select and adjust specific medications, dosage and timing of dosing for optimal effectiveness of remediation.

Effects of medication-induced changes in the brain's chemistry can be considered at three different levels, each of which has its own value and limitations. One approach is the use of brain imaging to observe brain functioning directly while the participants are receiving a specific treatment and compare those results with a control group. Modern imaging techniques make it possible to assess brain regions and functions impacted by medication treatment. A second level is an experimental trial of individuals with ADHD who are provided a specific treatment under controlled conditions for specific experimental tasks; their responses can then be compared to those of an appropriate control group. The third and most common level of assessment is to focus simply on self-report of behavioral symptoms such as are included in the rating scales discussed in Chapter 4. Clinical trials usually use such rating scales for DSM-IV criteria and/or executive functions to test medications used for ADHD.

Evidence of Effectiveness of Medication Treatment for ADHD

Imaging Studies

Some examples of brain imaging studies of the impact of medication for treatment of ADHD have been described in Chapter 2; others follow here. Rubia and colleagues used functional MRI (2009) to assess activation and functional connectivity deficits in attention and motivation networks of brain in children diagnosed with ADHD and matched controls. They found that, when on placebo, medication-naïve children with ADHD showed significantly less activation and reduced functional inter-connectivity in several areas of brain important for an attention task, but when offered a reward, they showed excessive activation in the relevant brain regions. When on methylphenidate, these children with ADHD showed normalization in both of these networks so they were not significantly different from normal controls. This demonstrated that methylphenidate improves both activation and motivation functional networks in children with ADHD.

Another study by the Rubia group (2011) demonstrated that methylphenidate can normalize activation of the frontal-striatal regions of brain which facilitate inhibition of distraction by interfering stimuli during task performance. In a double-blind, placebo-controlled study they showed that, while on placebo, boys with ADHD had reduced activation of the right inferior prefrontal cortex, left striatum, and thalamus as well as other areas typically active in normal controls when the brain is trying to control task interference and inhibit distracted behaviors. When those participants with ADHD were on a single dose of methylphenidate, the level of activation in those brain regions was fully comparable to that of healthy, age-matched controls. These researchers noted that while the methylphenidate normalized frontal-striatal functioning in participants with ADHD, it did not appear to affect medial frontal or temporal dysfunction. This led them to claim that methylphenidate has region-specific up-regulation effects that turn on needed network connections specifically in the frontal-striatal region of the brain.

Improved functional connectivity in response to stimulant medication was also demonstrated by Wong and Stevens (2012) in a placebo-controlled study of youths aged 11 to 17 years with ADHD doing working memory tasks. When on stimulant medication, participants showed improved performance on encoding, maintenance or retrieval phases of the Sternberg task for assessing working memory using fMRI. They found hemodynamic responses in six fronto-parietal networks/components when participants were medicated; three of these networks showed increased activation in that condition. Functional connectivity analysis showed that medication also produced recruitment of additional brain networks that were not engaged when participants were on placebo. These results provide evidence that stimulant medication has widespread and adaptive effects on the functional connectivity of the fronto-parietal brain networks, components of brain closely associated with working memory.

Peterson and colleagues (2009) have shown that stimulant medications can improve the ability of youths with ADHD to "put the lid" on their excessive mind-wandering so that their wayward thoughts are not disrupting their attention much more than occurs in normal controls. Their fMRI scans showed that stimulant medication suppressed excessive default-mode activity in the ventral anterior cingulate and posterior cingulate cortices, circuits that have been shown to correlate with the degree of mind-wandering during attention tasks.

Tomasi, et al. (2011) demonstrated that methylphenidate has double impact on brain activity for task performance. They showed suppression/deactivation of default-mode activity in insula and posterior cingulate cortex (resulting in reduced distractibility). They also demonstrated activation of the dorsal attention network including parietal and prefrontal cortex (resulting in improved performance on visual attention and working memory tasks). Both of these changes in brain function occurred when participants were given a 20 mg dose of methylphenidate; such results were not obtained from controls who did not receive the methylphenidate.

There is some evidence that use of stimulant medication may help to improve not only the functioning of brain components, but also the brain structures themselves. Using MRI, Sobel, et al. (2010) presented evidence that stimulant medication tends to normalize structural abnormalities, specifically large inward deformations of the surface of the basal ganglia in limbic circuitry that is important for associative learning. This measure was correlated with severity of ADHD symptoms and was associated with changes in the physical structure and surfaces of these regions.

Impact of stimulant medication on motivation was demonstrated by Volkow and colleagues (2004). They used PET scans to show that methylphenidate can increase the amount of dopamine released in the synapse and thereby increase motivation of participants to persist in a boring academic task. Imaging showed that methylphenidate increased dopamine in the striatum during the uninteresting math task. As the dopamine in the striatum increased, participants reported increased interest in doing that task. It had become more salient in a way not found during placebo trials.

In a subsequent study, this research group (Volkow, et al., 2012) used PET scans to demonstrate the direct linkage between regional brain changes induced by methylphenidate treatment and longer term improvement in symptoms of inattention and hyperactivity in adults with ADHD. At baseline they demonstrated that methylphenidate significantly enhanced dopamine signaling in the reward/motivation regions of the brain (ventral striatum). They continued consistent treatment of those patients with methylphenidate over the course of 12 months and then did follow-up PET scans at the end of the year as well as rating scale assessment of ADHD symptoms. Results indicated not only that the medication improved ADHD symptoms; the follow-up scans showed that methylphenidate-induced increased dopamine release in the ventral striatum as well as in the prefrontal and temporal cortices which was associated with significant reductions in both hyperactivity/impulsivity and inattention impairments in adults with ADHD.

Taken together, these various imaging studies demonstrate that stimulant medications used to treat ADHD can reduce impairment and, in some cases, normalize functioning of multiple aspects of the infrastructure for executive functioning in the brain. In controlled studies, these PET, MRI and fMRI studies indicate that stimulants can improve functional connectivity and increase activity in activation and motivational networks, can normalize capacity to inhibit distractibility, can activate additional aspects of brain needed for specific task performance, can reduce wanderings of mind associated with default-mode activity, can improve visual attention and working memory, and can increase motivation for boring tasks.

Experimental Studies

A second level of analysis of how stimulants impact executive function impairments associated with ADHD is found in experimental studies, many of which were done and reported prior to availability of modern imaging techniques. Typically, these studies compared groups of individuals diagnosed with ADHD on their performance of specific experimental tasks while on stimulant medication and while on placebo or in comparison to a control group.

An early study by Abikoff and Gittelman (1985) did a controlled observational study to assess a wide variety of classroom behaviors in children with ADHD. They used trained and blinded observers to compare classroom behavior of children with ADHD paired with gender-matched children without ADHD who were reported by the teacher to have average classroom behavior. Prior to medication only 45% of the ADHD children were rated as normal in their overall classroom behavior; most were conspicuously different from their matched controls. After eight weeks of treatment with MPH, more than 80% of the ADHD children were classified by the blinded raters as displaying normal classroom behavior.

Effects of medication on more specific cognitive tasks have been reported by numerous researchers. With paired controls Carlson, et al. (1991) found that methylphenidate improved speed and accuracy of boys with ADHD asked to solve arithmetic problems significantly more than when on placebo; though they compromised speed for accuracy when asked to attend to two tasks simultaneously. An experiment by Milich and colleagues (1991) showed that MPH improved willingness and ability of boys with ADHD to persist in trying to solve unsolvable problems.

In a crossover study of children with ADHD Bedard and colleagues (2004) found that MPH improved visual-spatial memory in children with ADHD. A previous study by the Bedard group (2003) demonstrated that, relative to community controls, children with ADHD showed significant impairment in selective inhibition of responses on a modified stop-signal task. When on MPH the participants with ADHD demonstrated improved performance on selective inhibition and in response execution on the task. When signaled during their time on medication, they held themselves back more effectively and performed the task more adequately.

Effects of methylphenidate on motivation in children with ADHD were demonstrated in a study by Chelonis, et al. (2011). They compared task performance by a group of children with ADHD while those children were off medication and while they were on medication. Findings indicated that MPH enhanced motivation to perform and execute more adequately on a wide variety of tasks associated with executive functions.

Taken together, these examples of experimental studies of medication treatment for ADHD demonstrate that stimulant medication can improve classroom behavior in children with ADHD, can improve processing speed on certain cognitive tasks, can increase persistence of effort for tasks in the face of frustration, can improve some types of working memory, and can enhance motivation for task performance.

In the past there have been questions raised about whether stimulant medications work as effectively for individuals with predominantly inattentive type as they do for those with combined type. Solanto, et al. (2009) reported a double-blind crossover study of children rigorously diagnosed with ADHD in either combined or predominantly inattentive subtype. Each was exposed to treatment with placebo and three different dose levels of short-acting methylphenidate administered three times daily and evaluated after each treatment regimen. Results indicated that both groups responded equally well to medication treatment with a linear increase in improvement with increasing dose.

Clinical Trials of Medication Treatment for ADHD

Faraone and Buitelaar (2010) have provided a meta-analysis of 23 double-blind, placebo-controlled studies of stimulant medication treatments for children and adolescents with ADHD as defined by DSM-II, DSM-III, DSM-III-R, or DSM-IV. This study produced 99 effect sizes which were categorized into three subgroupings: total ADHD symptom scores, inattention subscale scores, and hyperactivity-impulsivity subscale scores for treatments with methylphenidate or amphetamine formulations. Data analysis indicated robust, statistically significant effects for all stimulant medication treatments assessed. Results for amphetamine were generally somewhat stronger than results for methylphenidate. Comparisons based on number needed to treat successfully (NNT) indicated that when using amphetamine, clinicians need to treat two patients for each positive outcome for alleviation of total ADHD symptoms; the NNT for methylphenidate was just slightly higher, indicating that 2.6 patients needed to be treated for a positive outcome.

A different approach was taken by Newcorn and colleagues (2008) who used a placebo-controlled study to compare responses of a large group of children diagnosed with ADHD to two different types of medications. Their sample of children aged 6 to 16 years were randomly assigned to be treated with atomoxetine, a non-stimulant, noradrenergic medication for ADHD (n=220), osmotically released methylphenidate (n=220), or a placebo (n=74) for six weeks. After six weeks those treated with atomoxetine were switched to osmotically released methylphenidate and vice versa.

Response rates for atomoxetine (45%) and for methylphenidate (56%) were both clearly superior to placebo (24%). Each medication was well-tolerated and neither medicated group had more discontinuations than the group of patients on placebo. Of the 70 who did not respond to methylphenidate 43% subsequently responded to atomoxetine. Among the 69 who did not respond to atomoxetine, 42% had responded to osmotically released methylphenidate. Although the osmotically released methylphenidate had a somewhat greater response rate, this study clearly showed that some children respond better to a non-stimulant while others have a better response to osmotically released methylphenidate.

A meta-analysis of effect sizes for studies of medication treatment of adults with ADHD was presented by Faraone and Glatt (2010). This analysis included 18 published studies that met inclusion criteria, yielding 60 effect sizes. The mean effect size for long-acting stimulants was found to be 0.73 with no significant heterogeneity among effect sizes. For short-acting stimulants, the mean effect size was 0.96, though there was significant heterogeneity among effect sizes which, when corrected, yielded an effect size of 0.86. For non-stimulants the mean effect size was considerably lower, just 0.39, though there was no significant heterogeneity. All of these effect sizes were statistically significant. The NNT for stimulants was ranged from two to four while the non-stimulant medications had an NNT of four to five; in this analysis higher NNT indicates fewer successful treatments.

These efficacy findings are similar to those obtained by Faraone, Biederman and Spencer in a 2006 review of comparative efficacy of medications for youths with ADHD (Faraone, et al., 2006c). There too, the effects of non-stimulants were considerably less than those of methylphenidate or amphetamine which tended not to differ significantly from one another. However, it should be noted that such findings are describing the average of responses of groups of individuals. Some individuals respond much better to non-stimulants such as atomoxetine than to stimulants, either because they have adverse responses to stimulants or simply because their specific body chemistry is more responsive to noradrenergic medications than to the dopamine targeted stimulants.

These comparative studies yield impressive findings of the efficacy of medications for treating ADHD, but it should be kept in mind that all of the studies included in these meta-analyses assessed effects of medication on ADHD as defined by existing DSM diagnostic criteria. None of these assessments were designed to assess the broader range of ADHD described in this book. To assess impact of medication treatment on the wider phenotype of ADHD described here, assessment would require rating scales that query the broader range of symptoms included in the new model. One study by Brown, et al. (2011a) compared the sensitivity and specificity of a rating scale based on the DSM-IV-TR definition of ADHD with the Brown ADD Rating Scale for Adults, a rating scale that assesses for the new model of ADHD described in

Chapter 2. Overlap between these two measures was just 20%. This finding highlights the importance of using both the DSM diagnostic criteria and an additional rating scale for the modern broader concept of ADHD for assessing treatment effects.

Brown and colleagues have published data from two large studies assessing the impact of medication treatments for ADHD on the wide range of EF impairments in adults assessed with the Brown ADD Scale. A double-blind, placebo-controlled study tested the effects of atomoxetine on EF impairments in 501 adults diagnosed with ADHD (Brown, et al., 2011b). The Brown ADD Scale for Adults was administered to participants at baseline and again after six months of treatment with either placebo or atomoxetine. After six months of treatment, mean scores were significantly improved on all five clusters of the Brown ADD Scale for Adults for those treated with atomoxetine compared to those treated with placebo.

Two placebo-controlled studies assessed the impact of atomoxetine on executive function impairments in children with ADHD. The Brown ADD Scale for Children was administered at baseline and endpoint. Results indicated statistically significant improvement in EF impairments in response to treatment (Brown, et al., 2005).

The Brown ADD Scale for Adults was also used in an open-label study to test the effectiveness of lisdexamfetamine for alleviation of executive function impairments in 142 adults diagnosed with ADHD and treated with optimized doses over a period of four weeks (Brown, et al., 2010). Statistically significant improvement was shown in all five clusters of EF impairments assessed by the Brown ADD Scale for Adults. This same rating scale was also used to assess medication impact on executive functions in two large placebo-controlled studies of adults (n=280, 411) with ADHD using a triple-bead formulation of mixed amphetamine salts (Brown, et al., 2007). Results in both studies found significant improvement on the Brown rating scale for treated participants versus those on placebo.

These studies suggest that medications approved to treat ADHD and found effective for alleviating ADHD symptoms measured by rating scales based on DSM-IV diagnostic criteria are also effective in treating the wider range of ADHD-related impairments of executive function included in the new model of ADHD described in Chapter 2.

Age Considerations in Use of Stimulant Medications for ADHD

Some children show significant ADHD impairments in their preschool years. Children brought for assessment at this early age may manifest serious behavior problems such as severe tantrums, physical aggression against others, including younger siblings, or impulsive behavior that may risk serious injury, e.g. running out into traffic, climbing in places where they are likely to fall and get injured, and placing eating utensils in electric sockets.

In 2011 the American Academy of Pediatrics published new guidelines for care of children and adolescents with ADHD. Those guidelines recommend that preschool-aged children (4 to 5 years old) with ADHD should first be treated with behavior therapy and should also be carefully assessed for other possible developmental problems such as language impairments. However, if those interventions are not effective and the ADHD problems persist in moderate or severe form for at least nine months, the American Academy of Pediatrics guidelines suggest cautious use of prescription medications such as dextro-amphetamine or methylphenidate (American Academy of Pediatrics, 2011).

To assess the impact of stimulant medications on these very young children, a study of stimulant treatment for 532 preschool children aged 3 to 5.5 years, the Preschool ADHD Treatment Study (PATS), was sponsored by the U.S. National Institute of Mental Health. Results reported by Greenhill, et al. (2006) and Kollins, et al., (2006) indicated that 85% of those preschoolers, all of whom had been diagnosed with moderate to severe ADHD, showed improvement while taking medication, a much better response than was reported for placebo. Details on treatment for ADHD in preschoolers are provided in a chapter by Posner, Pressman and Greenhill (2009). Adverse effects in that study were minimal, though slightly more common than is usually reported for older children.

Longer Term Effects of Medication Treatment on Academic Functioning

Efforts to begin active treatment of ADHD in young children who show significant impairments from ADHD seem quite reasonable, given that risks of adverse effects from medications used to treat ADHD tend to be small while adverse effects of untreated ADHD can cause considerable long-persisting impairment. Massetti, et al. (2008) followed 125 children diagnosed with ADHD at four to six years and compared them with a sample of 130 non-ADHD comparison children. Over eight years they tracked academic achievement seven times for these children and found that children diagnosed with predominantly inattentive type ADHD by age six years had significantly lower reading, spelling and math scores than comparison children, even when IQ scores were controlled for. Interestingly, children diagnosed with combined type ADHD at ages four to six years did not show the lower scores that were seen in those with predominantly inattentive type of ADHD.

A different, population-based study of 370 children with ADHD followed from birth up through age 18 years found no significant difference between subtypes of ADHD or between boys and girls in the severity of their impairment in long-term educational achievement as measured by school records and a nationally-normed reading test (Barbaresi, et al., 2007a, 2007b). In comparison of their ADHD sample with matched controls without ADHD, the researchers found that those with ADHD had significantly lower scores for reading achievement and increased rates of absenteeism, grade retention, and school dropout. Those children with ADHD complicated by a specific learning disorder and/or a comorbid psychiatric disorder had lower grade averages and more than triple the likelihood of dropping out of school prior to high school graduation.

School records indicated that those children treated with stimulant medication in this sample had higher scores for reading achievement, lower rates of grade retention, and decreased rates of absenteeism, relative to students with ADHD who did not receive medication treatment.

The Barbaresi (2007b) study also reported important findings regarding modifying factors that impact outcome, factors other than just whether or not stimulant medication was provided. There was a positive correlation between amount of stimulant dose and reading achievement scores; those students with ADHD who received higher doses of stimulants tended to have higher reading scores. They also found that students with ADHD whose mothers had more education were less likely to drop out of school. Dropout rate for those with ADHD whose mothers had not completed high school was 59.1%; for those whose mothers graduated from high school, the rate of dropout was 31.7%. For students with ADHD whose mothers had some college education the dropout rate was much lower, 12.6%, while children of mothers who were college graduates dropped out at a rate of 13.5%. Not surprisingly, those students with ADHD who also suffered from comorbid learning or psychiatric disorders were more likely to drop out of high school than those with ADHD who did not have a comorbid disorder (25.4% versus 11.3%). While medication may significantly improve school performance for those with ADHD, there are also many other factors which can significantly impact outcome.

Benefits of treatment with stimulant medication for improving academic achievement and classroom performance were also shown by Powers, et al., (2008). They compared children diagnosed with ADHD at age 7 to 11 who received at least a year of treatment with stimulant medication with a group of children diagnosed with ADHD in the same age group who did not receive such medication treatment for at least a year versus a matched control group.

Results indicated that those who received at least a year of medication treatment achieved better academic outcomes as measured by scores for reading, math and written expression on a nationally-normed academic achievement test; they also achieved a higher high school grade point average. However, even those who received treatment for their ADHD did not fare as well on these measures as students in the control group who had never received an ADHD diagnosis. These researchers noted, however, that medication did not produce normalization of academic functioning and that long-term academic improvement is likely to vary as a result of multiple factors.

Another population-based study of children showed that an earlier start with medication treatment can reduce escalating academic problems in children with ADHD. Zoega, et al. (2012) showed that children with ADHD who began medication treatment for ADHD sometime relatively soon after taking their required fourth grade math and language arts exams tended to do better on their seventh grade exams than did those children with ADHD who did not start medication treatment for ADHD until more than a year after their fourth grade exams. Exam scores of students who started ADHD medications within 12 months of the fourth grade exams showed significantly less decline in their required seventh grade academic exams than did those who started ADHD medications more than a year after completing their fourth grade exams. Results showed that, for both boys and girls, later start of stimulant medications for ADHD is associated with more academic decline in math. Boys who started medication treatment earlier showed less decline also in their seventh grade exam scores for language arts.

Persistence in Use of Medication Treatments for ADHD

Medication treatments for ADHD do not cure the disorder as an antibiotic may cure an infection. For most patients with ADHD, treatment with approved medications will reduce symptoms and decrease impairment while not curing the underlying causes of the disorder. This is comparable to eyeglasses or contact lenses that improve vision while not curing the underlying problems with the visual system. And, like eyeglasses which improve vision only while they are being worn, medications used to treat ADHD do not bring symptom improvement when they are not taken. Once the chemical action of the medication in the brain has worn off, usually a period in the range of 4 to 12 hours, depending on the formulation, the benefits of medication treatment quickly wear off as well.

Despite the loss of effectiveness when these medications are not taken on an ongoing basis, research data indicate that many individuals with ADHD who begin medication treatment do not persist in taking it on a regular basis for very long. Palli and colleagues (2012) reported a retrospective study of records of prescriptions for ADHD written for a population-based sample of 46,135 children aged 6 to 19 years over a one year period in four different states of the U.S. They classified the prescriptions according to three types of stimulants: short-acting stimulants (lasting 4 to 6 hours); intermediate-acting stimulants (lasting 6 to 8 hours); and long-acting stimulants (lasting 10 to 14 hours).

Results indicated that the average number of days of persistent use of stimulants was 79.97 days in a year for short-acting users; 76.59 days for intermediate-acting users, and 104.96 days for users of long-acting. Probably the convenience of once-a-day dosing for long-acting stimulants contributed to the increased persistence among those using longer-acting formulations, but even those patients persisted in use for less than four months in one year. Additional data indicated that patients who received an additional psychotropic medication concurrent with their stimulant treatment for ADHD tended to persist longer. It should be noted, however, that these data about early discontinuation are derived from insurance and prescription data which may not adequately reflect the full reality of patterns of use. Although there are many patients who prematurely discontinue use of their medications, there are also many who miss getting refills or who take a break from it, e.g. over summer vacation from school, and then resume use. These studies do not adequately reflect those patterns.

There were some factors that increased the length of time patients continued in use of their ADHD medications. When the stimulant was administered with atomoxetine or another psychotropic medication, e.g. an antidepressant, or mood stabilizer, the persistence rate for the combined medication increased by 15% to 50%. The authors of the study suggested that combined pharmacotherapy may make the ADHD symptoms more manageable, thus increasing motivation for further persistence. Or, the increased persistence of the combined treatments might have been successfully directed at management of adverse side effects such as stimulant induced patterns of irritability, insomnia or anxiety, particularly as the stimulant may "rebound" late in its duration of action.

There are many possible reasons for any given patient to discontinue use of medications prescribed to treat ADHD. The patient and/or family may not see any significant improvement resulting from medication use. This often occurs when a child is treated with medication that provides coverage only while the child is in school; this may cause the teachers to observe improvement in symptoms during the school day while parents see no significant change at home, particularly in late afternoon or early evening when the student needs to be doing homework. Even for so-called "all day" medications, the benefits may not persist beyond the end of the school day. This wearing off in late afternoon may also involve "rebound" where the patient taking the ADHD medication experiences a "crash" reaction of excessive fatigue or irritability for a couple of hours or more as the medication is wearing off. Although rebound can often be alleviated by adding a short-acting dose of the same ADHD medication shortly before the crash occurs, some clinicians do not recognize this problem when it occurs and may not take effective action to alleviate it.

Another possible cause of a patient ceasing use of a prescribed medication after a short trial may be minimal side effects such as reduced appetite, difficulty falling asleep, being "too serious" and not wanting to interact much with others, or feeling excessively restless or irritable. Often such side effect problems can be alleviated by careful fine-tuning of dose and/or timing or by change of medication in consultation with the patient and family. However, in order to recognize that such problems are present, the clinician needs to follow the patient carefully encouraging prompt communication of any experienced difficulties so they can be addressed and managed.

Another potential cause of premature discontinuation of medication treatment for ADHD may be excessive fears of patients or parents that some more substantial adverse effects might emerge with longer term use, even though, as is shown in the next section of this chapter, research data indicate minimal risk of serious adverse effects from such treatments. In other cases medication treatment may be discontinued because of conflict between parents and an adolescent where refusing to take prescribed medication may be one of many ways in which the teenager attempts to win increased independence from parental authority. Sometimes there is conflict between parents over whether or not their child should be taking such medication at all. It is not uncommon, especially for divorced parents, to polarize over such a question as it becomes entangled in their ongoing conflicts over other matters. In cases of excessive fears of the medication or excessive conflict between family members over medication, the clinician may be able to engage in conversation with the patient and/or family members to try to clarify realistic versus unrealistic fears and to help all involved understand the potential risks of leaving ADHD untreated or inadequately treated.

Among adults taking stimulant medication for ADHD, adherence to the prescribed regimen seems to be somewhat higher, at least according to a review of the few published studies of this issue. Caisley and Müller (2012) reported a mean adherence rate of 52% to 87% for adults with ADHD. They noted some evidence that longer-acting formulations of stimulant medication seem to yield better adherence than do shorter-acting regimens which require dosing two or three times daily. This may be due to forgetfulness of many adults with ADHD regarding any daily tasks which are not prompted by external reminders. Their review also observed that many adults tend to use medications for ADHD on an "as needed" basis, taking the medication when they are doing a task for which they expect the medication to be quite useful and not taking it when they feel they are able adequately to meet task demands. More research is needed to assess the effectiveness of "as needed" dosing for adults. However, many of the worries and concerns that may cause parents to be reluctant to continue their children on prescribed medications for ADHD can also apply to adults, even when they have sought out the medication treatment for themselves.

Risks and Safety of Medications Used to Treat ADHD

Any parent considering the possibility of their son or daughter beginning a regimen of medication for ADHD, and any adult considering such medication for himself/herself has important and usually quite reasonable questions about whether the medication regimen being considered is likely to have any risk of adverse effects in addition to whatever benefits are being sought. It is important for clinicians to respond to these questions honestly and with facts, not to dismiss them with a blanket reassurance that these medications will never cause any adverse effects.

The first point to be made is that no one can ever promise that any particular medication given to any specific person is 100% guaranteed to have no adverse effects. Some medications, even widely used medications such as antibiotics used to treat infections or analgesics used to treat fever and headaches can be associated with serious, potentially fatal adverse reactions in a very small number of persons who use them. Such reactions are extremely rare and generally occur only in individuals whose health is seriously impaired, but they do occasionally occur.

The active ingredients of most medications currently approved to treat ADD/ADHD have been in use for decades by very large numbers of children, adolescents and adults. Amphetamine has been available since the 1930s and methylphenidate was introduced in the 1950s. The first reports of the beneficial effects of amphetamine on learning and behavior of children were provided by Bradley (1937) who discovered these benefits accidentally in his research with emotionally and behaviorally disturbed children. These medications initially received widespread use by adults as a treatment for depression and to induce weight loss. They were officially issued and used by American, British, German and Japanese soldiers, sailors and airplane crews during the Second World War and are still officially issued to some pilots in the U.S. Air Force to help them to stay alert during long flights. Iversen (2008) has provided a history of the development of amphetamines and related drugs, describing both licit and illicit patterns of use.

Both methylphenidate and amphetamines are controlled by the U.S. and most other federal governments in the same way opiate pain medications are controlled; this is because when misused, they have the potential for abuse when taken in excessive doses or when administered in other than oral modalities. In the 1940s there were numerous reports of stimulants being abused as treatments for weight loss. That is no longer considered an appropriate use of stimulants.

Common side effects to stimulants are not persistent or dangerous. It is not unusual for patients starting these medications to report some difficulty with headache, stomach ache, reduced appetite, or occasional difficulty in falling asleep (Aagaard & Hansen, 2011). Usually such reactions are generally not severe, tend to be quite transient, and usually respond to adjustment of dose and/or timing. Some adverse reactions may occur because the patient is given a dose too high for that individual. As was mentioned earlier, there is wide variation among patients in all age groups regarding what is the most effective dose of stimulant for them.

Stimulant medications cannot be effectively prescribed using weight-based formulas; the question is how sensitive is the individual's body to that particular medication. Most very young, small children respond to very small doses, but others of the same age, size and symptom severity do not respond until they are treated with much higher doses such as might be used for most adults. Among adults with ADHD, most are taking fairly substantial doses of stimulants, but some just as old with comparable body mass and similar symptom severity respond well to doses of stimulant which would usually be prescribed for a preschooler. Usually it is wise for dosing to start at a very minimal level with gradual increments in dose at intervals of several days or a week until an effective dose is found, a maximum dose is reached, or significant adverse effects intervene.

Recent years have brought several studies seeking to identify the risks of potentially more severe adverse effects. One concern is the potential for cardiovascular adverse events. Vitiello and colleagues (2012) reported on a 10-year follow-up of the 579 children in the Multimodal Treatment Study of Children with ADHD (MTA) study. Those children, all carefully diagnosed with combined type ADHD, were randomly assigned to treatment conditions, some with medications for ADHD, others with only behavioral treatments. After following those children for ten years, these researchers reported: that no evidence could be found that intensive, sustained, and continuous treatment with stimulant medication starting at ages seven to nine years increased the risk for prehypertension or hypertension over a period of ten years observation. They did find, however, that there were some indications of a slightly elevated heart rate while children were on stimulant medications. There were no symptomatic events in this ten-year study that led to medical attention and no patient was discontinued from stimulant as a result of cardiovascular adverse events. However, this elevated heart rate effect may have clinical implications for individual patients with underlying heart abnormalities.

A large study comparing children aged 3 to 17 years exposed and not exposed to ADHD medications, methylphenidate, amphetamine or atomoxetine, was published by Schelleman, et al. (2011). They studied the rate of cardiovascular events (sudden death or ventricular arrhythmia, stroke, myocardial infarction, and endpoint of stroke or MI) and found that the rate of these cardiovascular events in children who had taken any of these medications was very low and no higher than their sample of children who had never been exposed to any ADHD medications.

Assessment of cardiovascular risks that might be associated with stimulants was also done by Olfson, et al. (2012). They reviewed insurance records of over 89,000 young people aged 6 to 21 years treated for ADHD with stimulants and compared them with over 82,000 patients in the same age group who had never taken stimulants. No significant differences were found in risk for cardiovascular events and there were no differences between those treated with methylphenidate versus amphetamine.

Likewise, Cooper, et al. (2011) found no evidence that current use of any ADHD drugs by children brought any increased risk of cardiovascular problems. They did a large retrospective study of 1,200,438 children and young adults between the ages of 2 and 24 years. Their study included 373,667 person years of current use of any ADHD drugs. This large study showed no evidence that current use of an ADHD medication was associated with an increased risk of serious cardiovascular events.

Studies focused specifically on adults have reported similar findings. Habel, et al. (2011) reported a study from four sites involving 443,198 total users and non-users of ADHD medications. Results indicated that among those young and middle-aged adults, current or new use of ADHD medications was not associated with an increased risk of serious cardiovascular events.

Schelleman, et al., (2012) studied a cohort 43,999 new methylphenidate users whom they compared to a matched group of 175,955 of non-users. Hazard ratios for stroke, myocardial infarction, and the composite endpoint of stroke or heart attack did not differ statistically. There was a slight increase in risk of sudden death or ventricular arrhythmia, but since this was not linked to dose-response, the researchers suggested that the association is probably not causal.

Another concern of many parents and their children is whether stimulant medication might cause slowing of a child's growth trajectory for height or weight. Faraone, et al. (2008) published a review of the literature of studies assessing possible slowing of growth trajectory for height and weight in children with ADHD treated with stimulants. Findings from that literature review indicated that stimulant medication is sometimes associated with delays in achieving full height and full weight during childhood. These researchers argue that these delays are generally minor and not clinically significant for most patients, but in some cases where a child is exceptionally small for his or her age, this may become a problem.

There are some data that indicate that growth delays found in ADHD children may be an aspect of their ADHD rather than a direct result of stimulant medication treatment, but this is not adequately sorted out at this time. Data from these studies also indicate that these delays tend not to persist into late adolescence or adulthood. Eventually most children with ADHD, with or without treatment with stimulant medication, tend to attain their full predicted growth.

In their long-term longitudinal studies of boys and girls with ADHD versus matched controls, Biederman and colleagues (2010c) assessed longer term height and weight variables. They followed these children for 10 or 11 years into early adulthood (the mean age of participants in the study at follow-up was 22 years). Most of the participants had been treated with stimulants with a mean age of onset of 8.4 years with a mean duration of stimulant medication of 7.4 years. They reported that there was no evidence that stimulant medication for ADHD was associated with any deficits in growth outcomes at follow-up in adulthood.

Another concern expressed by some parents considering the possibility of stimulant medication to treat their child's ADHD is the question of whether longer term use of methylphenidate or another medication for ADHD might cause some longer term damage, possibly genetic damage. This issue was addressed by Morris, et al. (2012) in an article reviewing the current literature. That review confirmed the initial safety testing of methylphenidate completed by the FDA in the 1950s. In reviewing both animal and human studies completed in recent years, these researchers found no evidence that methylphenidate treatment increases the risk of genetic damage in ADHD patients.

Taken together, these various studies indicate that risks of serious adverse events from appropriate use of medications currently approved for ADHD are extremely small in both children and adults, so long as the treated individual is in reasonable health.

Practice parameters developed by the American Academy of Child and Adolescent Psychiatry for the use of stimulant medications were published by the American Academy of Child and Adolescent Psychiatry (2002). A comprehensive discussion of the appropriate uses and limitations of various medication treatments for ADHD and various comorbid disorders is provided by Prince and Wilens (2009).

Psychosocial Interventions for ADHD

A variety of psychosocial treatments have been utilized in efforts to provide effective treatment for children with ADHD. These include training parents to use more effective reinforcement strategies in managing their children and instituting daily report forms for teachers to rate the child's performance on specific targeted behavioral problems and then communicate that information daily to parents who are expected to reward good performance with or without negative consequences for poor performance. Another psychosocial intervention is summer treatment programs which include parent training, behavior modification strategies in a classroom setting, academic and sports skills practice and tutoring, social skills training, and, sometimes, stimulant medication.

In a review of psychosocial interventions for ADHD Antshel and Barkley (2008) found evidence supporting the effectiveness of three types of psychosocial interventions:

1   training parents to manage behavior of their children more effectively using operant conditioning techniques such as rewards for appropriate behaviors and rational punishment for inappropriate behaviors;

2   training for teachers in managing classroom behavior problems, which has also been shown to be effective for reducing excessive activity or disruptive behavior and for increasing attention to class activities;

3   intensive summer treatment programs providing behavior modification structures such as token economies, response cost and time out from

reinforcement in an integrated program of summer school and recreational activities augmented by parent training, peer relationship training, and follow-up sessions after the summer program is concluded.

Despite the demonstrated effectiveness of these methods, Antshel and Barkley emphasize that there is little evidence that beneficial effects of such treatments persist after the treatment is concluded or that positive effects in one domain of activity will generalize to other domains. They describe such behavioral methods as "prostheses—means of rearranging environments by artificial means so as to yield improved participation in major life activities" (2008, p. 432). They challenge earlier assumptions that behaviors reinforced in such intervention will be "internalized" and continued after the structure of the behavioral intervention is eventually removed.

It should be noted that although these psychosocial interventions have been demonstrated effective for alleviation of behavioral problems in ADHD, there is no substantial evidence that they are effective in improving cognitive functions recognized in the new model as the primary problems of most individuals with ADHD. Psychosocial interventions are not likely to improve working memory, ability to sustain focus or other cognitive functions described in the forgoing pages as effectively as adequate medication treatment.

The review by Antshel and Barkley (2008) and a more recent meta-analysis by Sonuga-Barke, et al. (2013) indicate a significant lack of adequate scientific evidence, at present, for non-pharmacological interventions for ADHD such as behavioral interventions, neurofeedback, cognitive training, and elimination diets. Much of the "evidence" offered for these interventions thus far is unblinded, without adequate protection from reporter bias. This is not to say that such treatments are never helpful for any children. In some cases they might be useful for treatment of other emotional or behavioral problems. However, at present, none of these treatments is supported by substantial evidence of effectiveness for alleviating impairments of ADHD.

Comparisons of Effectiveness of Medication and/or Psychosocial Treatments for ADHD

Two major studies have compared effectiveness of psychosocial treatments for ADHD with and without medication treatment for ADHD. One study conducted between 1990 and 1995 in New York City and in Montreal compared 103 children divided into three experimental groups. One group received only carefully managed medication treatment, specifically short-acting methyl-phenidate given three times daily for two years, but no psychosocial treatments.

Another group received the same program of carefully managed medication supplemented by a rich program of multimodal psychosocial interventions that included parent training and counseling, academic assistance, psychotherapy and social skills training. A third group received the carefully managed medication supplemented only with a limited attention control treatment program (Abikoff, et al., 2004a, 2004b; Hechtman, et al., 2004a, 2004b).

Participants in all three programs improved after the first year of treatment and maintained their improvement over the second year of treatment. However, the expectations of those conducting the study were not confirmed by obtained results. The assumption at the outset was that those children who received both medication and the full package of psychosocial treatments would improve significantly more and would be able to sustain their improvements, even after the treatments had been stopped, more than would children treated only with the carefully monitored medication. In fact, those children treated with the combination of psychosocial interventions and carefully managed medication for ADHD showed no better improvement than those children who received only carefully managed medication three times daily for seven days each week. Nor did the addition of psychosocial treatments increase the length of time participating children could function before relapsing after active treatment was concluded with substitution of placebo. Children in all three groups deteriorated in their functioning and had to resume taking methylphenidate again to recapture and continue the benefits of treatment (Abikoff, et al., 2004a, 2004b; Hechtman, et al., 2004a, 2004b).

The other major study designed to assess the relative effectiveness of medication and psychosocial treatment for ADHD was the six-site MTA study of 579 children aged seven to nine years at outset, diagnosed with ADHD, who were randomly assigned to one of four arms of treatment for 14 months (MTA Cooperative Group, 1999):

1   medication management without any psychosocial treatment;

2   behavioral treatment which included individual and group parent training, classroom behavioral management with a trained paraprofessional working with the teacher, and an intensive eight-week summer treatment program, with no medication treatment;

3   combined treatment including all of the treatments in 1 and 2 above;

4   referral to community care treatment resources.

Similar to the findings of the Montreal-New York study described above, this study demonstrated that for the core symptoms of ADHD being assessed, there were no significant differences in the mean scores for outcome measures between those with the combined medication and psychosocial treatment versus those who received medication treatment alone. There were indications that the combined treatment had some advantages in alleviating non-core symptoms associated with ADHD. The MTA study reported follow-up assessments of the participants for several years after cessation of controlled treatments, but results of those studies are not very useful given that there was no adequate monitoring or control of continuing treatment. It should also be noted that applicability of findings from these two studies cannot reasonably be generalized to other age groups or to those whose ADHD impairments are of the predominantly inattentive type.

In reviewing these two major studies Jensen, Abikoff, and Brown (2009) noted: "One important finding from the two multimodal studies is that medication treatment seems to be the critical ingredient for alleviating ADHD symptoms in most patients with ADHD" (p. 416). Hinshaw's review (2009) made a similar point in noting that "Although individual differences are clearly the rule, on average, medication treatments yield stronger effects than do behavioral interventions" (p. 388).

Another problem in psychosocial treatments that involve parent participation is the difficulty some parents with ADHD have in following through consistently with planned interventions. Hinshaw (2009) observed that, given the high rate of heritability of this disorder, in many families of children with ADHD it is very difficult for parents to implement behavioral interventions effectively and with the consistency which is essential to successful treatment.

> Implementing behavioral contingencies for a child or an adolescent with ADHD is a formidable task; when the caregivers who implement those procedures have problems with organization, impulse control and emotion regulation themselves, it is little wonder that consistent performance may be problematic (p. 389).

Another important limitation of both psychosocial treatments and medication treatments for ADHD was noted by Hinshaw (2009). Neither type of intervention cures the disorder!

> A key limitation of both medication and behavioral treatments for ADHD is that the effects of both tend to dissipate rapidly when the

medication is terminated or the contingencies are lifted. Thus, a key implication is that both behavioral and medication treatments are best viewed as palliative rather than curative... recommendations for extended treatment are now viewed as the rule rather than the exception (p. 389).

There have been some studies of psychosocial treatments for ADHD in adults. McDermott (2009) has reviewed key concepts and research on cognitive therapy for adults with ADHD; and Safren, et al. (2005) have published a treatment manual for cognitive-behavioral treatment of adults with ADHD. An extensive review of non-medication treatments for ADHD in adults has been provided by Ramsay (2010). Another approach to psychosocial treatment for adults with ADHD is a program designed by Solanto (Solanto, et al., 2008; Solanto, 2011) to assist adults with ADHD in learning more effective executive function skills such as time management, organizational and planning skills. Since 70% of adults participating in this program were also medicated for their ADHD symptoms, it is difficult to know how much of the progress observed in this study was due to the medication and how much to other aspects of the intervention.

Increasingly research has highlighted the advantages of psychosocial treatments in combination with medication treatments for ADHD. Rostain and Ramsay (2006) reported a study of 43 patients treated with both medication and cognitive-behavioral methods in an integrated program. Ramsay and Rostain have also provided a manual (2008) that describes how such integrated treatment can be accomplished. A study by Safren, et al. (2005) found that 56% of study participants responded to combined treatment while only 13% did not.

Some educators have recognized the critical importance of executive functions for students in school and have put forward programs to teach executive functions to students of various ages (Meltzer, 2007, 2010; Dawson & Guare, 2004, 2010). Many of these programs propose useful strategies for helping students to develop skills that facilitate executive functioning in learning and school settings. However, such programs often do not distinguish adequately between helping individuals whose executive functions are developing within the usual range for their age, and assisting students who are significantly impaired in development of their executive functions. For the former group, the majority of students, such interventions can be useful additions to the curriculum to help students improve their executive skills and enhance their learning and productive work.

But the latter group, those individuals whose executive functions are developmentally impaired, whose brain infrastructure has not yet developed executive function capacity to within the normal range for their age, those are the students with ADHD. Instructional programs to develop their executive function skills are not likely to be successful without medication treatment of their underlying impairments.

Cognitive impairments of ADHD are not likely to be significantly improved simply by coaching or didactic instruction in relevant skills. Quite often students with ADHD know quite well what they should be doing to plan, prioritize and organize and start their work, to focus and to shift focus, to keep in mind what they have just read or heard, to sustain effort for completion of a necessary task, etc. They are simply not able to get themselves to do these things.

For individuals with ADHD, repeated instruction in what they should be doing to exercise executive skills for their academic work is comparable to repeatedly explaining and demonstrating to an individual with paralysis of both legs how they should be moving their legs in order to walk. This analogy implies an all-or-nothing division between those with ADHD and those whose development of the capacity for learning and exercising executive skills is within normal range. In fact, there is considerable variability in severity of impairment among those with ADHD and there are many individual differences in profiles of strengths and weaknesses.

The point here is not that instruction in how to develop and exercise adaptive executive skills is useless for anyone with an ADHD diagnosis. Such instruction may be quite useful, even to persons with significant ADHD impairments, but usually effective medication treatment for ADHD is prerequisite to those with ADHD being able to make effective use of such instruction and being able to retain and practice with some consistency the executive skills they are being taught. A similar point might be made for approaches to "coaching" adolescents or adults with ADHD without their receiving concurrent support from effective medication.

These instructional approaches to ADHD might do well to review the history of cognitive training interventions for children with "hyperactivity," the syndrome now known as ADHD. In 1985 Abikoff reviewed a decade of research efforts designed to develop "self-control skills and reflective problem-solving strategies" by instructing the child and modeling how this should be done.

It was hypothesized that training the children to use appropriate, task relevant, reflective cognitive strategies would result in positive behavior changes. To this end, cognitive modeling and self-instructional techniques were employed with a variety of psychoeducational tasks... that emphasized the importance of defining the task problem, focusing attention, evaluating performance, and correcting errors.... Finally the child worked silently, using covert self-instructions to guide his or her performance (Abikoff, 1985, pp. 480–481).

After reviewing 23 studies of this approach, Abikoff observed: "The expectation that the development of internalized self-regulation skills would facilitate generalization and maintenance has not been realized" (1985, p. 508). Five years later Abikoff and Hechtman began their large two-year study that demonstrated the essential importance of medication for alleviation of ADHD symptoms and the necessity of ongoing treatment to sustain treatment effects.

Accommodations for Individuals with ADHD

In addition to medication and/or psychosocial treatment, some, but not all, individuals with ADHD need accommodations in their school or workplace in order to have a fair chance to learn and work productively. One accommodation needed by many students is extended time for taking tests or examinations. Although some individuals with ADHD rush too much when taking tests, often making careless errors that go unnoticed and uncorrected, there are also many with ADHD who suffer from slow processing speed and impairments of working memory that make it necessary for them to re-read texts in order to adequately grasp the meaning, who need to recheck their calculations to catch careless errors, who struggle to choose between multiple choice question responses, or who are painstakingly slow to write sentences and paragraphs. Brown, Reichel and Quinlan (2011d) have demonstrated the significant improvement in scores that a modest extension of time for taking tests requiring reading comprehension can provide for students with ADHD.

Other accommodations and supports may include special education services or classroom modifications for students in school. Information about how parents can collaborate with their child's school to obtain needed accommodations available for those with ADHD under relevant laws is provided in a book by Jensen (2004). Ramsay (2010) has described academic support and accommodations for post-secondary students with ADHD. And Latham and Latham (2007) have provided comprehensive information about legal aspects of accommodations for those with learning disabilities and/or ADHD in higher education and employment.

Comprehensive guidelines for assessment and treatment of ADHD have been published by the American Academy of Child and Adolescent Psychiatry (1997, 2007), by the American Academy of Pediatrics (2011), and by the Canadian Attention Deficit Hyperactivity Disorder Resource Alliance (2011).

This chapter began with the observation that medical/psychological treatment usually seeks to minimize suffering and impairment and to improve functioning. It also noted that such treatment also has two primary constraints: availability of knowledgeable persons and resources necessary for treatment, and willingness of the patient to engage in the necessary procedures. At present, the reality is that many individuals suffering from ADHD do not have access to knowledgeable persons and resources necessary for treatment. This is especially true of adolescents and adults living in countries that still will not allow treatment of anyone over 16 years with medications for ADHD. It is also true that many are reluctant to engage and sustain effective treatment because of lack of adequate understanding of the disorder and its treatment or because of exaggerated and unrealistic fears or prejudices about the disorder.

6

WHY MANY LEARNING AND PSYCHIATRIC DISORDERS SO OFTEN CO-OCCUR WITH ADHD

The term "comorbidity" is medical jargon for having one or more disorders co-occurring with another. For example, if a child has ADHD concurrent with an anxiety disorder, the anxiety disorder would be considered comorbid with the ADHD. Likewise, an adolescent who has ADHD along with Oppositional Defiant Disorder who then develops a substance use disorder, or an adult who has ADHD concurrent with Obsessive-Compulsive Disorder. When one or more disorders occurs with ADHD, it is important that each and all of the disorders are recognized and taken into account in planning and evaluating treatment. Comorbid combinations of disorders are quite different from pure forms of any of the disorders involved (Angold, et al., 1999). Some comorbid combinations require additional treatments while some others narrow the range of treatments that should be used for the ADHD.

This chapter summarizes some of the research on various combinations of ADHD comorbid with other disorders. More comprehensive information about these and various other combinations is available in the volume on ADHD comorbidities edited by Brown (2009). The initial chapter of that book includes a detailed discussion of the developmental complexities of comorbidities in combination with the new model of ADHD described in the chapters of this current book.

In trying to understand comorbidities, it is helpful to keep in mind that psychological/psychiatric disorders are not substantial entities like a tumor or clogged artery. Unlike diagnoses for bodily ills, these disorders are conceptual "pigeon holes" used to identify persisting and problematic patterns of emotions, thinking and behaving that often occur together. Over recent years researchers have increasingly recognized that many disorders are better understood as dimensional rather than "all-or-nothing" categorical classifications, on a wide spectrum of impairment, often overlapping with other disorders. This has led many to agree with Cloninger (1999) who asserted that "there is no empirical evidence" for "natural boundaries between major syndromes"; and that "no one has ever found a set of symptoms, signs or tests that separate mental disorders into non-overlapping categories"; and that "the categorical approach is fundamentally flawed" (p. 184).

Despite the substantial reasons for questioning the validity of diagnostic categories as currently conceived, these categories do serve a useful purpose. Kendell and Jablensky (2003) have helpfully distinguished between the questionable validity and the clinical utility of psychiatric diagnoses:

> Diagnostic categories provide invaluable information about the likelihood of future recovery, relapse, deterioration, and social handicap; they guide decisions about treatment; and they provide a wealth of information about similar patients encountered in clinical populations or community surveys throughout the world (p. 9).

Usefulness of such information is substantial, so long as the clinician does not lose sight of the individuality of each patient and the likelihood that each individual is likely to have some unique characteristics which may distinguish him or her from others with similar diagnoses.

Following an initial summary of research on broad patterns of comorbidity associated with ADHD, this chapter describes seven specific clusters of disorders often comorbid with ADHD. Each of those sections includes some discussion about specific aspects of the new model of ADHD that play an important role in that specific comorbid configuration.

Research reports on comorbidity are not all consistent in the way they classify comorbidities. Some studies are cross-sectional, counting only disorders occurring within the past six months or the past year. Other research reports include as comorbid any disorder that has occurred within the lifetime of the individual. Each approach has its own values and limitations.

Two additional ways of categorizing comorbidity can also be useful. Lahey and colleagues (2002) have used the term "dynamic comorbidity" to refer to comorbidities that wax and wane over an individual's lifetime, possibly in response to situational influences such as the presence or absence of specific stressors and supports, or the unfolding of developmental factors. For example, some patients with ADHD suffer from Obsessive-Compulsive Disorder symptoms or substance abuse problems that worsen when they are under stress and virtually disappear when their life situation is less stressful.

Another useful category of comorbidity is "subthreshold comorbidity" described by Lewinsohn, et al., (2004) which refers to situations where a person may have multiple impairing symptoms of a particular disorder, possibly over a long time, yet those symptoms do not fully meet the official diagnostic criteria of that particular disorder. An example would be an individual who has significant anxiety problems without fully meeting diagnostic criteria for an anxiety disorder.

Numerous studies have shown that most children, adolescents and adults who meet diagnostic criteria for ADHD also meet criteria for at least one additional psychiatric disorder. Some meet criteria for several different disorders at the same time; others suffer from one comorbid disorder at one point in their life which gradually becomes more or less problematic. Rates of these comorbid disorders among persons with ADHD are much greater than among others who do not have ADHD.

In a retrospective birth cohort study of 343 children diagnosed with ADHD before age 19 years, 62% had at least one additional psychiatric disorder; only 19% of 712 controls had any psychiatric disorder by the same age. This is a threefold increased risk of a comorbid disorder for those with ADHD. The percentage of children in that study having two or more disorders was 34% for those with ADHD and just 8% for controls. The most common comorbidities among patients with ADHD in that study are listed below:

	ADHD %	Non-ADHD %
Adjustment disorders	34.5	10.2
Mood disorders	22.9	7.2
Oppositional Defiant/Conduct Disorder	22.5	2.7
Substance use disorders	21.2	6.3
Anxiety disorders	9.6	3.5

The category of adjustment disorders shown above is not often used in studies of comorbidities; generally it refers to problems with mood, anxiety and/or conduct that seem related to specific environmental stressors. That 2012 study also showed that rates of comorbidity were not significantly different for boys and girls with ADHD or between genders of the non-ADHD children (Yoshimasu, et al., 2012a).

High incidence of comorbid disorders has been found even among very young children with ADHD. Among the 579 children aged seven to nine years who were enrolled in the MTA study, 70% met full diagnostic criteria for at least one other psychiatric disorder in the year prior to their enrollment (Jensen, et al., 2001). In that sample of children, all of whom were diagnosed with ADHD, the most common comorbid disorders were:

- Oppositional Defiant Disorder   40%
- Anxiety Disorder   34%
- Conduct Disorder   14%
- Tic Disorder   11%
- Mood Disorder   4%

One variable which affects comorbidity patterns is age. Some disorders do not usually onset until late childhood or adolescence. This is illustrated in the very low percentage of young children in the MTA study diagnosed with a mood disorder as contrasted with the 14% of adolescents diagnosed with a mood disorder in a subsequent epidemiological study.

Among adolescents in the general population seen for assessment of lifetime psychiatric disorders (only 8.7% of whom were diagnosed with ADHD) the median age of onset was earliest for anxiety disorders (6 years) followed by 11 years for behavior disorders (including ADHD), 13 years for mood disorders, and 15 years for substance use disorders. In that sample, 49.5% had been diagnosed with at least one class of psychiatric disorder, 27.6% suffered severe impairment from that diagnosed disorder. (Merikangas, et al., 2010).

Impact of comorbidity on academic, family and social functioning was assessed by parent report in a national study of over 61,000 children aged 6 to 17 years (Larson, et al., 2011). The reported incidence of ADHD in that sample was 8.2%. Comorbid disorders reported in those children with ADHD compared to children without ADHD are listed below.

	ADHD %	Non-ADHD %
Learning disability	46.1	5.3
Conduct disorders	27.4	1.8
Anxiety	17.8	2.1
Depression	13.9	1.4
Speech problem	11.8	2.5
Autism Spectrum Disorder	6.0	0.6

Most children with ADHD in this 2007 study had at least one comorbid disorder: 33% had one comorbid disorder, 16% had two, and 18% had three or more. Stress from socioeconomic limitations was found to be a significant complicating factor. Children from economically deprived families had a 3.8 times higher rate of comorbidity than did children from affluent families (30% versus 8%).

Functional impairments in this sample included 29% of ADHD children having repeated a grade in school; children with ADHD also had lower scores for social competence, and higher scores reporting parental aggravation than those without ADHD. For children with ADHD, the odds of poorer functioning increased in a step-wise fashion with increasing numbers of comorbid disorders.

There are certainly differences between these three data sets of comorbidities observed in children and adolescents with ADHD. One is a retrospective review of charts in a medical center, another is based on exhaustive diagnostic evaluations done by specialists, and the third is based on parental report of diagnoses made by professionals. One listing includes adjustment disorders, the others do not; another includes learning disabilities, speech problems and Autism Spectrum Disorder while the other two omit these three important categories. Despite these differences, these three studies taken together clearly indicate than most children and adolescents diagnosed with ADHD are also suffering with one or more comorbid disorders. Those disorders tend to increase their impairment and complicate development of effective treatment plans.

Some of the limitations of individual studies of comorbidity are compensated for in a meta-analysis which compares multiple studies. In a meta-analysis of 21 general population studies of comorbidity among children with ADHD, Angold, Costello and Erkanli (1999) found that the likelihood of anxiety disorders, depressive disorders, or conduct/oppositional disorders among children with ADHD is respectively about 3 times, 5.5 times and 10.7 times the prevalence of those disorders in the general population of children. However, it should be noted that this meta-analysis put Oppositional Defiant Disorder and Conduct Disorder together in a single category, despite the fact that those two disorders are not equivalent, thus that high prevalence rate should not be taken as valid for either disorder separately.

Comorbidity of other disorders with ADHD may sometimes modify ADHD symptoms. For example, clinical experience indicates that many individuals who have ADHD with comorbid anxiety disorders tend to do better in completing homework and other schoolwork because their exaggerated fear of getting into trouble with teachers and/or parents may counteract excessive procrastination and motivate them to work harder and more consistently than most other children with ADHD. More often, comorbidity exacerbates impairments caused by ADHD. Booster, et al. (2012) demonstrated that children with ADHD and both externalizing (e.g. behavioral disorders like Oppositional Defiant Disorder or Conduct Disorder) and internalizing (e.g.

anxiety or depressive disorders) comorbid disorders tend to display more severe problems with homework completion and poorer social skills than children with ADHD alone. The Larson (2011) study discussed above provided clear evidence of how increasing numbers of comorbid disorders tend to bring increased overall impairment in children and adolescents with ADHD.

Adults with ADHD also have elevated rates of comorbid disorders. Kessler and colleagues reported data from the National Comorbidity Study Replication (Kessler, et al. 2005, 2006) indicating that adults with ADHD in the community, not referred for treatment, had more than six times the likelihood of having at least one additional psychiatric disorder at some point in their lifetime up to age 44 years when compared with the general population. The numbers below show the lifetime prevalence of categories of comorbid disorders in adults with ADHD aged 18 to 44 years; the column under Odds Ratio (OR) shows the odds ratio for that disorder compared to the general population. An OR of 1.0 indicates that persons with ADHD have the same prevalence as the general population, 3.0 indicates three times the base rate in the general population.

Disorder	Lifetime Prevalence %	Odds Ratio
Mood disorders	38.3	5.0
Anxiety disorders	47.1	3.7
Substance use disorders	15.2	3.0
Impulse disorders	19.6	3.7
Any psychiatric disorder	88.6	6.3

The specific comorbid disorder most frequently reported in adults with ADHD studied by Kessler and colleagues (2006) was social anxiety (29.3%). This is a substantial increase from the rate of social anxiety found in a national epidemiological study which was 11.7% for adolescents aged 13 to 18 years (Burstein, et al., 2011). Many adolescents and even more adults with ADHD suffer from excessive worries about how others view them and/or are often irritable or argumentative with others.

Another aspect of comorbidity among adults with ADHD, one less discussed, is comorbidity with personality disorders, persistent patterns of personality functioning that tend to be maladaptive in interpersonal functioning. Miller, Nigg and Faraone (2007) studied three composite types of personality disorders among 363 adults with combined type or inattentive type ADHD in comparison to non-ADHD controls. They found that adults with combined type of ADHD tended to manifest more severe overall impairment than adults with predominantly inattentive type. They also assessed the frequencies of three composite types of personality disorder in this sample of adults. The clusters of disorders studied were:

A   Paranoid, schizoid and/or schizotypal personality disorders

B   Borderline, antisocial, histrionic, and/or narcissistic personality disorders

C   Avoidant, dependent, and/or obsessive compulsive personality disorders

This study found that adults with ADHD tended to have a higher incidence of both Cluster B and Cluster C personality disorders independent of whether the ADHD participant was of the predominantly inattentive or combined type. Frequency distributions of the types are listed below.

	Controls %	*ADHD (any subtype) %*
Cluster A	No significant difference between ADHD and controls	
Cluster B	9.5	24.4
Cluster C	4.3	21.0

Data from that study indicated no significant difference between controls and persons with ADHD in the frequency of Cluster A personality disorder. However, in comparison to controls, those with ADHD had 3.1 increased likelihood of a Cluster B disorder and 6.48 increased likelihood of a Cluster C disorder.

The most frequent Cluster B personality disorder seen in the ADHD group was Borderline Personality Disorder which is characterized by "a pervasive pattern of instability in interpersonal relationships, self-image and affects, and marked impulsivity... in a variety of contexts" (DSM-IV, p. 706). In Cluster C, the most frequent was Obsessive-Compulsive Personality Disorder which involves "preoccupation with orderliness, perfectionism, and mental and interpersonal control, at the expense of flexibility, openness and efficiency" (American Psychiatric Association, 2000, p. 725). These two types of personality disorder seen most frequently among patients with ADHD could be seen as sharply contrasting patterns of reacting to and coping with underlying impairments of executive function implicated in ADHD.

As shown above, rates of co-occurrence or comorbidity of other psychiatric disorders with ADHD in both children and adults are very high, ranging from two to ten times higher than the incidence of these disorders in the general population. One might reasonably ask why persons with ADHD are so vulnerable to additional psychiatric impairments. It is not likely that this is due to persons with ADHD simply being unlucky. It is more likely that the high incidence of comorbidity is due to limitations of our current conceptual system for classifying psychiatric disorders. The pigeon holes of the present classification system do not adequately capture the complex hybrids and overlaps of many psychiatric disorders.

It seems likely that the impairments of executive function implicated in ADHD are underlying factors in many other disorders as well. Sergeant, et al. (2002) observed that executive function impairments are not specific to ADD, but are characteristic of many other disorders as well. Brown (2009) has argued that the syndrome of impairments currently known as ADHD should be seen not as just one of many psychiatric disorders, but as a foundational disorder that cuts across many different disorders and renders affected individuals more vulnerable to environmental stressors that increase the risk of incurring another disorder. He also notes that ADHD is associated with genetic vulnerability to other disorders.

Brown (2009) suggested that most psychiatric disorders could be compared to software problems in a computer that impact only one or two specific domains of functioning without compromising operation of other software programs. He proposed that, in contrast, ADHD could be compared to a significant problem in the operating system of the computer, a problem that can impact multiple domains of functioning. From this view, comorbidity between ADHD and other disorders is seen as a more general problem underlying many other disorders, each of which also has its own unique and specific impairments.

One consequence of the high rates of comorbidity that accompany ADHD is that sometimes when persons with ADHD seek treatment for their difficulties, their comorbid disorder is recognized and treated while their underlying ADHD remains unrecognized and untreated. This occurs because many physicians, psychologists and other mental health professionals have not received sufficient education about the new understandings of ADHD. Many are more familiar with depression, anxiety, Obsessive-Compulsive Disorder, substance abuse and other disorders and are therefore quicker to recognize and treat these more familiar problems. Barkley and Brown (2008) and Fischer, et al. (2007) have described this problem and the importance of clinicians assessing for ADHD when they are assessing for other disorders that may be comorbid.

ADHD with Learning Disorders

For decades specific learning disorders (LD), e.g. reading disorder (dyslexia), math disorder (dyscalculia) and disorder of written language have been seen as totally separate from ADHD. More recent research has found that while there are certainly differences between LD and ADHD, impairments of executive function associated with the new model of ADHD play an important role in each of the primary learning disorders.

In a review of clinical data from children diagnosed with ADHD, Mayes, Calhoun and Crowell (2000) found that children with LD and ADHD had more severe learning problems than children who had LD without ADHD, and that those with LD and ADHD also had more severe attention problems than children who had ADHD without LD. They concluded that "learning and attention problems are on a continuum, are interrelated and usually coexist" (p. 417).

Among a large sample of children aged 6 to 16 years (mean age=9 years) diagnosed with ADHD, 76% met diagnostic criteria for one or more specific learning disorders (Mayes & Calhoun, 2007). The most frequent LD in this group of 678 children was disorder of written expression (65%); frequency for math disorder was 20% to 30% while frequency for LD in reading was 30% to 52%. These researchers found that the best predictors of LD in reading, math and written expression were the students' WISC-III or IV index scores for working memory and processing speed, two important aspects of executive functioning.

Similarly, among adolescents with ADHD, working memory, a primary executive function associated with the new model, especially auditory verbal working memory, is strongly associated with achievement in reading and math, while spatial working memory and inattention are significantly associated specifically with math achievement (Rogers, et al., 2011).

Two executive functions, working memory and processing speed, have been shown in multiple studies to be central to reading as well as to ADHD. In a sample of 145 adolescents aged 13 to 18 years, Brown, Reichel and Quinlan (2011d) demonstrated that reading comprehension difficulties of adolescent students with ADHD are related not so much to weak verbal abilities or weak basic reading skills, as to impairments of working memory and processing speed. The importance of working memory, particularly verbal working memory, for reading comprehension has been supported also in meta-analytic studies by Swanson, Zheng and Jerman (2009) and Carretti, et al. (2009). Evidence for a central role of processing speed in reading and ADHD has been provided by Shanahan and colleagues (2006) and by McGrath, et al. (2011).

Working memory and processing speed, are not so important when the child is asked to decode and pronounce single words, but they are critical for comprehension of sentences and paragraphs. This was described by Sesma and colleagues (2009):

> Reading comprehension is inherently more complex than single word reading, with demands that go beyond phonological decoding and word identification and include higher order cognitive processing of meaning conveyed through sentences and paragraphs... executive control skills such as planning and working memory become more necessary as the length and complexity of written text increases (p. 8).

Comprehension of more complex text requires the ability to retain the central ideas or information presented in the text, in its segments and as a whole, and continually to update understanding of connections between these elements, building and revising a mental representation of the primary ideas or actions in the passage. Miller, et al. (2012b) compared children with ADHD and matched controls with comparable basic reading skills. They found that those with ADHD were significantly impaired relative to controls in these reading comprehension processes; they identified this problem as "centrality deficit," a difficulty in recall of central information of passages read. After testing for a variety of ADHD symptoms that might cause this deficit, their data identified impairment of working memory as the primary underlying cause of this inability to identify accurately the major points of the text.

Importance of attentional mechanisms for reading comprehension has also been emphasized by dyslexia researchers, Shaywitz and Shaywitz, (2008) as they noted that reading is not simply a modular process dependent only on phonological processing needed to decode words. They argued that, given recent research in dyslexia, reading must now be understood as involving also attention mechanisms that are essential to fluency and automaticity in reading. "The critical requirement for automaticity is for the reader to encode the relevant items in memory and to retrieve them on a subsequent encounter... for both encoding and retrieval, attention is central" (p. 1332). To address impairments in attention for dyslexic readers, Shaywitz and Shaywitz suggested treatment with medications used for treatment of ADHD.

Math is another academic area in which impairment of working memory has been found to be important. A study of 209 children divided students in first and second grade according to their having low math achievement or typically developing math achievement. Results indicated that performance on tests of working memory was a better predictor of typical achievement in math than was mastery of basic math skills (Toll, et al., 2011).

Recent research has demonstrated that math fluency, i.e. processing speed for calculating simple math problems, is largely independent of ability to compute math problems without time limits. Two-thirds of the variance in math fluency was independent from untimed math measures in a study done by Petrill, et al. (2012).

Berninger and Richards (2002) have highlighted the complex role of executive functions in math computations. They discuss the brain doing math as "the Computing Brain."

> The Computing Brain keeps the executive/government system very busy... (it) recruits the Reading Brain during written math word problem solving and the Writing Brain during written computation. During problem solving, the Computing Brain recruits the executive system to create goals and plans, coordinate multiple operations, and exert control over the working memory system... the executive governing, attentional and memory systems work together (p. 208).

ADHD-related executive function impairments are also strongly associated with written language disorder. In a large study of children with ADHD, Mayes and Calhoun reported that 65% met diagnostic criteria for disorder of written expression (2006). Brown, Reichel, and Quinlan reported that in a study of adolescents with ADHD aged 13 to 25 years, for 70% of the adolescents disorder of written expression was the lowest of their achievement test scores, significantly below their scores for reading and math (2010). Both of these studies showed that impairments of working memory and processing speed were strongly associated with obtained weaknesses in written expression.

High levels of overlap between ADHD and disorder of written language (written expression) were also found in a population-based, non-referred, sample of boys and girls with and without ADHD (Yoshimasu, et al., 2012b). Comparison of the ADHD sample and controls indicated that 46.9% of children with ADHD also suffered from disorder of written language while only 9.6% of children without ADHD manifested that learning disorder.

Berninger and Richards (2002) have described how written expression places greater demands on executive functions than does reading or math.

Writing may place a greater burden on working memory than does reading comprehension. Writing is an immense juggling act, with many more jobs to do than reading. The writing jobs include planning (generating ideas and setting goals), translating those ideas into text, transcribing the text, and reviewing and revising it.... Reading may also require multiple executive functions... however, writing may require more work on the part of those executive processes than reading does. Control processes for extracting the meaning from a finished text (reading) are not as taxing as the executive processes that go into generating and repairing a text until it is deemed a final product (writing) (p. 173–174).

In their discussion of brain functions involved in reading, writing and math, Berninger and Richards (2002) also note the fundamental importance of arousal and attention, for example:

Brains that are asleep do not respond to the stimuli that feed into the reading process.... The reading brain also needs an attentional system. Too much is happening in the external environment for learning to pay attention to everything.... The posterior attentional system allows the Reading Brain to select the most relevant information in the external environment for the target of its attention (p. 155).

This emphasis upon arousal, activation and selective attention points to the critical, but often neglected, problem of motivation for reading, writing and math. In a study of junior high students reading social studies texts Anmarkrud and Braten (2009) found that the value the individual assigns to a reading task tends to be a more important determinant of reading comprehension than the individual's cognitive capacity to read well. They noted that the question of "Can I understand what I read?" may be less important than the question "Do I want to understand what I read and why?" Their study of junior high students' reading of a social studies text led them to observe that:

comprehension of challenging text seems to require not only cognition, but also motivation... beliefs about how important it is to do well on given tasks, how useful those tasks are in relationship to current and future goals, and how intrinsically interesting they are to the individual (p. 252).

These findings are consistent with the observations of Brown about the situational variability of ADHD-related executive function impairments described in Chapter 2. Absence of adequate motivation for reading has been described in Brown's discussion of "passive reading" (2005a). It is illustrated in the comment of a college student who observed:

> If I'm reading some text that doesn't really interest me, it's as though I'm just licking the words and not chewing them. My eyes go over each word and I understand what all of it means as I'm reading it, but I'm just not engaged enough to get the information to stick inside my head.

How ADHD is Related to Learning Disorders

Taken together, research on comorbidity between ADHD and LD highlights the critical role of executive functions in learning and its disorders. Most important are abilities to focus and sustain attention, to engage with the task, and to utilize working memory. This comorbidity involves general impairments of executive function in combination with impairments of more specific skills related to reading, writing and/or math.

A dimensional view of this overlap is also important. While some with ADHD also suffer sufficient impairment in reading, writing and/or math to warrant an additional diagnosis of learning disorder, many others whose difficulties in these domains are not severe enough to warrant an LD diagnosis, do suffer significant impairment in their learning and academic work due to the executive function impairments of their ADHD.

ADHD with Anxiety and Depressive Disorders

High rates of comorbidity between ADHD and anxiety, as well as between ADHD and depressive disorders are reported in the initial section of this chapter. Both children and adults with ADHD tend to have markedly elevated rates of anxiety and depressive disorders when compared with the general population. In samples of ADHD children comorbid anxiety rates range from 9.6% to 34% (Jensen, et al., 2001; Yoshimasu, et al., 2012a); among ADHD adults reported rates range from 27.9% to 47.1% (Kessler, 2011; Van Ameringen, et al., 2011). Rates for depression in children with ADHD range from 13.9% to 22.9%; estimates for adults with ADHD are in the 38% to 63% range (Millstein, et al., 1997; Kessler, et al., 2006). While many with ADHD have none or just one of these two comorbid disorders, it is also true that these two categories of disorder often occur together in a given individual.

Both anxiety symptoms and depressive symptoms occur in a variety of forms. Two major types of anxiety disorders are:

- those characterized by "anxious-misery", usually focused on worrying in preparation for a dreaded state or event that is expected to occur in the future;
- those characterized by fear that occurs in response to an immediate threat of perceived danger.

Examples of the first type are chronically excessive worry and anxiety about many things (generalized anxiety disorder), and intense stress reactive to personal experience with a life-threatening stressor (post-traumatic stress disorder). Examples of the second type are unexpected, recurrent attacks of panic followed by persistent concern about having additional attacks (panic disorder), persistent fear of being embarrassed in a social situation which leads to avoidance (social phobia), excessive fear of being in a place where escape is impossible or where help might be unavailable during a panic attack (agoraphobia), and circumscribed fear of specific objects or situations accompanied by extreme fear of being in such a situation (specific phobia) (Craske, et al., 2009).

Depressive disorders include low grade chronically depressed mood, where one can still carry on most necessary functions, but has low self-esteem and little pleasure in most activities (dysthymia); and more severe, extremely depressed mood nearly every day with severely diminished pleasure in most activities, disturbance of eating and/or sleeping, and persisting feelings of worthlessness (Major Depressive Disorder). The depressive mood involved in each of these tends to reflect hopeless preoccupation with past losses, disappointments or failures, assuming that this is or will become a persisting pattern. Attention here is often focused recurrently upon images or thoughts of these gloomily recalled aspects of the past, as though none of this is likely ever to get any better. Hope is largely diminished.

Research over the past two decades has confirmed strong correlations among these two types of anxiety and depression, components of the "tripartite model" (Craske, et al., 2009). That model proposes that anxiety and depression share some symptoms while there are also some symptoms specific to each. The shared symptoms comprise a general distress factor and pervasive negative emotion. In both of these types of disorder, the individual tends to feel chronically unhappy, burdened, stressed and inadequate. Specific symptoms of depression include loss of interest or pleasure in most activities and lack of positive affect; specific symptoms of anxiety are physiological hyperarousal (fear) and excessive worry.

A new addition to the classification of depressive disorders appears in DSM-V: Disruptive Mood Dysregulation Disorder. This diagnosis was proposed to describe children or adolescents who tend to have persistently irritable mood and demonstrate severe recurrent temper outbursts on an almost daily basis. These outbursts are not episodic, as in Bipolar Disorder, and they are much more severe than the irritability associated with Oppositional Defiant Disorder. Those with this disorder tend to react to even minor disappointments or frustrations with disproportionately intense anger (Leibenluft, 2011). While most persons who are depressed become sad and less active, those with Disruptive Mood Dysregulation tend to get more agitated and irritable in their reactions. Longitudinal data suggest that children and adolescents with the syndrome of severe Disruptive Mood Dysregulation tend to qualify also for the diagnosis of ADHD; as they get older they tend to suffer from anxiety and/or depressive disorders (Rich, et al., 2011).

How ADHD is Related to Anxiety and Depressive Disorders

One way to integrate understanding of why individuals with ADHD tend to be more susceptible to problems with anxiety, depression and/or irritability than those without ADHD is to recognize that these difficulties can be seen as particular instances of a core aspect of ADHD as it is described in Chapter 2: chronic difficulty with regulation of emotion. Seymour, et al. (2012) have demonstrated that children diagnosed with ADHD tended to have impaired capacity to regulate emotion and that this usually preceded the onset of depression in students with ADHD, much more than in matched controls. Two important components of this impairment of emotional regulation in those with ADHD are chronic problems with working memory and attention bias toward fearful or depressing thoughts.

One important reason for the high rates of comorbidity between ADHD, anxiety and depression is chronic difficulty of affected persons in shifting their focus away from excessive attention on what interests or concerns them. Recent research has recognized the critical role of biased attention in both anxiety and depressive disorders. Review articles highlight studies showing that anxious individuals tend to be exceptionally alert to potential threats in ways that bias their information processing at several levels—in what they focus their attention on (orienting), how they size up situations they encounter in terms of likely impact on them (appraisal), and what patterns of response they have found helpful for them (learning) (Britton, et al., 2010; Shechner, et al., 2012).

Very anxious persons tend to be perpetually scanning for thoughts or perceptions that, for them, signal potential danger. Anxious persons tend also to be very quick to assess thoughts and situations as potentially threatening, even in circumstances of considerable ambiguity. And they tend to learn by repeated conditioning that they can reduce their anxiety by avoiding situations linked to these perceived threats. Such avoidance is a powerful reinforcer. Each time avoidance reduces anxiety, it increases the likelihood of further avoidance and reinforces the tendency of the individual to continue to give priority attention to potential dangers in daily life. These patterns then can become quite resistant to change, particularly in individuals who have excessive difficulty in shifting focus from emotionally charged stimuli, as do many with ADHD.

Capacity to regulate emotions such as anxiety or depression and their associated thoughts also depend, in part, on working memory capacity, a function often relatively weak in individuals with ADHD (Martinussen, et al., 2005; Quinlan & Brown, 2003). Multiple experiments have shown that people higher in working memory capacity suppressed emotion better than people with lower working memory capacity. Those with greater working memory capacity also were more effective in appraising emotional stimuli without getting too caught up in them (Schmeichel, et al., 2008). Perhaps the larger working memory capacity makes it easier for the individual to keep in mind more hopeful memories that may counter or modulate anxious or depressive thoughts.

A biological explanation for elevated rates of anxiety disorders in individuals with ADHD has been offered by Levy (2004). She has described how reduction of synaptic gating at the accumbens section of the brain in persons with ADHD coupled with insufficient gating of anxiety by the prefrontal cortex may be neural routes for less adequate gating of anxiety in individuals with ADHD.

ADHD with Bipolar Disorders

For many years the diagnosis of Bipolar Disorder has been classified with depressive disorders as though they were all just variations of the same processes. More recent research has highlighted differences which make it important to conceptualize depression and Bipolar Disorder as two separate categories of problems with mood. Although incidence rates of Bipolar Disorder in the general population are quite low, about 1% in adults, individuals with this disorder have extremely high rates of premature death due to suicide and associated medical conditions, as well as substantial role impairments and elevated rates of hospitalization. Moreover, when the full spectrum of Bipolar syndromes, including subthreshold cases, is considered, incidence in the general population increases to almost 6% (Merikangas, et al., 2007).

The two main types of Bipolar Disorder are:

- Bipolar I which includes one or more episodes of mania or episodes of mania interspersed with baseline depression or euthymia;
- Bipolar II which is characterized by one or more major depressive episodes accompanied by at least one hypomanic episode.

The primary difference between manic and hypomanic episodes is the level of severity of impairment. Manic episodes and hypomanic episodes are both defined as distinct periods during which there is abnormally and persistently elevated or irritable mood, accompanied by at least three other symptoms from a list including decreased need for sleep, flight of ideas, and excessive involvement in pleasurable activities with a high potential for painful consequences. Mania might be compared to having a car's accelerator pedal fully pushed to the floor and getting stuck there while driving—cognitive processes are severely speeded up and become very difficult to control. Hypomania is a similar process, somewhat less severe and less likely to require hospitalization.

Various studies have reported high rates of comorbidity between ADHD and Bipolar Disorder, but these rates tend to be widely divergent from one another, depending upon how Bipolar Disorder is operationally defined. Reported incidence rates of Bipolar Disorder in clinical samples of adults with ADHD have ranged from 3% to 17% (Brown, 2011). In a large study of adults diagnosed with Bipolar Disorder, reported incidence of ADHD was 9.5%, well above the estimated incidence of ADHD in the general population of adults (Nierenberg, et al., 2005). Among children with ADHD estimated incidence of Bipolar Disorder has ranged from 2.4% to 21% (Arnold, et al., 2011).

Differences in these incidence rates may be explained largely by whether the researchers have included the requirement of episodicity as stipulated in the diagnostic manual definition of Bipolar Disorder. Several studies have now demonstrated that most of those whose mood tends to be consistently irritable, not dramatically worse for a brief period followed by intervals of non-agitated, euthymic mood, are likely to fit the new diagnostic category of Disruptive Mood Regulation Disorder described in the section on ADHD with anxiety and depressive disorders above. This new diagnostic category of Disruptive Mood Regulation Disorder was created to identify individuals who suffer from chronically severe mood problems that do not warrant a diagnosis of Bipolar Disorder.

Several studies have demonstrated the difference between Severe Mood Dysregulation (SMD) and Bipolar Disorder in children (Leibenluft, 2011; Rich, et al., 2011). Both of these classes of disorder carry considerable risk for serious impairments over the lifespan.

How ADHD is Related to Bipolar Disorders

Overlap between ADHD and Bipolar disorders involves not only insufficient ability to manage and modulate emotions. It also involves two additional executive functions often impaired in persons with ADHD: a) ability to inhibit and manage actions; and b) ability to regulate levels of arousal. Episodes of mania generally involve not only intense, poorly controlled emotions, but also intense, driven behavior, not modulated by the usual levels of self-control. During manic episodes persons with Bipolar Disorder not only talk much faster under more apparent pressure than usual, they also tend to engage in agitated behaviors, frequently intense and protracted outbursts of temper. During such episodes they also tend to be hyperalert and have great difficulty in slowing down to relax and to sleep. Bipolar episodes might be seen as limited periods of extreme intensifications of executive function impairments in regulating emotions, regulating alertness and modulating behavior. In many instances Bipolar episodes also involve cognitive disruptions that reflect failure to inhibit psychotic thought processes.

ADHD with Oppositional Defiant Disorder and/or Conduct Disorder

Oppositional Defiant Disorder (ODD) is defined as a recurrent pattern of defiant, disobedient, angry and resentful behavior that usually begins in childhood or adolescence. Recent evidence suggests that ODD symptoms are clustered into three distinct groupings: chronically angry/irritable mood, defiant/headstrong behavior, and vindictiveness (Rowe, et al., 2010). These impairments are manifest not simply in internal feelings, but in quite overt verbal and/or physical actions. These chronic behaviors may be quick, overt and impulsive—an immediate angry refusal when asked to do something, a verbal outburst of disrespectful expletives when confronted by a parent or other authority. Or they may be sullen and sustained refusals to comply with directions, often while doing more of what has been forbidden or deliberately escalating the misbehavior in question.

In the general population of the U.S., lifetime prevalence of ODD is estimated at about 10.2% to 12.6% (Nock, et al., 2007; Kessler, et al., 2010; Merikangas, et al., 2010). Among individuals with ODD more than 92% have at least one additional psychiatric disorder; approximately 35% of those in epidemiological samples also have ADHD. Among children with ADHD, the estimated prevalence of ODD ranges from about 35% to 50% with higher prevalence among those with combined type ADHD (Connor, et al. 2010). Usually onset of ODD occurs later than ADHD. ODD is generally less severe than Disruptive Mood Regulation Disorder in the intensity of temper outbursts and it does not involve the episodic mood changes associated with Bipolar Disorder.

Conduct disorder (CD) is a more severe behavior disorder characterized by seriously delinquent behavior in which basic rights of others are violated and/or major age-appropriate societal norms are violated, e.g. physical cruelty to people, theft while confronting a victim, deliberate fire setting with intent to cause serious damage, persistent truancy, and staying out at night despite parental prohibitions. Lifetime incidence of CD in the general population of adolescents is 6.8% (Merikangas, et al., 2010).

ODD usually onsets at about 12 years, but this pattern of severe, chronic oppositionality and irritability sometimes appears in preschoolers who greatly exceed the range of oppositional and defiant behavior typical among most of their peers (Burke, et al., 2010). For most affected children, ODD persists for approximately six years. More than 70% of those diagnosed with ODD do not continue to meet diagnostic criteria for that disorder by age 18 years and most never meet diagnostic criteria for CD. However, over the longer term ODD has been found to be associated with Major Depressive Disorder and higher rates of school suspension as well as, for some, elevated risk of CD (Biederman, et al., 2008a).

For those with ADHD and ODD who also met diagnostic criteria for CD, there was increased risk of drug or alcohol abuse or dependence, Bipolar Disorder, being expelled from school, being fired from a job, and being convicted of a crime. The greatest burden of impairment among youths diagnosed with ADHD and ODD is with those who also qualify for the more serious diagnosis of CD (Biederman, et al., 2008a).

How ADHD is Related to Oppositional Defiant Disorder
and Conduct Disorder

At first glance ODD might be considered simply another example of the executive function "difficulty in modulating emotions", similar to anxiety and depression. However, both ODD and CD involve not only emotions, but also actions. While ODD certainly involves chronic difficulty in managing frustration and anger, it also involves a larger behavioral component than is usually involved in most disorders of anxiety and depression.

ODD characteristically involves also recurrent patterns of "failure adequately to inhibit" defiant verbal outbursts and overt actions or failures to act which make considerable trouble for the individual with ODD and for those with whom he or she interacts, especially for parents, teachers and other caretakers. In CD, the defiance of authorities and social expectations may or may not be less weighted with emotions, but actions of CD are much more severe and likely to carry heavier penalties; those failures of inhibition of action are more destructive and more dangerous both to self and to others.

One important characteristic of individuals with ODD or CD is that they tend to be quite impulsive in their actions. Shapiro (1965) has described how impulsive persons tend to respond to their whims without thinking much about how acting on that whim in this moment is likely to work out, what potential consequences may be, given other interests and concerns that may be important to them in the longer term. They do not stop to think long enough to consider the longer term impact of swearing at their teacher or shouting rudely at their boss, of throwing their computer on the floor, of shoplifting an object they want to get, or of driving a car at excessive speed to get to their destination, etc.

While those with ODD and/or CD may be quite skilled in acting effectively in the moment to obtain their goals, e.g. expressing their frustration, getting quickly to where they want to go, they tend to be lacking in the executive function of inhibiting action sufficiently, even for just a few moments, for adequate planning and consideration of potential consequences before acting. Their attention is focused too much on satisfying their immediate whim, doing what they feel they want in that moment, and not enough on considering the immediate and longer term context. Their working memory does not bring to mind and sustain awareness of the related concerns that others less impaired in these executive functions would consider before acting on similar whims or impulses.

Shapiro (1965) noted that impulsive persons often tend to lack the more stable interests and relationships, the longer term aims and commitments experienced by many less impulsive persons. He wrote:

> The normal person "tolerates" frustration or postpones the satisfaction of his whim at least in part because he is also interested in other things... independent of the immediate frustration... the existence of these general goals and interests automatically provides a perspective... in which a passing whim or an immediate frustration is experienced... a whim is experienced as a whim, perhaps exciting, interesting or at least worth it, and perhaps not, rather than being experienced, immediately and automatically, as the only next thing to do (pp. 145-146).

This view of impulsivity—chronic lack of sufficient capacity to inhibit or defer action enough to sufficiently plan and weigh potential risks and benefits—is an example of how executive functions involve, as Lezak stated, questions of "Will you do it and, if so, how and when?" (Lezak, et al., 2004, p. 35). Adequate EF involves capacity to inhibit for consideration of such questions in light of longer term concerns, to set priorities in the moment, taking into account both immediate and longer term goals, avoiding potentially damaging action on whims of the moment.

ADHD with Obsessive-Compulsive Disorders and Hoarding Disorders

In DSM-IV Obsessive-Compulsive Disorder (OCD) was classified as an anxiety disorder. This was based on a psychoanalytic assumption that compulsive behaviors were efforts to neutralize anxiety associated with obsessional thoughts. A substantial body of more recent research has challenged that assumption by demonstrating that OCD involves primarily failures of cognitive and behavioral inhibition, that the main problem is impairment in the ability to inhibit or "put the lid on" thoughts and actions that are intrusive, irrational and/or "magical" and cause considerable distress to the affected individual.

Four main symptom dimensions of OCD are listed below; the number in parentheses next to each factor is the percentage of the variance that item accounted for in factor analyses of OCD symptoms. These dimensions derived from factor analysis by Leckman, et al. (1997). Each represents a range of related obsessional themes:

- Aggressive behavior toward self or others, sexual or religious obsessions, and related checking compulsions (30%);

- Need for symmetry or exactness, repeating rituals, counting, ordering/arranging compulsions (13.8%);
- Contamination obsessions and cleaning, washing compulsions (10.2%);
- Hoarding and collecting obsessions and compulsions (8.5%).

Similar factors have been reported in a paper by Stewart, et al. (2007).

Recent research also has demonstrated that OCD is a prototype for a number of related OCD spectrum disorders that also involve excessive difficulty in inhibiting patterns of thought such as obsessional worrying about health problems (hypochondriasis), excessive worrying about body appearance (body dysmorphic disorder), or compulsive actions such as compulsive hair pulling (trichotillomania), compulsive skin picking, and compulsive nail biting (Fineberg, et al., 2011).

Many of the worrisome thoughts and irrational behaviors seen in individuals with OCD are found also among many in the general population.

The differences between "normal" and "OCD" cognitions are that the latter are more frequent, more intense, and elicit more resistance and subjective discomfort, such that they may impair activities of daily living and quality of life... OCD cognitions might be best characterized as failure to inhibit, or shift attention from these ongoing thoughts or motor activities (Chamberlain, et al., 2005).

Obsessional and compulsive symptoms sufficient to meet diagnostic criteria for OCD have been reported to occur in about 2% to 4% among children and adolescents and about 2% to 3% of adults in the general population. OCD is comorbid with many other psychiatric disorders. Among children and adolescents diagnosed with OCD the incidence of ADHD ranges from 6% to 33% (Geller & Brown, 2009; Geller, et al., 2000, 2001; Storch, et al., 2008). Onset of OCD is usually in late adolescence or early adulthood, but many cases actually begin in childhood at about age ten years.

Over recent years, research has identified hoarding as a type of OCD that warrants a separate diagnosis. One study compared 217 adults meeting proposed diagnostic criteria for hoarding with 96 participants who met diagnostic criteria for OCD without any hoarding symptoms. Fewer than 20% of those participants who fully met hoarding diagnostic criteria actually met OCD diagnostic criteria. Among those with Hoarding Disorder, the most common comorbid disorder was Major Depressive Disorder (MDD); 50.7% of the hoarders, but only 33.3% of the OCD participants met diagnostic criteria for MDD. ADHD was diagnosed in 40% of the hoarders, but in only 9% of adults with OCD without hoarding (Frost, et al., 2011).

Proposed diagnostic criteria for Hoarding Disorder include:

- Persistent difficulty discarding or parting with possessions regardless of actual value.
- This difficulty is due to a perceived need to save the items and distress associated with discarding them.
- The symptoms result in accumulation of possessions that congest or clutter active living areas and substantially compromise their intended use.
- Hoarding is not attributable to another medical condition, e.g. brain injury.
- Hoarding is not better accounted for by symptoms of another DSM-V disorder.

A slightly modified version of these proposed criteria was used in a nationally representative sample of over 2000 persons. In that sample 5.8% of the respondents met the diagnostic criteria for hoarding; there was no difference in rates for men versus women. Hoarders were significantly more likely to buy items, acquire free things, and steal items they did not need, compared to non-hoarders. Perfectionism, indecision, and procrastination were all significantly associated with hoarding (Timpano, et al., 2011).

How is ADHD Related to OCD and Hoarding Disorder?

One of the most striking characteristics of persons with OCD is the sharp, intense focus of their concentration; most are quite attentive to details of whatever they are focusing on. This equips them well for technical tasks where very specific focus on details is important. However, this narrowed intensity can be problematic for many other tasks just as a narrow beam flashlight can be helpful for focusing on a small object, but not helpful for illuminating an overview of a dark room.

Many individuals with ADHD who also have OCD report that they tend to have chronic difficulty in shifting their focus, in moving flexibly from "micro view" to "macro view" and back. As a result, they often miss the bigger picture, the larger context within which any specific elements exist and need to be understood. Similar tendencies to get caught up in specifics while missing the context can occur in social interactions where persons with OCD may tend to focus on the verbal content of what others or they themselves are saying, while ignoring the non-verbal context in which the communication is taking place. They may listen to the words spoken while missing subtleties in tone of voice, facial expressions or other non-verbal behaviors which, in some situations carry important messages from and about persons with whom they are interacting. Overly focused on the manifest content of what is said, they are often too quick to assume that they understand what another person is saying and may be quite impatient with others who are not sufficiently concise in conversation. At times it seems that they might prefer all conversation to be in concise text messages, uncluttered with emotion or elaboration.

Shapiro (1965) has noted that persons with OCD tend not only to be narrow and rather inflexible in their focus; they also tend often to feel and act as though they are under persistent pressure to behave and think in specified ways.

> The obsessive-compulsive person functions like his own overseer issuing commands, directives, reminders, warnings, and admonitions concerning not only what is to be done and what is not to be done, but also about what is to be wanted, felt, and even thought... the obsessive-compulsive person tells himself, "I should..." almost continuously... he feels he is reminding himself of some objective necessity (pp. 34-39).

One example of the power of the "should" seen so much in OCD is perfectionism, a complex trait explicitly identified in DSM-IV as characteristic of Obsessive-Compulsive Personality Disorder, but also seen in OCD and in patients with other diagnoses and different personality profiles (Shafran & Mansell, 2001; Shafran, et al., 2002; Ayearst, et al., 2012). A specific example of perfectionism often seen in students with ADHD and comorbid OCD is perfectionism in writing tasks. Many university students with ADHD and OCD report that they struggle to take adequate notes in lectures, given their chronic problems with inattention and working memory, but then they are also impaired by their perfectionism so that if they make an error or cross over the margin of their notepad, they feel they must immediately discard that page and restart another so their notes can be perfectly formatted.

Another serious difficulty of many students with ADHD and comorbid OCD is that they are unable to write a rough draft of an essay and then go back to edit and elaborate on it. They feel compelled to get each sentence to sound "just right" to them before they can allow themselves to begin writing their next sentence. This process tends to be extremely time-consuming and often results in their not being able to get the assignment completed by deadline or they may simply give up the project in frustration.

Persons with ADHD and comorbid OCD tend to be exaggeratedly impaired in their ability to shift their focus of attention flexibly and to manage their activity in ways that allow adequate reprioritizing for changing situations. They often find it very difficult to respond to shifting emotions in interpersonal situations and to "let go" to enjoy and share emotions with others.

While some persons with ADHD have Hoarding Disorder with comorbid OCD, the study by Frost, Steketee and Tolin (2011) discussed above found that 80% of the hoarders in their sample did not also have OCD. Executive function impairments of those individuals tend to lie more in the domain of organizing and prioritizing of possessions, they tend to accumulate piles of unrelated objects ranging from worthless trash to extremely valuable papers and objects, all of which tend to be invested with a similar level of importance and emotional attachment (Hartl, et al., 2005). This is an exaggerated manifestation of impairment in the executive function of organizing and prioritizing included in the new model described in Chapter 2.

ADHD with Substance Use Disorders

What differentiates substance use disorders from other disorders often comorbid with ADHD is the role of the substance and context of usage in sustaining the disorder. Unlike anxiety, depression, OCD, Bipolar Disorder, etc., substance use disorders are shaped primarily by the actions of a chemical substance introduced into the body deliberately to modify mood, thought patterns and/or social interactions. Usually getting access to and use of these chemical agents also involves the individual in a social context which can also have a significant impact upon motivations, patterns of use, and self-understanding. Interacting with those who provide the substance and with others who use it can have a powerful effect on the individual's view of self and patterns of interacting with family, friends, and classmates or co-workers.

Substance use disorders need to be differentiated from substance use which is not disordered, which does not damage the person's health or disrupt the individual's adaptive functioning. Using coffee to get the day started or a reasonable amount of beer or wine in the context of a meal or social gathering would be considered an aspect of a substance use disorder only if those uses were part of a larger pattern that significantly damages the person's health or disrupts the individual's daily life. Likewise, taking prescribed medications in a medically appropriate way to combat a disease process, to alleviate pain, to reduce excessive anxiety or to control a serious mood disorder, even if the individual becomes dependent upon it, is not in itself a manifestation of a disorder. A diabetic may become dependent upon insulin injections, but this does not constitute a substance use disorder. DSM-V clarified this distinction in changing the terminology from "substance dependence" to "substance use disorder."

Substance use disorders involve patterns of addiction. Drug addiction is a chronically relapsing disorder characterized by: 1) compulsion to seek and take the drug; 2) loss of control in limiting intake; and 3) emergence of a negative emotional state (depressed mood, anxiety, irritability) which reflects a motivational withdrawal syndrome when access to the drug is prevented. Although approximately 15.6% of the U.S. adult population will engage in nonmedical or illicit drug use at some time in their lives, only about 2.9% develop substance dependence on illicit drugs. While slightly over 50% of adults are current users of alcohol, only about 7.7% of those current users meet criteria for substance abuse or dependence on alcohol (Koob & Volkow, 2010).

When substance use becomes a substance use disorder, the process of addiction is underway. This process is intimately involved with the brain's reward system, the brain functions that monitor and signal presence or absence of pleasure. Although drugs of abuse have very different mechanisms of action, they all tend to act upon the brain's reward pathways in similar ways. This is also true for so-called "natural rewards" such as food, sex, and social interaction (Nestler, 2005). One unified system is the register for pleasures of all sorts.

Many assume that addiction is essentially a persistent craving for pleasure obtained from use of a specific substance. This excessively simplistic view overlooks the complexity of addiction, particularly its "dark side" which involves chronic irritability, depression, emotional pain, sleep disturbances, and loss of motivation for natural rewards. This dark state emerges especially when the individual is in withdrawal following excessive use of the addictive drug and tends to persist in a protracted way during which the individual is impacted by a chronically intensified stress response that stimulates a compulsive drive to use the substance again (Koob & Le Moal, 2010). In trying to understand addiction, it is important to realize that addicts do not repeatedly seek to use the drug of abuse in order to gain pleasure, they urgently seek it in order to reduce their stress and pain.

These negative responses result from lasting changes in the brain's reward system into which the brain transitions after repeated episodes of excessive use. A landmark study reported:

> Work from imaging studies has provided evidence that this transition involves reprogramming of neuronal circuits that process 1) reward and motivation; 2) memory, conditioning and habituation; 3) executive

function and inhibitory control; 4) interoception and self-awareness; and 5) stress reactivity. This transition is influenced by genetic, developmental, and environmental factors and their dynamic interactions, which will determine the course and severity of the addiction (Koob & Volkow, 2010, pp. 225-226).

Substance	Study I*	Study II*
Nicotine	2.82	2.36
Alcohol	1.7	1.35
Marijuana	2.29	1.51
Cocaine	2.05	NA
Psychoactive drug use	NA	1.59
Overall drug use disorder	2.64	3.48 (non-alcohol)

* the number on each line above is the pooled odds ratio over multiple studies where 1.0 means the same as the non-ADHD sample and 2.0 means twice as likely as those in the non-ADHD comparison group.

There is considerable evidence that individuals with ADHD have a greater risk of developing a substance use disorder at some point in life than do most persons without ADHD. A meta-analysis of 27 studies found that individuals diagnosed with ADHD were more likely to develop each of the following substance use disorders when compared with a matched sample of persons without ADHD:

Statistics cited above under Study I are based on pooled samples of over 4,000 persons with ADHD and over 6,000 comparison persons without ADHD assessed at an average age of 18.9 years (Lee, et al., 2011). Those listed under Study II are from a meta-analysis of 13 studies involving children with or without ADHD followed into early adulthood. This was a sizable sample; the number of participants varied between 600 and 3,000 depending upon the various substances assessed (Charach, et al., 2011).

The high frequency of overlap between ADHD and substance use disorders can also be seen in studies of persons identified as having substance use disorder. A meta-analysis of 30 studies of over 4,000 adolescents and over 2,600 adults who sought treatment for substance use disorders found that the overall prevalence of ADHD in adolescents was 25.3% while it was 21% among adults (van Emmerik-van Oortmerssen, et al., 2011). These rates are three times the reported incidence for ADHD in the general population of adolescents in the U.S. and five times the reported incidence of ADHD among adults in the general population of the U.S. (Merikangas, et al., 2010; Kessler, et al., 2006).

Impact of substance use disorders in combination with ADHD can be substantial, particularly on educational achievement. A study of a U.S. national sample interviewed over 29,000 adults and found that failure to graduate from high school by the usual time of age 18 years was more common among those with any psychiatric or substance use disorders (18.1% to 33.2%) than among those with no such disorders (15.2%). Use of any tobacco, alcohol and illegal drugs and disorders associated with tobacco and illegal drugs was significantly associated with increased risk of failure to graduate from high school on time when these correlations were examined separately for each drug. However, when statistical adjustments were made to compensate for co-occurring disorders, only correlations with CD or ADHD remained significant (Breslau, et al., 2011).

How are ADHD and Substance Use Disorders Related?

Substance use disorders tend to have a negative impact upon many aspects of the affected individuals' daily life, particularly education and employment. Breslau, Miller, Chung and Schweitzer (2011) interpreted data from their large study described above with the suggestion that there are distinct pathways connecting CD and ADHD with educational attainment. They noted that:

> attention problems assessed at the time of school entry are associated with lower academic achievement, as measured by standardized tests, at the end of primary school and at the end of high school. This increased burden in students with ADHD to perform the tasks that underlie academic achievement (i.e. working memory, processing speed, organization of information) may have cumulative negative effects. Inefficiency in learning may enter into considerations that individuals and families make regarding the potential benefits of continuing education vs. pursuing alternative careers that do not demand HS graduation as a credential (p. 299).

The authors also noted that CD in itself was not statistically associated with failure to graduate from high school on time after the correlation of CD with ADHD was statistically controlled for. From this perspective, ADHD is seen as the primary underlying source of impairment contributing to elevated failure of those with other psychiatric or substance use disorders to graduate from high school at the usual time.

The importance of ADHD impairments in substance abuse is also seen in results from a study that prospectively followed children with ADHD and a comparison sample from ages 13 to 18 years (Molina & Pelham, 2003). These investigators looked not only at exposure to use of illicit substances, but also at the frequency and quantity of use. Results indicated that ADHD in childhood was associated with increased risk for elevated use and abuse of alcohol and heavier and earlier use of tobacco and other drugs by the teenage years. They also found that inattention symptoms of ADHD were better predictors of later substance abuse than were childhood antisocial behaviors, e.g. conduct disorders. Their data indicated that ADHD in childhood is as strong a risk factor of substance use and abuse as is having a positive family history of substance use disorder.

Molina and Pelham (2003) argued that:

> Executive functioning deficits associated with inattention, and not impulsivity-hyperactivity... may be at the root of this mediational chain to substance abuse... inattention may influence substance use through mediational variables such as poor academic achievement and peer difficulties... teacher ratings of inattention were more strongly related with grade point average than were ratings of impulsivity-hyperactivity and ODD... what may follow is gravitation away from conventional group values and behaviors that include academic success, and gravitation toward nonconformist peer groups where substance use is tolerated and modeled (p. 504).

Clinical experience and research indicate that social context often plays an important role in the substance use disorders. Those individuals who make excessive use of drugs of abuse often become more withdrawn from many of their previous social relationships and tend to spend more time with others with whom they can join comfortably in more excessive drug use. This can provide companionship with others less likely to be judgmental of their drug use; and it may also provide connections where they can more easily procure drugs not legally available to them.

A shift of social interaction patterns can be quite problematic if an individual suffering from a substance use disorder is seeking to recover from excessive drug use. One problem, particularly for adolescents and young adults, is that an individual who has severed relationships with former friends and developed a reputation as a "druggie" may not be welcome to return to the former friendship group. It may be quite difficult for them to gain access to friends who are not still actively using drugs of abuse. Sustaining recovery from drug abuse is extremely difficult if the recovering addict returns to the social context in which they were previously using, especially if former friends in that setting are still actively using. There is strong evidence that if a person who has been addicted to a substance returns to the context in which they practiced their addiction, even after a long period of abstinence, multiple cues intensify brain activity that produces intensified craving and a strong push toward seeking and resuming use of the habitual drug (Crombag, et al., 2010). For those who suffer from ADHD, avoiding relapse, even after a lengthy period of abstinence is particularly difficult because of weaknesses in inhibition and their tendency toward impulsive action.

An additional perspective on the high rates of comorbidity between ADHD and substance use disorders has been provided by genetic studies. A research team from the Medical Genetics Branch of the National Human Genome Research Institute has recently presented data to show that a common genetic network underlies substance use disorders and ADHD as well as ODD and CD. Many of these genes are associated with the development and guidance of neural pathways, regulation of synaptic transmission, and regulation of transmission of nerve impulses, among other functions (Arcos-Burgos, et al., 2012).

ADHD with Autistic Spectrum Disorders

Diagnostic guidelines in DSM-IV stipulate that the diagnosis of ADHD should not be made for persons diagnosed with Autistic or Pervasive Developmental Disorders, but this requirement has been challenged by numerous clinical and some epidemiological studies. Reviews of evidence have demonstrated that 20% to 50% of children with ADHD also meet diagnostic criteria for an Autistic Spectrum Disorder while 30% to 80% of children with an Autistic Spectrum Disorder also fully meet diagnostic criteria for ADHD. These reviews also include evidence of significant shared heritability between these two disorders (Reiersen, et al., 2007; Rommelse, et al., 2010). It is expected that DSM-V will not include Autistic Spectrum Disorders as an exclusion for ADHD diagnosis, but both similarities and differences between these two disorders need to be considered in research and in clinical practice.

Many, but not all, individuals with Autistic Spectrum Disorders also suffer from significant intellectual impairments. A review of 21 studies found that the median proportion of individuals on this spectrum who did not suffer from intellectual impairment (IQ of 70 or above) was about 29.6%; some of these actually have IQ scores in the superior range of 120 or above. About

29.3% suffered mild-to-moderate intellectual impairments (IQ of 35 to 69) and about 38% suffered from severe-to-profound mental retardation (IQ of 34 or below) (Fombonne, 2005).

The Autistic Spectrum includes a variety of different patterns of symptoms, but the core symptoms of disorders on this spectrum are: 1) persistent deficits in social communication and social interaction across contexts; and 2) restricted, repetitive patterns of behaviors, interests, or activities.

When these two disorders are considered in a longitudinal, rather than just cross-sectional perspective, a more complex relationship between ADHD and Autism Spectrum Disorders emerges. A birth cohort study of over 5,000 children with almost equal numbers of boys and girls followed from birth, repeatedly measured social communication impairments typical of Autistic Spectrum Disorders and problems of inattention and hyperactivity characteristic of ADHD up to age 17 years (St. Pourcain, et al., 2011).

Latent class growth modeling of the resulting data yielded two different trajectories of social communication traits and four trajectories of symptoms related to ADHD.

Impaired social communication traits:

- 10% were in a high risk trajectory with high probability of deficits in social reciprocity and verbal, non-verbal communication throughout development;
- 90% were in a low risk trajectory for those social communication impairments.

ADHD-related impairment traits:

- 3.9% were persistently impaired with high probability of hyperactivity-inattention symptoms;
- 8.1% showed intermediate probability of expressing hyperactivity-inattention symptoms;
- 5.3% showed hyperactivity-inattention symptoms that persisted only during childhood;
- 82.8% demonstrated low risk of hyperactivity-inattention symptoms at all.

There was considerable crossover between those with Autistic Spectrum traits and those with ADHD traits, particularly in the more severely impaired children in each group. Over 80% of the children included in the persistently high impairments of hyperactivity-inattention group were also in the persistently impaired social communication group. Most of the children in the impaired social communication group were in either the persistently impaired (32.3%) or intermediate impairment trajectory for hyperactivity-inattention (39%) (St. Pourcain, et al., 2011).

It should be noted, however, that this impressive study included measures of some important traits of each of these two disorders, but did not include assessment for the full range of impairments associated with either ADHD or Autistic Spectrum Disorders. Diagnosis with either ADHD or Autistic Spectrum Disorder was not required for inclusion. The study also excluded any participant with an IQ below 70, thus omitting a sizable percentage of children who might qualify for diagnosis of an Autism Spectrum Disorder.

Several cross-sectional studies have provided assessment of social impairments in children fully diagnosed with ADHD. A study that used peer ratings to compare 165 children with ADHD versus 1,298 of their same sex classmates aged seven to nine years found that both girls and boys with ADHD were significantly less preferred socially, had fewer dyadic friends, were more disliked by popular peers, and were more often rejected by peers (52% of the ADHD children were of rejected status) than classmates without ADHD. These patterns, not explained by comorbid disorders, were apparent by the age of seven years (Hoza, et al., 2005).

A different study compared 50 boys and girls with ADHD and 42 comparison children without behavior problems to assess capacity for empathy and social perspective taking, i.e. understanding a social situation from another person's perspective. Both of these abilities play an important role in developing and sustaining social relationships. Results showed that children with ADHD showed less parent-reported empathy than comparison children and more impaired social perspective taking (Marton, et al., 2009).

Some of these impairments in empathy were attributable to IQ and attentional problems, but impairments in pragmatic language were also a major contributing factor. In that study about 60% of the boys with ADHD suffered from significant problems with pragmatic language more than typically developing boys. Pragmatic language skills involve ability to recognize what information is needed by other participants in a specific situation, ability to find appropriate expressions to communicate what is needed via words, facial expressions, gestures, tone of voice, etc., and the ability to make rapid "on line" changes according to moment-by-moment changes in the interpersonal situation and how other participants react (Tannock & Schachar, 1996). Impairments in these aspects of language can significantly interfere with the child's ability to make and sustain relationships.

A 3-way comparison of pragmatic language skills found that children with ADHD demonstrated more difficulties with pragmatic language than typically developing children, while children on the Autistic Spectrum demonstrated more severe impairments on most, but not all measures, than those with ADHD and significantly more impairments than typically developing children (Geurts & Embrechts, 2008). This suggests that differences between ADHD children and children on the Autistic Spectrum may be quantitative rather than qualitative—that both groups manifest elevated rates of impairment in pragmatic language skills critical to social relationships relative to typically developing children, however those with Autistic Spectrum diagnosis tend to have more severe presentation of these symptoms. Since these studies are all reporting group data, usually means for the group, severity may vary considerably among individuals within each group. Some may have very substantial characteristics of the other group, while others have virtually no similarities.

In their review of multiple studies demonstrating a wide variety of ways in which children with ADHD have significantly impaired social functioning, Nijmeijer and colleagues observed:

> It is an intriguing question why some children with ADHD, despite having difficulties in performing tasks at school, have a healthy social life and why others appear to be unable to connect with peers and other people in a normal way" (Nijmeijer, et al., 2008).

They noted that adverse social environments and such comorbid disorders as ODD might also contribute to social dysfunction often found in those with ADHD. However, they also call attention to the fact that some with ADHD also manifest more specific symptoms of impairments in social communication associated with various Pervasive Developmental Disorders such as Asperger's and Autism, aspects of the Autistic Spectrum Disorder.

How are ADHD and Autistic Spectrum Disorders Related?

The elevated frequency of impairments in social interaction among many, but not all of those diagnosed with ADHD calls attention to the fact that some important impairments of Autistic Spectrum Disorder are also manifest in many with ADHD. Recently, van der Meer, et al. (2012) published a study questioning: "Are Autism Spectrum Disorder and Attention-Deficit/Hyperactivity Disorder different manifestations of one overarching disorder?" Using latent class modeling with a large sample, they found five classes that identified both overlapping and non-overlapping deficits, with no Autistic Spectrum children who were fully without at least some ADHD symptoms.

Ability to understand, communicate and interact effectively with others is critically important in multiple aspects of daily life. These skills develop initially in interactions with family members and other caretakers, they are gradually expanded in interactions with peers and others outside the family throughout childhood, adolescence, and adulthood. Interpersonal skills, sometimes referred to as "emotional intelligence" or "social intelligence," remain important in interactions not only with teachers and employers, classmates, co-workers and friends, but also in developing and sustaining more intimate relationships throughout life. Goleman (1996) has argued that a person's emotional and social intelligence may be far more important than his or her IQ in determining success in education, work, social relationships and family life. However, these abilities are not equally developed in everyone.

While capacities referred to as social or emotional intelligence are sometimes referred to as intelligences, they are clearly differentiated from cognitive intelligence as measured by IQ tests. These abilities are critically dependent upon executive functions described in our new model of ADHD, for example:

- Capacity to focus on the immediate situation without becoming excessively distracted
- Capacity to shift focus as needed for the changing dynamics of the situation
- Ability to hold in mind what is being said and done in the ongoing situation
- Ability to recall and use relevant memories from previous experiences
- Capacity to inhibit excessively impulsive responses and behave appropriately
- Ability to appropriately modulate expression of emotion
- Capacity to monitor verbal and non-verbal clues revealing others' reactions.

Given the chronic impairments of these executive functions experienced by those with ADHD relative to their age mates, it is not surprising that many with ADHD demonstrate significant difficulties in understanding, communicating, and interacting effectively with others. This does not mean that ADHD and Autistic Spectrum are fully overlapping disorders. There are both significant similarities and significant differences between the two disorders.

One important difference is that individuals with ADHD do not generally show the extreme disengagement from and lack of interest in social interactions which is characteristic of most children on the Autistic Spectrum. Nijmeijer and collaborators, have pointed out that:

> Although children with ADHD generally do not lack interest in other people, they often fail to properly attune their behavior to other persons and to constantly changing social environments. The key characteristic of a substantial number of children with ADHD can be described as an apparent lack of a full comprehension of the consequences of their behavior to others (Nijmeijer, et al., 2009).

In contrast, from their earliest years, children with Autism Spectrum disorders tend to show striking lack of interest in engaging with other persons. Recent research has shown that evaluations of children just 12 months old can often identify children at high risk of Autistic Spectrum Disorder based upon lack of an early-emerging capacity to join in shared attention activities with another person, and avoiding engagement with another person in directing interest to a specific object or activity (Macari, et al., 2012).

Despite such differences, it now seems clearly established by research that there is a subgroup of children diagnosed with ADHD who also have elevated ratings of Autistic Spectrum traits that are not accounted for by their ADHD or behavioral symptoms; the range of such cases reported is between 13% and 50%. For many of those with these combined symptoms, there is also an elevation of ODD symptoms, but not greater ADHD severity or more severe anxiety symptoms (Grzadzinski, et al., 2011).

Moreover, multiple studies with clinical and general population samples have found that the relationship between autistic traits and ADHD symptoms is familial and mostly accounted for by genetic influences (Ronald, et al., 2008; Nijmeijer, et al., 2009).

Data from their study led Grzadzinski and colleagues to suggest that a dimensional perspective may be the most useful way to think about overlap between traits of Autistic Spectrum Disorder and traits of ADHD. This approach assumes that both of these clusters of traits are found in the general population in varying levels of intensity from totally absent to the level required for a full clinical diagnosis of either or both of these disorders (Grzadzinski, et al., 2011).

Overview of Comorbidity between ADHD and Other Disorders

From the research on overlaps between ADHD and other disorders briefly summarized in this chapter, it seems clear that boundaries between ADHD and other disorders are not defined by clear borders. This was recognized by Sonuga-Barke and Sergeant (2005) who observed that recent clinical and neuroscientific research has described ADHD as "a disorder with a complex, heterogeneous and 'fuzzy' psychopathology that challenges current diagnostic conceptualizations regarding the internal structure of the disorder... and its distinctiveness from other disorders" (p. 104).

This notion was expanded by others who pointed out that many executive function deficits of ADHD are "shared with other disorders and some differences between ADHD and other disorders may be *quantitative* rather than *qualitative*" (Banaschewski, et al., 2005, p. 136, italics added).

To illustrate the quantitative distinction, an individual with ADHD may have considerable chronic difficulty, more than most peers, in managing emotions, in getting started on tasks, in regulating sleep and alertness, in utilizing working memory, etc. simply as an aspect of impaired executive functions of ADHD. Yet when some of those specific impairments reach a certain level of severity, an additional diagnosis of depression, may be warranted. The additional diagnosis might be appropriately made when another specific cluster of symptoms is sufficiently severe in terms of the quantity of impairment.

This could be the difference between oppositional symptoms associated with ADHD and those that might warrant an additional diagnosis of ODD or Bipolar Disorder. It could be the quantitative differentiating point between social awkwardness associated with ADHD impairments and the level of more severe social impairments that might warrant the additional diagnosis of Autism Spectrum Disorder.

Likewise, executive functions of ADHD such as impaired focus and chronic difficulties with working memory and processing speed may be seen as generalized impairments upon which, in some individuals, are superimposed severe specific problems with decoding and phonological processing which warrant an additional diagnosis of dyslexia. This might be compared to a symphony orchestra in which the conductor is impaired while the string section is also not functioning well—generalized impairments with additional specific impairments.

Operating from this perspective Brown (2009) suggested that ADHD is:

> not just one more among other psychiatric disorders; it may be foundational in the sense that a person with ADHD-related impairments of executive function is more vulnerable to other psychiatric disorders. One might compare ADHD to chronic problems

in the operating system of a computer that affect a wide range of software used, as distinguished from problems in a specific computer software program that impair a narrower range of functions. ADHD impairments can bring a cascade of additional problems in adaptation. It also may be linked to increased genetic vulnerability to other disorders that exacerbate problems in adaptation (p. 14).

This view is consistent with the view of neuroscientist Joaquin Fuster who described how the complex range of cognitive activity known as *attention* plays a critical underlying role in multiple overlapping cognitive operations:

Perception is part of the acquisition and retrieval of memory; memory stores information acquired by perception; language and memory depend on each other; language and logical reasoning are special forms of cognitive action; attention serves all the other cognitive functions (Fuster, 2003, p. 16).

REFERENCES

Aagaard, L., & Hansen, E. H. (2011). Occurrence of adverse drug reactions reported for attention deficit hyperactivity disorder (ADHD) medications in the pediatric population: a qualitative review of empirical studies. *Neuropsychiatric Disease and Treatment* 7, 729–744.

Abikoff, H. (1985). Efficacy of cognitive training interventions in hyperactive children. *Clinical Psychology Review*, 5, 479–512.

Abikoff, H., & Gittelman, R. (1985). The normalizing effects of methylphenidate on the classroom behavior of ADHD children. *Journal of Abnormal Child Psychology*, 13(1), 33–44.

Abikoff, H., Hechtman, L., Klein, R. G., et al. (2004a). Symptomatic improvement in children with ADHD treated with long-term methylphenidate and multi-modal psychosocial treatment. *Journal of the American Academy of Child & Adolescent Psychiatry.* 43(7), 802–811.

Abikoff, H., Hechtman, L., Klein, R. G., et al. (2004b). Social functioning in children with ADHD treated with long-term methylphenidate and multi-modal psychosocial treatment. *Journal of the American Academy of Child & Adolescent Psychiatry,* 43(7), 820–829.

American Academy of Child and Adolescent Psychiatry. (1997). Practice parameters for the assessment and treatment of children, adolescents, and adults with Attention-Deficit/Hyperactivity Disorder. *Journal of the American Academy of Child & Adolescent Psychiatry,* 36(10 (Supplement)), 85S–121S.

American Academy of Child and Adolescent Psychiatry. (2002). Practice parameters for the use of stimulant medications in the treatment of children and adolescents. *Journal of the American Academy of Child & Adolescent Psychiatry,* 41 (Supplement), 26S–49S.

American Academy of Child and Adolescent Psychiatry. (2007). Practice parameters for the assessment and treatment of children and adolescents with Attention-Deficit/Hyperactivity Disorder. *Journal of the American Academy of Child & Adolescent Psychiatry,* 46 (7 (Supplement)), 894–921.

American Academy of Pediatrics. (2011). ADHD: Clinical practice guideline for the diagnosis, evaluation, and treatment of Attention-Deficit/Hyperactivity Disorder in children and adolescents. *Pediatrics,* 128(5), 1–16.

American Psychiatric Association. (1980). *Diagnostic and statistical manual of mental disorders, 3rd edition.* Washington, DC: American Psychiatric Association.

American Psychiatric Association. (1987). *Diagnostic and statistical manual of mental disorders, DSM-III-R, text revision.* Washington, DC: American Psychiatric Association.

American Psychiatric Association. (1994). *Diagnostic and statistical manual of mental disorders, 4th edition.* Washington, DC: American Psychiatric Association.

American Psychiatric Association. (2000). *Diagnostic and statistical manual of mental disorders, 4th edition, text revision.* Washington, DC: American Psychiatric Association.

Angold, A., Costello, E. J., & Erkanli, A. (1999). Comorbidity. *Journal of Child Psychology and Psychiatry, and Allied Disciplines,* 40(1), 57–87.

Anmarkrud, O., & Braten, I. (2009). Motivation for reading comprehension. *Learning and Individual Differences,* 19, 252–256.

Antshel, K. A., & Barkley, R. A. (2008). Psychosocial interventions in Attention Deficit Hyperactivity Disorder. *Child and Adolescent Psychiatric Clinics of North America,* 17, 421–437.

Antshel K. M., Faraone S. V., & Maglione, K. (2008). Temporal stability of ADHD in the high-IQ population: results from the MGH longitudinal family studies of ADHD. *Journal of the American Academy of Child and Adolescent Psychiatry,* 47(7), 817–825.

Antshel K. M., Faraone S. V., Stallone, K, et al. (2007). Is attention deficit hyperactivity disorder a valid diagnosis in the presence of high IQ? Results from the MGH longitudinal family studies of ADHD. *Journal of Child Psychology and Psychiatry,* 48(7), 687–694.

Applegate, B., Lahey, B. B., Hart, E. L., et al. (1997). Validity of the age-of-onset criterion for ADHD: A report from the DSM-IV field trials. *Journal of the American Academy of Child & Adolescent Psychiatry,* 36(9), 1121–1221.

Arcos-Burgos, M., Velez, J. I., Solomon, B. D., et al. (2012). A common genetic network underlies substance use disorders and disruptive or externalizing disorders. *Human Genetics,* 131, 917–929.

Ardila, A., Pineda, D., & Rosselli, M. (2000). Correlation between intelligence test scores and executive function measures. *Archives of Clinical Neuropsychology,* 15, 31–36.

Arnold, L. E., Dementer, C., Mount, K., et al. (2011). Pediatric bipolar spectrum disorder and ADHD: comparison and comorbidity in the LAMS clinical sample. *Bipolar Disorders,* 13, 509–521.

Arnsten, A. F. (2011). Catecholamine influences on dorsolateral prefrontal cortical networks. *Biological Psychiatry,* 69(12), e89–e99.

Arnsten, A. F., & Li, B. (2005). Neurobiology of executive functions: Catecholamine influences on prefrontal cortical functions. *Biological Psychiatry,* 57, 1377–1384.

Arnsten, A. F., Paspalas, C. D., Gamo, N. J., et al. (2010). Dynamic network connectivity: A new form of neuroplasticity. *Trends in Cognitive Sciences,* 14(8), 365–375.

Ayearst, L. E., Flett, G. L., & Hewitt, P. L. (2012). Where is multidimensional perfectionism in DSM-5? A question posed to the DSM-5 personality and personality disorders work group. *Personality Disorders: Theory, Research, and Treatment,* 3(4), 458–469.

Backman, L., Small, B. J., Wahlin, A., et al. (2000). Cognitive functioning in very old age (2000), in *Handbook of aging and cognition* (2nd edition), edited by Craik, F. I. M., and Salthouse, T. A., Nahwah, NJ: Lawrence Erlbaum Associates Publishers.

Baird, A. L., Coogan, A. N., Siddiqui, A., et al. (2011). Adult attention-deficit hyperactivity disorder is associated with alterations in circadian rhythms at the behavioral, endocrine and molecular levels. *Molecular Psychiatry*, 1–8.

Banaschewski, T., Hollis, C., Oosterlaan, J., et al. (2005). Towards an understanding of unique and shared pathways in the psychopathophysiology of ADHD. *Developmental Science*, 8(2), 132–140.

Banerjee, T. D., Middleton, F., & Faraone, S. V. (2007). Environmental risk factors for attention-deficit hyperactivity disorder. *Acta Paediatrica*, 96, 1269–1274.

Barbaresi, W. J., Katusic, S. K, Colligan, R. C., et al. (2007a). Long-term school outcomes for children with Attention-Deficit/Hyperactivity Disorder: a population-based sample. *Journal of Developmental and Behavioral Pediatrics*. 28 (4), 265–273.

Barbaresi, W. J., Katusic, S. K, Colligan, R. C., et al. (2007b). Modifiers of long-term school outcomes for children with Attention-Deficit/Hyperactity Disorder: Does stimulant medication make a difference? Results from a population-based study. *Journal of Developmental & Behavioral Pediatrics*. 28, 274–287.

Bargh, J. A. (2005). Bypassing the will: Toward demystifying the nonconscious control of social behavior, in *The New Unconscious*, edited by Hassin, R., Uleman, J., & Bargh, J. A., New York: Oxford University Press.

Bargh, J. A., & Barndollar, K. (1995). Automaticity in action: The unconscious as repository of chronic goals and motives, in *The psychology of action: Linking cognition and motivation to behavior*. New York, NY: Guilford Press, 475–481.

Barkley, R. A. (1997). *ADHD and the nature of self-control*. New York, NY: Guilford Press.

Barkley, R. A. (2006) *Attention-Deficit Hyperactivity Disorder: A handbook for diagnosis and treatment, 3rd edition*. New York, NY: Guilford Press.

Barkley, R. A. (2010). Against the status quo: Revising the diagnostic criteria for ADHD. *Journal of the American Academy of Child & Adolescent Psychiatry*, 49(3), 205–206.

Barkley, R. A. (2011). *Barkley deficits in executive function scale (BDEFS)*. New York, NY: The Guilford Press.

Barkley, R. A. (2012a). Distinguishing sluggish cognitive tempo from Attention-Deficit/ Hyperactivity Disorder in adults. *Journal of Abnormal Psychology*, 121(4), 978–990.

Barkley, R. A. (2012b). *Executive functions: What they are, how they work, and why they evolved*. New York: The Guilford Press.

Barkley, R. A., & Biederman, J. (1997). Toward a broader definition of the age-of-onset criterion for attention-deficit hyperactivity disorder. *Journal of the American Academy of Child & Adolescent Psychiatry*, 36(9), 1204–1210.

Barkley, R. A., & Brown, T. E. (2008). Unrecognized Attention-Deficit/Hyperactivity Disorder in adults presenting with other psychiatric disorders. *CNS spectrums*, 13(11), 977–984.

Barkley, R. A., & Murphy, K. R. (2010). Impairment in occupational functioning and adult ADHD: The predictive utility of executive function (EF) ratings versus EF tests. *Archives of Clinical Neuropsychology*, 25, 157–173.

Barkley, R. A., Murphy, K. R., DuPaul, G. I., et al., (2002). Driving in young adults with attention deficit hyperactivity disorder: Knowledge, performance, adverse outcomes, and the role of executive functioning. *Journal of International Neuropsychological Society*, 8(5), 665–672.

Barkley, R. A., Murphy, K. R., & Fischer, M. (2008). *ADHD in adults: What the science says.* New York, NY: The Guilford Press.

Bedard, A., Ickowicz, A., Logan, G. D., et al. (2003). Selective inhibition in children with Attention-Deficit Hyperactivity Disorder off and on stimulant medication. *Journal of Abnormal Child Psychology,* 31(3), 315–327.

Bedard, A., Martinussen, R., Ickowicz, A., et al. (2004). Methylphenidate improves visuo-spatial memory in children with Attention-Deficit/Hyperactivity Disorder. *Journal of American Academy of Child and Adolescent Psychiatry,* 43(3), 260–268.

Berninger, V. W., & Richards, T. L. (2002). *Brain literacy for educators and psychologists.* San Diego, CA: Academic Press.

Biederman, J., Faraone, S. V., Mick, E., et al. (1995). High risk for Attention Deficit Hyperactivity Disorder among children of parents with childhood onset of the disorder: A pilot study. *American Journal of Psychiatry,* 152(3), 431–435.

Biederman, J., Faraone, S. V., Mick, E., et al. (1999). Clinical correlates of ADHD in females: Findings from a large group of girls ascertained from pediatric and psychiatric referral sources. *Journal of the American Academy of Child & Adolescent Psychiatry,* 38(8), 966–975.

Biederman, J., Faraone, S. V., Monteaux, M. C., et al. (2004). Gender effects on Attention-Deficit/Hyperactivity disorder in adults, revisited. *Biological Psychiatry,* 55(7), 692–700.

Biederman, J., Faraone, S. V., Spencer, T. J., et al. (2006). Functional impairments in adults with self-reports of diagnosed ADHD: A controlled Study of 1001 Adults in the Community. *Journal of Clinical Psychiatry,* 67(4), 524–540.

Biederman, J., Mick, E., Faraone, S. V. (2000). Age-dependent decline of symptoms of attention deficit hyperactivity disorder: Impact of remission definition and symptom type. *American Journal of Psychiatry,* 157(5), 816–818.

Biederman, J., Petty, C. R., Day, H., et al. (2012). Severity of aggression/anxiety-depression/attention child behavior checklist profile discriminates between different levels of deficits in emotional regulation in youth with Attention-Deficit Hyperactivity Disorder. *Journal of Developmental and Behavioral Pediatrics:* 33(3), 236–243.

Biederman, J., Petty, C. R., Dolan, C., et al. (2008a). The long-term longitudinal course of oppositional defiant disorder and conduct disorder in ADHD boys: findings from a controlled 10-year prospective longitudinal follow-up study. *Psychological Medicine,* 38(07), 1027–1036.

Biederman, J., Petty, C. R., Evans, M. et al. (2010a). How persistent is ADHD? A controlled 10-year follow-up study of boys with ADHD. *Psychiatry Research* 177, 299–304.

Biederman, J., Petty, C. R., Fried, R., et al. (2008b). Discordance between psychometric testing and questionnaire-based definitions of executive function deficits in individuals with ADHD. *Journal of Attention Disorders,* 12(1), 92–102.

Biederman, J., Petty, C. R., & Fried, R., et al. (2008c). Utility of an abbreviated questionnaire to identify individuals with ADHD at risk for functional impairments. *Journal of Psychiatric Research,* 42, 304–310.

Biederman, J., Petty, C. R., Monuteaux, M. C., et al. (2010b). Adult psychiatric outcomes of girls with Attention Deficit Hyperactivity Disorder: 11-year follow-up in a longitudinal case-control study. *American Journal of Psychiatry,* 167(4), 409–417.

Biederman, J., Petty, C. R., O'Connor, K. B., et al. (2011). Predictors of persistence in girls with attention deficit hyperactivity disorder: results from an 11-year controlled follow-up study. *Acta Psychiatrica Scandinavica*, 152(2), 1–10.

Biederman, J., Spender, T. J., Monuteaux, M. C., et al. (2010c). A naturalistic 10-year prospective study of height and weight in children with Attention-Deficit Hyperactivity Disorder grown up: Sex and treatment effects. *Journal of Pediatrics*, 157, 635–640.

Booster, G. D., DuPaul, G. J., Eiraldi, R., et al. (2012). Functional impairments in children with ADHD: Unique effects of age and comorbid status. *Journal of Attention Disorders*, 16(3), 179–189.

Bradley, C. (1937). Behavior of children receiving Benzedrine. *American Journal of Psychiatry*, 94(11), 577–585.

Breslau, J., Miller, E., Chung, W. J., et al. (2011). Childhood and adolescent onset psychiatric disorders, substance use, and failure to graduate high school on time. *Journal of Psychiatric Research*, 45(3), 295–301.

Britton, J., Lissek, S., Grillon, C., et al. (2010). Development of anxiety: The role of threat appraisal and fear learning. *Depression and Anxiety*, 28(1), 5–17.

Brown, T. E. (1996). *Brown Attention-Deficit Disorder Scales for Adolescents and Adults; Manual*. San Antonio, TX: The Psychological Corporation.

Brown, T. E. (2000a). *Attention-deficit disorders and comorbidities in children, adolescents, and adults*. Washington, DC: American Psychiatric Press.

Brown, T. E. (2000b). Emerging understandings of Attention-Deficit/Hyperactivity Disorder and comorbidities, in *Attention-deficit disorders and comorbidities in children, adolescents and adults*, edited by Brown, T. E., Washington, DC: American Psychiatric Publishing, 3–56

Brown, T. E. (2001). *Brown Attention-Deficit Disorder Scales for Children and Adolescents; Manual*. San Antonio, TX: The Psychological Corporation.

Brown, T. E. (2005a). *Attention Deficit Disorder: The unfocused mind in children and adults*. New Haven, CT: Yale University Press.

Brown, T. E. (2005b). Circles inside squares: A graphic organizer to focus diagnostic formulations. *Journal of the American Academy of Child & Adolescent Psychiatry*, 44(12), 1309–1312.

Brown. T. E. (2009). Developmental complexities of attentional disorders. In *ADHD Comorbidities Handbook for ADHD complications in children and adults*, edited by Brown, T. E., Washington, DC: American Psychiatric Publishing, 3–22.

Brown, T. E. (2011). Adult ADHD and mood disorders, in *Adult ADHD and mood disorders*, edited by Buitelaar, J. K., Kan, C., & Asherson, P. J., Cambridge, U.K.: Cambridge University Press, 121–129.

Brown, T. E., & McMullen, W. J. (2001). Attention deficit disorders and sleep arousal disturbance. *Annals of the New York Academy of Sciences*, 931, 271–286.

Brown, T. E., Brams, M., Gao, J., et al. (2010). Open-label administration of lisdexamfetamine demesylate improves executive function impairments and symptoms of Attention-Deficit/Hyperactivity Disorder in adults. *Postgraduate Medicine*, 122(5), 7–17.

Brown, T. E., Brams, M., Gasior, M., et al. (2011a). Clinical utility of ADHD symptom thresholds to assess normalization of executive function with lisdexamfetaminedimesylate treatment in adults. *Current Medical Research and Opinion*, 27(2), 23–33.

Brown, T. E., Holdnack, J., Saylor, K., et al. (2011b). Effect of atomoxetine on executive function in adults with ADHD. *Journal of Attention Disorders*, 15(2), 130–138.

Brown, T. E., Reichel, P. C., & Quinlan, D. M. (2009). Executive function impairments in high IQ adults with ADHD. *Journal of Attention Disorders*, 13(2), 161–167.

Brown, T. E., Reichel, P. C., & Quinlan, D. M. (August, 2010). Impairments of written expression in 13–25 year old students with ADHD. Presented at annual meeting of American Psychological Assn. in San Diego, CA.

Brown, T. E., Reichel, P. C., & Quinlan, D. M. (2011c). Executive function impairments in high IQ children and adolescents with ADHD. *Open Journal of Psychiatry*, 1, 56–65.

Brown, T. E., Reichel, P. C., & Quinlan, D. M. (2011d). Extended time improves reading comprehension test scores for adolescents with ADHD. *Open Journal of Psychiatry*, 1, 79–87.

Brown, T. E., Spencer, T. J., Silverberg, A., et al. (2007). Improved executive functions with triple-bead mixed amphetamine salts in adults with ADHD. Presented at the annual meeting of the New Drug Evaluation Unit (National Institute of Mental Health) in Boca Raton, FL.

Brown, T. E., Sutton, V. K., Rogers, A., et al. (May, 2005). Atomoxetine alleviates executive function impairments in children with ADHD. Presented at Annual Meeting of American Psychiatric Association, Atlanta, GA.

Burgess, P. W. (1997). Theory and methodology in executive function research, *Methodology of frontal and executive function*. Hove, East Sussex, U.K.: Psychology Press, 81–116.

Burke, J. D., Waldman, I., & Lahey, B. B. (2010). Predictive validity of childhood Oppositional Defiant Disorder and Conduct Disorder: Implications for the DSM-V. *Journal of Abnormal Psychology*, 119(4), 739–751.

Burstein, M., He, J., Kattan, G., et al. (2011). Social phobia and subtypes in the national comorbidity survey-adolescent supplement: Prevalence, correlates, and comorbidity. *Journal of the American Academy of Child & Adolescent Psychiatry*, 50(9), 870–880.

Bush, G. (2008). Neuroimaging of Attention Deficit Hyperactivity Disorder: Can new imaging findings be integrated in clinical practice?. *Child and Adolescent Psychiatric Clinics of North America*, 17, 385–404.

Bush, G. (2009). Attention-Deficit/Hyperactivity Disorder and attention networks. *Neuropsychopharmacology*, 35(1), 278–300.

Buzaki, G. (2006). *Rhythms of the Brain*. New York: Oxford University Press.

Caisley, H., & Müller, U. (2012). Adherence to medication in adults with attention deficit hyperactivity disorder and pro re nata dosing of stimulants: A systematic review. *European Psychiatry* 27, 343–349.

Campbell, S. B., & von Stauffenberg, C. (2009). Delay and inhibition as early predictors of ADHD symptoms in third grade. *Journal of Abnormal Child Psychology*, 37, 1–15.

Canadian Attention Deficit Hyperactivity Disorder Resource Alliance (2011). *Canadian ADHD Practice Guidelines. 3rd edition*, Toronto, Ontario.

Carlson, C. L., Pelham, W. E., Swanson, J. M., et al. (1991). A divided attention analysis of the effects of methylphenidate on the arithmetic performance of children with Attention-Deficit Hyperactivity Disorder. *Journal of Child Psychology and Psychiatry*, 32(3), 463–471.

Carretti, B., Borella, E., Cornoldi, C., et al. (2009). Role of working memory in explaining the performance of individuals with specific reading comprehension difficulties: A meta-analysis. *Learning and Individual Differences*, 19(2), 246–251.

Casey, B. J., Somerville, L. H., Gotlib, I. H., et al. (2011). Behavioral and neural correlates of delay of gratification 40 years later. *Proceedings of the National Academy of Sciences*, 108(36), 14998–15003.

Castellanos, F. X., & Tannock, R. (2002). Neuroscience of attention-deficit hyperactivity disorder: The search for endophenotypes. *Nature*, 3, 617–628.

Castellanos, F. X., Sonuga-Barke, E. J. S., Scheres, A., et al. (2005). Varieties of Attention-Deficit/Hyperactivity Disorder-related intra-individual variability. *Biological Psychiatry*, 57, 1416–1423.

Centers for Disease Control and Prevention (2010): Increasing prevalence of parent-reported Attention-Deficit/Hyperactivity Disorder among children—United States, 2003–2007, *Morbidity and Mortality Weekly*, 59(44), 1439–1443. November 12, 2010. www.cdc.gov/mmwr

Chamberlain, S. R., Blackwell, A. D., Feinberg, N. A., et al. (2005). The neuropsychology of obsessive compulsive disorder: the importance of failures in cognitive and behavioral inhibition as candidate endophenotypic markers. *Neuroscience and Biobehavioral Reviews*, 29, 399–419.

Charach, A., Yeung, E., Climans, T., et al. (2011). Childhood Attention-Deficit/Hyperactivity Disorder and future substance use disorders: Comparative meta-analyses. *Journal of the American Academy of Child & Adolescent Psychiatry*, 50(1), 9–21.

Chelonis, J. J., Johnson, T. A., Ferguson, S. A., et al. (2011). Effect of methylphenidate on motivation in children with Attention-Deficit/Hyperactivity Disorder. *Experimental and Clinical Psychopharmacology*, 19(2), 145–153.

Cloninger, C. R. (1999). A new conceptual paradigm from genetics and psychobiology for the science of mental health. *Australian & New Zealand Journal of Psychiatry*, 33(2), 174–186.

Cohen, M. J. (1997). *Children's memory scale*. San Antonio, TX: Psychological Corporation.

Connor, D., Steeber, J., & McBurnett, K. (2010). A review of Attention-Deficit/Hyperactivity Disorder complicated by symptoms of Oppositional Defiant Disorder or Conduct Disorder. *Journal of Developmental & Behavioral Pediatrics*, 31(5), 427–440.

Cools, R., & D'Esposito, M. (2011). Inverted-U-shaped dopamine actions on human working memory and cognitive control. *Biological Psychiatry*, 2011(69), e113–e125.

Cooper, W. O., Habel, L. A., Sox, C. M., et al. (2011). ADHD drugs and serious cardiovascular events in children and young adults. *The New England Journal of Medicine*, 365(20), 1896–1904.

Cortese, S., Faraone, S. V., Konofal, E., et al. (2009). Sleep in children with Attention-Deficit/Hyperactivity Disorder: Meta-analysis of subjective and objective studies. *Journal of the American Academy of Child Adolescence and Psychiatry*, 48(9), 894–908.

Cortese, S., Kelly, C., Chabernaud, C., et al. (2012) Toward Systems Neuroscience of ADHD: A Meta-Analysis of 55 fMRI Studies. *American Journal of Psychiatry*, 16 (10), 1038-1055.

Cowen, E. L., Pederson, A., Babigian, H., et al., (1973). Long-term follow-up of early detected vulnerable children. *J. Consulting & Clinical Psychology* 41, 438–446.

Craske, M., Rauch, S., Ursano, R., et al. (2009). What is an anxiety disorder? *Depression and Anxiety*, 26(12), 1066–1085.

Crombag, H. S., Bossert, J. M., Koya, E., et al. (2010). Context-induced relapse to drug seeking: A review. In *Neurobiology of Addiction: new vistas*, Robbins, T. W., Everitt, B. J., & Nutt, D. J., New York: Oxford University Press.

Das, D., Cherbuin, N., Butterworth, P., et al. (2012). A population-based study of Attention Deficit/Hyperactivity Disorder symptoms and associated impairment in middle-aged adults. *PLoS ONE* 7(2), e31500. Doi:10.1371/journal.pone.0031500.

Dawson, P., & Guare, R. (2004, 2010). *Executive skills in children and adolescents. 2nd edition.* New York: Guilford Press.

DeCaro, M. S., & Beilock, S. L. (2010). Benefits and perils of attentional control. In *Effortless attention: A new perspective in the cognitive science of attention and action*, edited by Bruya, B. Cambridge, MA: MIT Press, 51–73.

de Graaf, R., Kessler, R. C., Fayyad, J., et al. (2008). The prevalence and effects of adult Attention-Deficit/Hyperactivity Disorder (ADHD) on the performance of workers: Results from the WHO World Mental Health Survey Initiative. *Occupational Environmental Medicine*, 65, 835–842.

Del Campo, N. D., Chamberlain, S. R., Sahakian, B. J., et al. (2011). The roles of dopamine and noradrenaline in the pathophysiology and treatment of Attention-Deficit/Hyperactivity Disorder. *Biological Psychiatry*, 69, e145–e157.

Delis, D. C., Lansring, A., Houston, W. S., et al. (2007). Creativity lost: The importance of testing higher-level executive functions in school-age children and adolescents. *Journal of Psychoeducational Assessment*, 25(1), 29–40.

Diamond, A. (2005). Attention-Deficit Disorder (Attention-Deficit/Hyperactivity Disorder without hyperactivity): A neurobiologically and behaviorally distinct disorder from Attention-Deficit/Hyperactivity Disorder (with hyperactivity). *Development and Psychopathology*, 17, 807–825.

Dickstein, S. G., Bannon, K., Castellanos, F. X., et al. (2006). The neural correlates of Attention Deficit Hyperactivity Disorder: An ALE meta-analysis. *Journal of Child Psychology and Psychiatry* 47, 1051–1062.

Douglas, V. I. (1988). Cognitive deficits in children with Attention-Deficit Disorder with hyperactivity. In *Attention Deficit Disorder: Criteria, cognition, intervention*, edited by Bloomingdale, L. M., & Sergeant, J. Book supplement to *Journal of Child Psychology and Psychiatry*, New York: Pergamon Press, Supplement 5, 65–81.

Ducharme, S., Hudziak, J., Botteron, K., et al. (2012). Decreased regional cortical thickness and thinning rate are associated with inattention symptoms in healthy children. *Journal of the American Academy of Child and Adolescent Psychiatry*, 51(1), 18–27.

Eigsti, I., Zayas, V., Mischel, W., et al. (2006). Predicting cognitive control from preschool to late adolescence and young adulthood. *Psychological Science*, 17(6), 478–484.

Epperson, C. N., Pittman, B., Czarkowski, K. A., et al. (2011). Impact of amoxetine on subjective attention and memory difficulties in perimenopausal and postmenopausal women. *Menopause*, 18(5), 1–8.

Epstein, J. N., Casey, B. J., Tonev, S., et al. (2007). ADHD and medication-related brain activation effects in concordantly affected parent-child dyads with ADHD. *Journal of Child Psychology and Psychiatry*, 48(9), 899–913.

Famularo, R., Kinscherff, R., & Fenton, T. (1992). Psychiatric diagnoses of maltreated children: Preliminary findings. *Journal American Academy Child Adolescent Psychiatry*, 31, 863–867.

Faraone, S. V., & Buitelaar, J. (2010). Comparing the efficacy of stimulants for ADHD in children and adolescents using meta-analysis. *European Child and Adolescent Psychiatry*, 19, 353–364.

Faraone, S. V., & Glatt, S. J. (2010). A comparison of the efficacy of medications for adult Attention-Deficit/Hyperactivity Disorder using meta-analysis of effect sizes. *Journal of Clinical Psychiatry*, 71(6), 754–763.

Faraone, S. V., Biederman, J., Chen, W. J., et al. (1992). Segregation analysis of attention deficit hyperactivity disorder. *Psychiatric Genetics*, 2, 257–275.

Faraone, S. V., Biederman, J., Doyle, A., et al. (2006a). Neuropsychological studies of late onset and subthreshold diagnoses of adult Attention-Deficit/Hyperactivity Disorder. *Biological Psychiatry*, 60, 1081–1087.

Faraone, S. V., Biederman, J., Mick, E., et al. (2000). Family study of girls with Attention Deficit Hyperactivity Disorder. *American Journal of Psychiatry*, 157, 1077–1083.

Faraone, S. V., Biederman, J., Mick, E. (2006b). The age-dependent decline of attention deficit hyperactivity disorder: A meta-analysis of follow-up studies. *Psychological Medicine*, 36, 159–165.

Faraone, S. V., Biederman, J., Morley, C. P., et al. (2008). Effect of stimulants on height and weight: A review of the literature. *Journal of the American Academy of Child & Adolescent Psychiatry*, 47(9), 994–1009.

Faraone, S. V., Biederman, J., Spencer, T. J., et al. (2006c). Comparing the efficacy of medications for ADHD using meta-analysis. *MedScape General Medicine*, 8(4), 4. Published online October 5, 2006.

Faraone, S., Biederman, J., Spencer, T., et al. (2006d). Diagnosing adult Attention Deficit Hyperactivity Disorder: Are late onset and subthreshold diagnoses valid? *American Journal of Psychiatry*, 163(10), 1720–1729.

Faraone, S. V., Biederman, J., & Spencer, T. (2010). Diagnostic efficiency of symptoms for identifying adult Attention-Deficit/Hyperactivity Disorder. *Journal of ADHD & Related Disorders*, 1(2), 38–48.

Faraone, S. V., Perlis, R. H., Doyle, A. E., et al. (2005). Molecular genetics of attention-deficit/hyperactivity disorder. *Biological Psychiatry*, 57(11), 1313–1323.

Fassbender, C., Zhang, H., Buzy, W. M., et al. (2009). A lack of default network suppression is linked to increased distractibility in ADHD. *Brain Research*, 1273, 114–128.

Fineberg, N. A., Saxena, S., Zohar, J., et al. (2011). Obsessive-Compulsive Disorder: boundary issues. In *Obsessive-compulsive disorders: Refining the research agenda for DSM-V* edited by Hollander, E., Washington, DC: American Psychiatric Association, 1–32.

Fombonne, E. (2005). Epidemiological Studies of Pervasive Developmental Disorders. In *Handbook of Autism and pervasive developmental disorders, 3rd edition*, edited by Volkmar, F. R., Paul, R., Klin, A., et al. Hoboken, NJ, 42–69.

Fischer, A. G., Bau, C. H., Grevet, E. H., et al. (2007). The role of comorbid major depressive disorder in the clinical presentation of adult ADHD. *Journal of Psychiatric Research*, 41, 991–996.

Frazier, T. W., Demaree, H. A., & Youngstrom, E. A. (2004). Meta-analysis of intellectual and neuropsychological test performance in Attention-Deficit/Hyperactivity Disorder. *Neuropsychology*, 18, 543–555.

Frazier, T. W., Youngstrom, E. A., Glutting, J. J. et al. (2007). ADHD and achievement: Meta-analysis of the child, adolescent, and adult literatures and a concomitant study with college students. *Journal of Learning Disabilities*, 40, 49–65.

Froehlich, T. E., Lamphear, B. P., Epstein, J. N., et al. (2007). Prevalence, recognition, and treatment of Attention-Deficit/Hyperactivity Disorder in a national sample of U.S. children. *Archives of Pediatric Adolescent Medicine*, 161(9), 857–864, 207

Frost, R. O., Steketee, G., & Tolin, D. F. (2011). Comorbidity in hoarding disorder. *Depression and Anxiety*, 28, 876–884.

Fuster, J. M. (2003). *Cortex and mind: Unifying cognition*, Oxford, U.K.: Oxford University Press.

Gau, S. S., & Chiang, H. L. (2009). Sleep problems and disorders among adolescents with persistent and subthreshold Attention-Deficit/Hyperactivity Disorders. *Sleep*, 32(5), 671–679.

Gaub, M., & Carlson, C. L. (1997). Gender differences in ADHD: A meta-analysis and critical review. *Journal of the American Academy of Child & Adolescent Psychiatry*, 36(8), 1036–1045.

Geller, D. A., & Brown, T. E. (2009). ADHD with Obsessive-Compulsive Disorder. In *ADHD comorbidities: Handbook for ADHD complications in children and adults*, edited by Brown, T. E., Washington, DC: American Psychiatric Publishing, 177–187.

Geller, D. A., Biederman, J., Faraone, S. V., et al. (2000). Clinical correlates of obsessive compulsive disorder in children and adolescents referred to specialized and non-specialized clinical settings. *Depression and Anxiety*, 11, 163–168.

Geller, D. A., Biederman, J., Faraone, S. V., et al. (2001). Developmental aspects of obsessive compulsive disorder: Findings in children, adolescents, and adults. *The Journal of Nervous and Mental Disease*, 189(7), 471–477.

Geurts, H. M., & Embrechts, M. (2008). Language profiles in ASD, SLI, and ADHD. *Journal of Autism and Developmental Disorders*, 38, 1931–1943.

Gioia, G., Isquith, P. K., Guy, S. C., et al. (2000). *BRIEF: Behavior rating inventory of executive function; Parent form.* Lutz, FL: Psychological Assessment Resources.

Golan, N., Shahar, E., Ravid, S., et al. (2004). Sleep disorders and daytime sleepiness in children with Attention-Deficit/Hyperactive Disorder. *Sleep*, 27(2), 261–266.

Goleman, D. (1996). *Emotional intelligence: Why it can matter more than IQ.* London: Bloomsbury Press.

Greenhill, L. L., Kollins, S., & Abikoff, H. (2006). Efficacy and safety of immediate-release methylphenidate treatment for preschoolers with ADHD. *Journal of the American Academy of Child & Adolescent Psychiatry*, 45, 1284–1293.

Grzadzinski, R., Martino, A. D., Brady, E., et al. (2011). Examining Autistic traits in children with ADHD: Does the Autism Spectrum extend to ADHD? *Journal of Autism and Developmental Disorders*, 41(9), 1178–1191.

Guy, S. C., Isquith, P. K., & Gioia, G. A. (2004). *BRIEF-SR: behavior rating inventory of executive function–self-report version: professional manual.* Lutz, FL: Psychological Assessment Resources.

Habel, L. A., Cooper, W. O., Sox, C. M., et al. (2011). ADHD medications and risks of serious cardiovascular events in young and middle-aged adults. *JAMA*, 306 (24), 2673–2683.

Halmoy, A., Klungsoyr, K., Skjaerven, R., et al. (2012). Pre- and perinatal risk factors in adults with Attention-Deficit/Hyperactivity Disorder. *Biological Psychiatry*, 71, 474–481.

Hartl, T. L., Duffany, S. R., Allen, G. J., et al. (2005). Relationships among compulsive hoarding, trauma, and Attention-Deficit/Hyperactivity Disorder. *Behavior Research and Therapy*, 43, 269–276.

Heaton, R. K. (1981). *Wisconsin Card-Sorting Test Manual*. Odessa, FL: Psychological Assessment Resources.

Hechtman, L., Abikoff, H., Klein, R. G., et al. (2004a). Children with ADHD treated with long-term methylphenidate and multimodal psychosocial treatment: Impact on parental practices. *Journal of the American Academy of Child & Adolescent Psychiatry*, 43(7), 830–838.

Hechtman, L., Abikoff, H., Klein, R. G., et al. (2004b). Academic achievement and emotional status of children with ADHD treated with long-term methylphenidate and multimodal psychosocial treatment. *Journal of the American Academy of Child & Adolescent Psychiatry*, 43(7), 812–819.

Heiligenstein, E., Guenther, G., Levy, A., et al. (1999). Psychological and academic functioning in college students with Attention Deficit Hyperactivity Disorder. *Journal of American College Health*, 47(4), 181–185.

Hervey, A. S., Epstein, J. N., & Curry, J. F. (2004). Neuropsychology of adults with Attention-Deficit/Hyperactivity Disorder: A meta-analytic review. *Neuropsychology*, 18(3), 485–503.

Hinshaw, S. P. (2002). Preadolescent girls with Attention-Deficit/Hyperactivity Disorder: I. Background characteristics, comorbidity, cognitive and social functioning, and parenting practices. *Journal of Consulting and Clinical Psychology*, 70(5), 1086–1098.

Hinshaw, S. P. (2009). Psychosocial interventions for ADHD and comorbidities. In *ADHD comorbidities: Handbook for ADHD complications in children and adults*, edited by Brown, T. E., Washington, DC: American Psychiatric Publishing, 385–398.

Hinshaw, S. P., Carte, E. T., Fan, C., et al. (2007). Neuropsychological functioning of girls with Attention-Deficit/Hyperactivity Disorder followed prospectively into adolescence: Evidence for continuing deficits. *Neuropsychology*, 21(2), 263–273.

Hinshaw, S. P., Carte, E. T., Sami, N., et al. (2002). Preadolescent girls with Attention-Deficit/Hyperactivity Disorder: II. Neuropsychological performance in relation to subtypes and individual classification. *Journal of Consulting and Clinical Psychology*, 70(5), 1099–1111.

Hinshaw, S. P., Owens, E. B., Zalecki, C., et al. (2012). Prospective follow-up of girls with Attention-Deficit/Hyperactivity Disorder into early adulthood: Continuing impairment includes elevated risk for suicide attempts and self-injury. *Journal of Consulting and Clinical Psychology*, 80(6), 1041–1051.

Hoza, B. (2007). Peer functioning in children with ADHD. *Ambulatory Pediatrics*, 7, 101–106.

Hoza, B., Mrug, S., Gerdes, A. C., et al. (2005). What aspects of peer relationships are impaired in children with Attention Deficit/Hyperactivity Disorder? *Journal of Consulting and Clinical Psychology*, 73(3), 411–423.

Huang-Pollock, C., Karalunas, S. L., Tam, H., et al. (2012). Evaluating vigilance deficits in ADHD: A meta-analysis of CPT performance. *Journal of Abnormal Psychology*, 11(2), 360–371.

Iversen, L. (2008). *Speed>Ecstasy>Ritalin: The Science of Amphetamines*. Oxford, U.K.: Oxford University Press.

Jensen, P. S. (2004). *Making the system work for your child with ADHD*. New York: Guilford Press.

Jensen, P. S., Abikoff, H., & Brown, T. E. (2009). Tailoring treatments for individuals with ADHD and their families. In *ADHD comorbidities: Handbook for ADHD complications in children and adults*, edited by Brown, T. E., Washington, DC: American Psychiatric Publishing, 415–428.

Jensen, P. S., Hinshaw, S. P., Kraemer, H. C., et al. (2001). ADHD comorbidity findings from the MTA study: Comparing comorbid subgroups. *Journal of the American Academy of Child & Adolescent Psychiatry*, 40(2), 147–158.

Katusic, M. Z., Voigt, R. G., Colligan, R. C., et al. (2011). Attention-Deficit Hyperactivity Disorder in children with high intelligence quotient: Results from a population-based study. *Journal of Developmental Behavioral Pediatrics*, 32, 103–109.

Kahneman, D. (2011). *Thinking, fast and slow*, New York: Farrar, Straus and Giroux.

Kent, K. M., Pelham, W. E., Molina, B. S., et al. (2011). The academic experience of male high school students with ADHD. *Journal of Abnormal Child Psychology*, 39, 451–462.

Kendell, R., & Jablensky, A. (2003). Distinguishing between the validity and utility of psychiatric diagnoses. *American Journal of Psychiatry*, 160, 4–12.

Kessler, R. C., Adler, L., Barkley, R., et al. (2006). The prevalence and correlates of adult ADHD in the United States: Results from the National Comorbidity Survey Replication. *American Journal of Psychiatry*, 163(4), 716–723.

Kessler, R. C., Adler, L. A., Ustun, T. B., et al. (2005). Patterns and predictors of attention-deficit/hyperactivity disorder persistence into adulthood: Results from the National Comorbidity Survey Replication. *Biological Psychiatry*, 57(11), 1442–1451.

Kessler, R. C., Green, J. G., Adler, L. A., et al. (2010). Structure and diagnosis of Adult Attention-Deficit/Hyperactivity: Analysis of expanded symptom criteria from the adult ADHD clinical diagnostic scale. *Archives of General Psychiatry*, 67(11), 1168–1178.

Kollins, S., Greenhill, L. L., & Swanson, J. (2006). Rationale, design, and methods of the Preschool ADHD Treatment Study (PATS). *Journal of the American Academy of Child & Adolescent Psychiatry*, 45, 1275–1283.

Konrad, K., & Eickhoff, S. B. (2010). Is the ADHD brain wired differently? A review on structural and functional connectivity in Attention Deficit Hyperactivity Disorder. *Human Brain Mapping*, 31, 904–916.

Konrad, K., Dielentheis, T. F., El Masri, D., et al. (2010). Disturbed structural connectivity is related to inattention and impulsivity in adult attention deficit hyperactivity disorder. *European Journal of Neuroscience*, 31, 912–919.

Konrad, K., Neufang, S., Fink, G. R., et al. (2007). Long-term effects of methylphenidate on neural networks associated with executive attention in children with ADHD: Results from a longitudinal functional MRI study. *Journal of the American Academy of Child & Adolescent Psychiatry*, 46(12), 1633–1641.

Koob, G. F., & Le Moal, M. (2010). Neurobiological mechanisms for opponent motivational processes in addiction. In *Neurobiology of Addiction: New Vistas*, edited by Robbins, T. W., Everitt, B. J., & Nutt, D. J., New York: Oxford University Press, 7–23.

Koob, G., & Volkow, N. (2010). Neurocircuitry of addiction. *Neuropsychopharmacology*, 35(1), 217–238.

Lahey, B. B., Loeber, R., Burke, J., et al. (2002). Waxing and waning in concert: Dynamic comorbidity of conduct disorder with other disruptive and emotional problems over 17 years among clinic-referred boys. *Journal of Abnormal Psychology*, 111(4), 556–567.

Larson, K., Russ, S. A., Kahn, R. S., et al. (2011). Patterns of comorbidity, functioning, and service use for US children with ADHD,. *Pediatrics*, 127(3), 462–470.

Larsson, H., Dilshad, R., Lichtenstein, P., et al. (2011). Developmental trajectories of DSM-IV symptoms of attention-deficit/hyperactivity disorder: genetic effects, family risk and associated psychopathology. *Journal of Child Psychology and Psychiatry*, 52(9), 954–963.

Latham, P. S., & Latham, P. H. (2007). *Learning disabilities/ADHD and the law in higher education and employment*. Washington, DC: JKL Communications.

Lecendreux, M., Konofal, E., Bouvard, M., et al. (2000). Sleep and alertness in children with ADHD. *Journal of Child Psychology and Psychiatry*, 41(6), 803–812.

Leckman, J. F., Grice, D. E., Boardman, J., et al. (1997). Symptoms of Obsessive-Compulsive Disorder. *American Journal of Psychiatry*. 154(7), 911–917.

Lee, S. S., Humphreys, K. L., Flory, K., et al. (2011). Prospective association of childhood Attention-Deficit/Hyperactivity Disorder (ADHD) and substance use and abuse dependence: A meta-analytic review. *Clinical Psychology Review*, 31, 328–341.

Leibenluft, E. (2011). Severe mood dysregulation, irritability, and the diagnostic boundaries of Bipolar Disorder in youths. *American Journal of Psychiatry*, 168(2), 129–142.

Levy, F. (2004). Synaptic gating and ADHD: A biological theory of comorbidity of ADHD and anxiety. *Neuropsychopharmacology*, 29, 1589–1596.

Lewinsohn, P. M., Shankman, S. A., Gau, J. M., et al. (2004). The prevalence and co-morbidity of subthreshold psychiatric conditions. *Psychological Medicine*, 34, 613–622.

Lezak, M. D., Howieson, D. B., Loring. D. W. (2004). *Neuropsychological Assessment, 4th edition*, New York: Oxford University Press.

Liddle, E. B., Hollis, C., Batty, M. J., et al. (2011). Task-related default mode network modulation and inhibitory control in ADHD: Effects of motivation and methylphenidate. *Journal of Child Psychology and Psychiatry*, 52(7), 761–771.

Lowe, C., & Rabbitt, P. (1997). Cognitive models of ageing and frontal lobe deficits. In *Methodology of frontal and executive function*, Hove, UK: Psychology Press Publishers, 39–60.

Luman, M., Oosterlaan, J., Sergeant, J. A. (2005). The impact of reinforcement contingencies on AD/HD: A review and theoretical appraisal. *Clinical Psychology Review*, 25(2), 183–213.

Macari, S. L., Campbell, D., Gengoux, G. W., et al. (2012). Predicting developmental status from 12 to 24 months in infants at risk for Autism Spectrum Disorder: A preliminary report. *Journal of Autism and Developmental Disorders*, Doi 10.1007/s10803–012–1521–0.

Manor, I., Rozen, S., Zemishlani, Z., et al. (2011). When does it end? Attention-Deficit/Hyperactivity Disorder in the middle aged and older populations. *Clinical Neuropharmacology*, 34(4), 148–154.

Marner, L., Nyengaard, J. R., Tang, Y., et al. (2003). Marked loss of myelinated nerve fibres in the human brain with age. *Journal of Comparative Neurology* 462(2), 144–152.

Martinussen, R., Hayden, J., Hogg-Johnson, S., et al. (2005). A meta-analysis of working memory impairments in children with Attention-Deficit/Hyperactivity Disorder. *Journal of the American Academy of Child & Adolescent Psychiatry*, 44(4), 377–384.

Marton, I., Wiener, J., Rogers, M., et al. (2009). Empathy and social perspective taking in children with Attention-Deficit/Hyperactivity Disorder. *Journal of Abnormal Child Psychology*, 37, 107–118.

Massetti, G. M., Lahey, B. B., Pelham, W. E., et al. (2008). Academic achievement over 8 years among children who met modified criteria for Attention-Deficit/Hyperactivity Disorder at 4–6 years of age. *Journal of Abnormal Child Psychology*, 36(3), 399–410.

Mayes, S., & Calhoun, S. (2006). Frequency of reading, math, and writing disabilities in children with clinical disorders. *Learning and Individual Differences*, 16(2), 145–157.

Mayes, S. D., & Calhoun, S. L. (2007). Wechsler Intelligence Scale for children, 3rd–4th edition, Predictors of academic achievement in children with Attention-Deficit/Hyperactivity Disorder. *School Psychology Quarterly*, 22(2), 234–249.

Mayes, S., Calhoun, S., & Crowell, E. (2000). Learning disabilities and ADHD: Overlapping spectrum disorders. *Journal of Learning Disabilities*, 33(5), 417–424.

McDermott, S. P. (2009). Cognitive therapy for adults with ADHD. In *ADHD comorbidities: Handbook for ADHD complications in children and adults*, edited by Brown, T. E., Washington, DC: American Psychiatric Publishing, 399–414.

McGough, J. J., & Barkley, R. A. (2004). Diagnostic controversies in adult Attention Deficit Hyperactivity Disorder. *American Journal of Psychiatry*, 161(11), 1948–1956.

McGrath, L. M., Pennington, B. F., Shanahan, M. A., et al. (2011). A multiple deficit model of reading disability and attention-deficit/hyperactivity disorder: searching for shared cognitive deficits. *Journal of Child Psychology and Psychiatry*, 52(5), 547–557.

Meltzer, L., ed. (2007). *Executive function in education: From theory to practice*. New York: Guilford Press.

Meltzer, L. (2010). *Promoting executive function in the classroom*. New York: Guilford Press.

Merikangas, K., Akiskal, H., Angst, J., et al. (2007). Lifetime and 12-month prevalence of Bipolar Spectrum Disorder in the National Comorbidity Survey Replication. *Arch Gen Psychiatry*, 64(5), 543–552.

Merikangas, K. R., He, J. P., Burstein, M., et al. (2010). Lifetime prevalence of mental disorders in U.S. adolescents: Results from the National Comorbidity Survey Replication – Adolescent supplement (NCS-A). *Journal of the American Academy of Child & Adolescent Psychiatry*, 49(10), 980–989.

Mick, E., & Faraone, S. V. (2008). Genetics of Attention Deficit Hyperactivity Disorder. *Child and Adolescent Psychiatric Clinics of North America*, 17, 261–284.

Milich, R., Carlson, C. L., Pelham, W. E., et al. (1991). Effects of methylphenidate on the persistence of ADHD boys following failure experiences. *Journal of Abnormal Child Psychology*, 19(5), 519–536.

Miller, A. C., Keenan, J. M., Betjemann, R. S., et al. (2012b). Reading comprehension in children with ADHD: Cognitive underpinnings of the centrality deficit. *Journal of Abnormal Child Psychology*, Doi: 10.1007/s10802–012–9686–8.

Miller, M., & Hinshaw, S. P. (2010). Does childhood executive function predict adolescent functional outcomes in girls with ADHD. *Journal of Abnormal Child Psychology*, 38, 315–326.

Miller, M., Ho, J., & Hinshaw, S. P. (2012a). Executive functions in girls with ADHD followed prospectively into young adulthood. *Neuropsychology*, 26(3), 278–287.

Miller, M., Nevado-Montenegro, A. J., & Hinshaw, S. P. (2011). Childhood executive function continues to predict outcomes in young adult females with and without childhood-diagnosed ADHD. *Journal of Abnormal Child Psychology*, 38, 315–326.

Miller, T., Nigg, J., & Faraone, S. (2007). Axis I and II comorbidity in adults with ADHD. *Journal of Abnormal Psychology*, 116(3), 519–528.

Millstein, R. B., & Wilens, T. E. et al. (1997). Presenting ADHD symptoms and subtypes in clinically referred adults with ADHD. *Journal of Attention Disorders* 2 (3), 159–166.

Molina, B. S., & Pelham, W. E. (2003). Childhood predictors of adolescent substance use in a longitudinal study of children with ADHD. *Journal of Abnormal Psychology*, 112(3), 497–507.

Morris, S. M., Petibone, D. M., Lin, W., et al. (2012). The genetic toxicity of methylphenidate: A review of the current literature. *Journal of Applied Toxicology*, 32(10), 756–764.

MTA Cooperative Group (1999). A 14 month randomized clinical trial of treatment strategies for Attention-Deficit/Hyperactivity Disorder. *Archives of General Psychiatry*. 56, 1073–1086.

Murphy, K., & Barkley, R. A. (1996). Prevalence of DSM-IV symptoms of ADHD in adult licensed drivers: Implications for clinical diagnosis. *Journal of Attention Disorders*, 1(3), 147–161.

Murray-Close, D., Hoza, B., Hinshaw, S. P., et al. (2010). Developmental processes in peer problems of children with ADHD in the MTA study: Developmental cascades and vicious cycles. *Developmental Psychopathology*, 22(4), 785–802.

Nagel, B. J., Bathula, D., Herting, M., et al. (2011). Altered white mater microstructure in children with Attention-Deficit/Hyperactivity Disorder. *Journal of the American Academy of Child and Adolescent Psychiatry*, 50(3), 283–292.

Naglieri, J. A., & Goldstein, S. (2013). *Comprehensive executive function inventory*. North Tonawanda, NY: Multi Health Systems.

Nakao, T., Radua, J., & Rubia, K. (2011). Gray matter volume abnormalities in ADHD: Voxel-based meta-analysis exploring the effects of age and stimulant medication. *American Journal of Psychiatry*, 168(11), 1154–1163.

Neale, B. M., Medland, S. E., & Ripke, S. (2010) Meta-analysis of genome-wide association studies of Attention-Deficit/Hyperactivity Disorder. *Journal of the American Academy of Child and Adolescent Psychiatry*, 49(9), 884–897.

Nestler, E. J. (2005). Is there a common molecular pathway for addiction? *Neurobiology of Addiction*, 8(11), 1445–1449.

Newcorn, J. H., Kratochvil, C. J., Allen, A. J., et al. (2008). Atomoxetine and osmotically released methylphenidate for the treatment of attention deficit hyperactivity: Acute comparison and differential response. Atomoxetine/Methylphenidate Comparative Study Group. *American Journal of Psychiatry*, 165 (6), 721–730.

Nierenberg, A. A., Miyahara, S., Spencer, T., et al. (2005). Clinical and diagnostic implications of lifetime Attention-Deficit/Hyperactivity Disorder comorbidity in adults with Bipolar Disorder: Data from the first 1000 STEP-BD participants. *Biological Psychiatry*, 57, 1467–1473.

Nigg, J., Nikolas, M., & Burt, S. A. (2010). Measured gene-by-environment interaction in relation to Attention-Deficit/Hyperactivity Disorder. *Journal of the American Academy of Child and Adolescent Psychiatry*, 49(9), 836–873.

Nijmeijer, J. S., Hoekstra, P. J., Minderaa, R. B., et al. (2009). PDD symptoms i n ADHD, an independent familial trait? *Journal of Abnormal Child Psychology*, 37, 443–453.

Nijmeijer, J. S., Minderaa, R. B., Buitelaar, J. K., et al. (2008). Attention-Deficit/ Hyperactivity Disorder and social dysfunctioning. *Clinical Psychology Review*, 28, 692–708.

Nock, M. K., Kazdin, A. E., Hiripi, E., et al. (2007). Lifetime prevalence, correlates, and persistence of oppositional defiant disorder: results from the National Comorbidity Survey Replication. *Journal of Child Psychology and Psychiatry*, 48 (7), 703–713.

Olfson, M., Huang, C., Gerhard, T., et al. (2012). Stimulants and cardiovascular events in youth with Attention-Deficit/Hyperactivity Disorder. *Journal of the American Academy of Child & Adolescent Psychiatry*, 51 (2), 147–156.

Palli, S. R., Kamble, P. S., Chen, H., et al. (2012). Persistence of stimulants in children and adolescents with Attention-Deficit/Hyperactivity Disorder. *Journal of Child & Adolescent Psychopharmacology*, 22 (2), 139–148.

Pelham, W. E., & Bender, M. E. (1982). Peer relationships in hyperactive children: Description and treatment. *Advances in Learning & Behavioral Disabilities*, 1, 365–436.

Pennington, B. F. (1991). *Diagnosing learning disorders: A neuropsychological perspective*. New York: Guilford Press.

Peterson, B. S., Potenza, M. N., Wang, Z., et al. (2009). An fMRI study of the effects of psychostimulants on default-mode processing during Stroop task performance in youths with ADHD. *American Journal of Psychiatry*, 166(11), 1286–1294.

Petrill, S., Logan, J., Hart, S., et al. (2012). Math fluency is etiologically distinct from untimed math performance, decoding fluency, and untimed reading performance: Evidence from a twin study. *Journal of Learning Disabilities*, 45(4), 371–381.

Philipsen, A., Hornyak, M., & Riemann, D. (2006). Sleep and sleep disorders in adults with Attention Deficit/Hyperactivity Disorder. *Sleep Medicine Reviews*, 10, 399–405.

Pingault, J. B., Tremblay, R. E., Vitaro, F., et al. (2011). Childhood trajectories of inattention and hyperactivity and prediction of educational attainment in early adulthood: A 16-year longitudinal population-based study. *American Journal of Psychiatry*, 168, 1164–1170.

Pliszka, S. R., Liotti, M., Bailey, B. Y., et al. (2007). Electrophysiological effects of stimulant treatment on inhibitory control in children with Attention-Deficit/ Hyperactivity Disorder. *Journal of Child and Adolescent Psychopharmacology*, 17(3), 356–366.

Poelmans, G., Pauls, D. L., Buitelaar, D. L., et al. (2011). Integrated genome-wide association study findings: Identification of a neurodevelopmental network for Attention Deficit Hyperactivity Disorder. *American Journal of Psychiatry*, 168, 365–377.

Polanczyk, G., Caspi, A., Houts, R., et al. (2010). Implications of extending the ADHD age-of-onset criterion to age 12: Results from a prospectively studied birth cohort. *Journal of the American Academy of Child & Adolescent Psychiatry*, 49(3), 210–216.

Polanczyk, G., Silva de Lima, M., Horta, B. L., et al. (2007). The worldwide prevalence of ADHD: A systematic review and meta-regression analysis. *American Journal of Psychiatry*, 164, 942–948.

Polderman, T. J. C., Boomsma, D. I., Bartels, M., et al. (2010). A systematic review of prospective studies on attention problems and academic achievement. *Acta Psychiatrica Scandinavica*, 122, 171–284.

Posner, J., Nagel, B. J., Maia, T. V., et al. (2011). Abnormal amygdalar activation and connectivity in adolescents with Attention-Deficit/Hyperactivity Disorder. *Journal of the American Academy of Child and Adolescent Psychiatry*, 50(8), 828–837.

Posner, K., Pressman, A. W., & Greenhill, L. L. (2009). ADHD in preschool children. In *ADHD comorbidities: Handbook for ADHD complications in children and adults*, edited by Brown, T.E. Washington, DC: American Psychiatric Association, 37–53.

Posner, M. I., & Petersen, S. E. (1991). The attention systems of the human brain. *Annual Review of Neuroscience*, 13, 25–42.

Powers, R. L., Marks, D. J., Miller, C. J., et al. (2008). Stimulant treatment in children with Attention-Deficit/Hyperactivity Disorder moderates adolescent academic outcome. *Journal of Child and Adolescent Psychopharmacology*, 18(5), 449–459.

Prince, J. B., & Wilens, T. E. (2009). Pharmacotherapy of ADHD and comorbidities. In *ADHD comorbidities: Handbook for ADHD complications in children and adults*, edited by Brown, T.E. Washington, DC: American Psychiatric Publishing, 339–384.

Proal, E., Reiss, P. T., Klein, R. G., et al. (2011). Brain gray matter deficits at 33-year follow-up in adults with Attention-Deficit/Hyperactivity Disorder established in childhood. *Archives of General Psychiatry*, 68(11), 1122–1134.

Quinlan, D. M., & Brown, T. E. (2003). Assessment of short-term verbal memory impairments in adolescents and adults with ADHD. *Journal of Attention Disorders*, 6(4), 143–152.

Rabbitt, P. (1997). *Methodologies and models in the study of executive function. Methodology of frontal and executive function.* Hove, U.K.: Psychology Press Publishers, 1–38.

Ramsay, J. R. (2010). *Nonmedication treatments for adult ADHD.* Washington DC: American Psychological Association.

Ramsay, J. R., & Rostain, A. L. (2008). *Cognitive behavioral therapy for adult ADHD: An integrative psychosocial and medical approach.* New York: Routledge.

Reiersen, A., Constantino, J. N., Volk, H. E., et al. (2007). Autistic traits in a population-based ADHD twin sample. *Journal of Child Psychology and Psychiatry and Allied Disciplines*, 48(5), 464–472.

Rich, B. A., Carver, F. W., Holroyd, T., et al. (2011). Different neural pathways to negative affect in youth with pediatric bipolar disorder and severe mood dysregulation. *Journal of Psychiatric Research*, 45(10), 1283–1294.

Robbins, T. W., James, M., Owen, A. M., et al. (1997). A neural systems approach to the cognitive psychology of ageing using the CANTAB battery. *Methodology of frontal and executive function*. Hove, East Sussex, U.K.: Psychology Press, 215–250.

Rogers, M., Hwang, H., Toplak, M., et al. (2011). Inattention, working memory, and academic achievement in adolescents referred for attention deficit/hyperactivity disorder (ADHD). *Child Neuropsychology*, 17(5), 444–458.

Rommelse, N. N., Altink, M. E., Oosterlaan, J., et al. (2008). Support for an independent familial segregation of executive and intelligence endophenotypes in ADHD families. *Psychological Medicine*, 38(11), 1595–1606.

Rommelse, N., Franke, B., Geurts, H., et al. (2010). Shared heritability of Attention-Deficit/Hyperactivity Disorder and Autism Spectrum Disorder. *European Child & Adolescent Psychiatry*, 19(3), 281–295.

Ronald, A., Simonoff, E., Kuntsi, J., et al. (2008). Evidence for overlapping genetic influences on Autistic and ADHD behaviors in a community twin sample. *Journal of Child Psychology and Psychiatry and Allied Disciplines*, 49(5), 535–542.

Rostain, A. L., & Ramsay, J. R. (2006). A combined treatment approach for adults with ADHD: Results of an open study of 43 patients. *Journal of Attention Disorders*. 10 (2), 150–159.

Roth, R. M., Isquith, P. K., & Gioia, G. A. (2005). *BRIEF-A: Behavior rating inventory of executive function—adult version: professional manual*. Lutz, FL: Psychological Assessment Resources.

Rowe, R., Costello, E. J., Angold, A., et al. (2010). Developmental pathways in Oppositional Defiant Disorder and Conduct Disorder. *Journal of Abnormal Psychology*, 119(4), 726–738.

Rubia, K., Halari, R., Cubillo, A., et al. (2009). Methylphenidate normalizes activation and functional connectivity deficits in attention and motivation networks in medication-naïve children with ADHD during a rewarded continuous performance task. *Neuropharmacology*, 57, 640–652.

Rubia, K., Halari, R., Cubillo. A., et al. (2011). Methylphenidate normalizes fronto-striatal underactivation during interference inhibition in medication-naïve boys with Attention-Deficit Hyperactivity Disorder. *Neuropsychopharmacology*, 36, 1575–1586.

Rucker, J. J., & McGuffin, P. (2012). Genomic structural variation in psychiatric disorders. *Developmental Psychopathology*, 24(4), 1335–1344.

Rutter, M., Cox, A., Tupling, C., et al. (1975). Attainment and adjustment in two geographical areas. I—the prevalence of psychiatric disorder. *British Journal of Psychiatry*, 126, 493–509.

Rybak, Y. E., McNeely, H. E., Mackenzie, B. E., et al. (2007). Seasonality and circadian preference in adult attention-deficit/hyperactivity disorder: clinical and neuropsychological correlates. *Comprehensive Psychiatry*, 48(6), 562–571.

Safren, S. A., Perlman, C. A., Sprich, S., et al. (2005). *Mastering your adult ADHD*. New York: Oxford University Press.

St. Pourcain, B. S., Mandy, W. P., Heron, J., et al. (2011). Links between co-occurring social-communication and hyperactive-inattentive trait trajectories. *Journal of the American Academy of Child & Adolescent Psychiatry*, 50(9), 892–902.

Schelleman, H., Bilker, W. B., Kimmel, S. E., et al. (2012). Methylphenidate and risks of serious cardiovascular events in adults. *American Journal of Psychiatry*, 169(2), 178–185.

Schelleman, H., Bilker, W. B., Strom, B. L., et al. (2011). Cardiovascular events and death in children exposed and unexposed to ADHD agents. *Pediatrics*, 127, 1102–1110.

Scheres, A., Milham, M. P., Knutson, B., et al. (2007). Ventral striatal hyporesponsiveness during reward anticipation in Attention-Deficit/Hyperactivity Disorder. *Biological Psychiatry*, 61, 720–724.

Schmeichel, B. J., Volokhov, R. N., & Demaree, H. A. (2008). Working memory capacity and the self-regulation of emotional expression and experience. *Journal of Personality and Social Psychology*, 95(6), 1526–1540.

Schuck, S. E., & Crinella, F. M. (2005). Why children with ADHD do not have low IQs. *Journal of Learning Disabilities*, 38(3), 262–280.

Seidman, L. J., Doyle, A., Fried, R., et al. (2004). Neuropsychological functions in adults with Attention-Deficit/Hyperactivity Disorder. *Psychiatric Clinics of North America*, 27(2), 261–282.

Sergeant, J. A. (2005). Modeling Attention-Deficit/Hyperactivity Disorder: A critical appraisal of the cognitive-energetic model. *Biological Psychiatry*, 57, 1248–1255.

Sergeant, J. A., Guerts, H., & Oosterlaan, J. (2002). How specific is a deficit of executive functioning for Attention-Deficit/Hyperactivity Disorder? *Behavioural Brain Research*, 130, 3–28.

Sesma, H. W., Mahone, E. M., Levine, T., et al. (2009). The contribution of executive skills to reading comprehension. *Child Neuropsychology*, 15(3), 232–246.

Seymour, K. E., Chronis-Tuscano, A., Halldorsdottir, T., et al. (2012). Emotion regulation mediates the relationship between ADHD and depressive symptoms in youth. *Journal of Abnormal Child Psychology*, 40, 595–606.

Shafran, R., & Mansell, W. (2001). Perfectionism and psychopathology: A review of research and treatment. *Clinical Psychology Review*, 21(6), 879–906.

Shafran, R., Cooper, Z., & Fairburn, C. G. (2002). Clinical Perfectionism: A cognitive behavioral analysis. *Behavior Research and Therapy*, 40, 663–791.

Shallice, T. (1982). Specific impairments of planning. *Philosophical Transactions of the Royal Society of London*, 298, 199–209.

Shallice, T., & Burgess, P. W. (1991). Deficits in strategy application following frontal lobe damage in man. *Brain*, 114, 727–741.

Shanahan, M., Pennington, B., Yerys, B., et al. (2006). Processing speed deficits in Attention Deficit/Hyperactivity Disorder and reading disability. *Journal of Abnormal Child Psychology*, 34(5), 585–602.

Shapiro, D. (1965). *Neurotic styles*. New York: Basic Books.

Shaw, P., Eckstrand, K., Sharp, W., et al. (2007) Attention-Deficit/Hyperactivity Disorder is characterized by a delay in cortical maturation. *Proceedings of the National Academy of Sciences*, 104(49), 19649–19654.

Shaw, P., Lerch, J., Greenstein, D., et al. (2006). Longitudinal mapping of cortical thickness and clinical outcome in children and adolescents with Attention-Deficit/Hyperactivity Disorder. *Archives of General Psychiatry*, 63, 540–549.

Shaw, P., Malek, M., Watson, B., et al. (2012). Development of cortical surface area and gyrification in Attention-Deficit/Hyperactivity Disorder. *Biological Psychiatry*, 72(3), 191–197.

Shaywitz, S. E., & Shaywitz, B. A. (2008). Paying attention to reading: The neurobiology of reading and dyslexia. *Development and Psychopathology*, 20, 1329–1349.

Shechner, T., Britton, J. C., Perez-Edgar, K., et al. (2012). Attention biases, anxiety, and development: Toward or away from threats or rewards. *Depression and Anxiety*, 29, 282–294.

Sheridan, M. A., Hinshaw, S., & D'Esposito, M. (2007). Efficiency of the prefrontal cortex during working memory in Attention-Deficit/Hyperactivity Disorder. *Journal of the American Academy of Child and Adolescent Psychiatry*, 46(10), 1357–1366.

Shoda, Y., Mischel, W., & Peake, P.K. (1990) Predicting adolescent cognitive and self-regulatory competencies from preschool delay of gratification: Identifying diagnostic conditions. *Developmental Psychology*, 26 (6), 978–986.

Smalley, S. L., McGough, J. J., Del'Homme, M., et al. (2000). Familial clustering of symptoms and disruptive behaviours in multiplex families with Attention-Deficit/Hyperactivity Disorder. *Journal of the American Academy of Child and Adolescent Psychiatry*, 39(9), 1135–1143.

Sobanski, E., Banaschewski, T., Asherson, P., et al. (2010). Emotional liability in children and adolescents with Attention Deficit/Hyperactivity Disorder (ADHD): Clinical correlates and familial prevalence. *Journal of Child Psychology and Psychiatry*, 51(8), 915–923.

Sobel, L. J., Bansal, R., Maia, T. V., et al. (2010). Basal ganglia surface morphology and the effects of stimulant medications in youth with Attention Deficit Hyperactivity Disorder. *American Journal of Psychiatry*, 167, 997–986.

Solanto, M. V. (2011). *Cognitive-behavioral therapy for adult ADHD: Targeting executive dysfunction*. New York: Guilford Press.

Solanto, M. V., Marks, D. J., Mitchell, K. J., et al. (2008). Development of a new psychosocial treatment for adult ADHD. *Journal of Attention Disorders*, 11(6), 728–736.

Solanto, M., Newcorn, J., Vail, L., et al. (2009). Stimulant drug response in the predominantly inattentive and combined subtypes of Attention-Deficit/Hyperactivity Disorder. *Journal of Child and Adolescent Psychopharmacology*, 19(6), 663–671.

Sonuga-Barke, E. J. (2005). Causal models of Attention-Deficit/Hyperactivity Disorder: From common simple deficits to multiple developmental pathways. *Biological Psychiatry*, 57, 1231–1238.

Sonuga-Barke, E. J., & Castellanos, F. X. (2007). Spontaneous attentional fluctuations in impaired states and pathological conditions: A neurobiological hypothesis. *Neuroscience & Biobehavioral Reviews*, 31(7), 977–986.

Sonuga-Barke, E. J., & Sergeant, J. (2005). The neuroscience of ADHD: Multidisciplinary perspectives in a complex developmental disorder. *Developmental Science*, 8(2), 102–104.

Sonuga-Barke, E. J., Bitsakou, P., & Thompson, M. (2010a). Beyond the dual pathway model: evidence for the dissociation of timing, inhibitory, and delay-related impairments in Attention-Deficit/Hyperactivity Disorder. *Journal of the American Academy of Child and Adolescent Psychiatry*, 49(4), 345–355.

Sonuga-Barke, E. J. S., Brandeis, D., Cortese, S., et al. (2013). Nonpharmacological interventions for ADHD: Systematic review and meta-analyses of randomized controlled trials of dietary and psychological treatments. *American Journal of Psychiatry*, 170(3), 275–289.

Sonuga-Barke, E., Wiersema, J. R., van der Meere, J. J., et al. (2010b). Context-dependent dynamic processes in Attention Deficit/Hyperactivity Disorder: Differentiating common and unique effect of state regulation deficits and delay aversion. *Neuropsychological Review*, 20, 86–10.

Sprich, S., Biederman, J., Crawford, M. H., et al. (2000). Adoptive and biological families of children and adolescents with ADHD. *Journal of the American Academy of Child and Adolescent Psychiatry*, 39(11)0, 1432–1437.

Stavro, G. M., Ettenhofer, M. L., & Nigg, J. T. (2007). Executive functions and adaptive functioning in young adult Attention-Deficit/Hyperactivity Disorder. *Journal of the International Neuropsychological Society*, 13, 324–334.

Stergiakouli, E., Hamshere, M., Holmans, P., et al. (2012). Investigating the contribution of common genetic variants to the risk and pathogenesis of ADHD. *American Journal of Psychiatry*, 169(2), 186–194.

Stewart, S. E., Rosario, M. C., Brown, T. A., et al. (2007). Principal components analysis of Obsessive-Compulsive Disorder symptoms in children and adolescents. *Biological Psychiatry*, 61, 285–291.

Storch, E. A., Merlo, L. J., Larson, M. J., et al. (2008). Impact of comorbidity on cognitive-behavioral therapy response in pediatric Obsessive–Compulsive Disorder. *Journal of the American Academy of Child & Adolescent Psychiatry*, 47(5), 583–592.

Strang-Karlsson, S., Raikkonen, K., Pesonen, A., et al. (2008). Very low birth weight and behavioral symptoms of attention-deficit hyperactivity disorder in young adulthood: The Helsinki study of very low birthweight adults. *American Journal of Psychiatry*, 165, 1345–1353.

Stuss, D. T., Murphy, K. J., Binns, M. A., et al. (2003). Staying on the job: The frontal lobes control individual performance variability. *Brain*, 126(11), 2363–2380

Swanson, H. L., Zheng, X., & Jerman, O. (2009). Working memory, short-term memory, and reading disabilities a selective meta-analysis of the literature. *Journal of Learning Disabilities*, 42(3), 260–287.

Swanson, J., Baler, R. D., & Volkow, N. D. (2011). Understanding the effects of stimulant medications on cognition in individuals with attention-deficit/hyperactivity disorder: a decade of progress. *Neuropsychopharmacology* 36 (1), 207–226.

Tannock, R., & Schachar, R. (1996). Executive dysfunction as an underlying mechanism of behavior and language problems in attention-deficit/hyperactivity disorder. In *Language, learning and behavior disorders: Developmental, biological and clinical perspectives*, edited by Beitchman, J. H., Cohen, N. J., Konstantareas, M. M., et al., New York: Cambridge University Press, 28–155.

Timpano, K. R., Exner, C., Glaesmer, H., et al. (2011). The epidemiology of the proposed DSM-5 hoarding disorder: Exploration of the acquisition specifier, associated features, and distress. *Journal of Clinical Psychiatry*, 72(6), 780–786.

Toll, S. W., Van der Ven, S. G., Kroesbergen, E. H., et al. (2011). Executive functions as predictors of math learning disabilities. *Journal of Learning Disabilities*, 44(6), 521–532.

Tomasi, D., & Volkow, N. D. (2012). Abnormal functional connectivity in children with Attention-Deficit/Hyperactivity Disorder. *Biological Psychiatry*, 71, 443–450.

Tomasi, D., Volkow, N. D., Wang, G. J., et al. (2011). Methylphenidate enhances brain activation and deactivation responses to visual attention and working-memory tasks in healthy controls. *NeuroImage*, 54, 3101–3110.

Torrente, F., Lischinsky, A., Torralva, T., et al. (2010). Not always hyperactive? Elevated apathy scores in adolescents and adults with ADHD. *Journal of Attention Disorders*, 7, 545–556.

Tripp, G., & Wickens, J. R. (2008). Research review: Dopamine transfer deficit: a neurobiological theory of altered reinforcement mechanisms in ADHD. *Journal of Clinical Psychology and Psychiatry*, 49(7), 691–704.

Van Ameringen, M., Mancini, C., Simpson, W., et al. (2011). Adult Attention Deficit Hyperactivity Disorder in an anxiety disorders population. *CNS Neuroscience & Therapeutics*, 17, 221–226.

Van der Meer, J. M. J., Oerlemans, A. M., van Steijn, D. J., et al. (2012). Are Autism Spectrum Disorder and Attention-Deficit/Hyperactivity Disorder Different manifestations of one overarching disorder? Cognitive and symptom evidence from a clinical and population-based sample. *Journal of American Academy of Child & Adolescent Psychiatry*, 51 (11), 160–1172.

Van Emmerik-van Oortmerssen, K., van de Glind, G., van den Brink, W., et al. (2011). Prevalence of attention-deficit/hyperactivity disorder in substance use disorder patients: A meta-analysis and meta-regression analysis. *Drug & Alcohol Dependence*, 122(1–2), 11–19. Doi 10.1016/drugalcdep.2011.12007.

Van Ewijk, H., Heslenfeld, D. J., Zwiers, M. P., et al. (2012). Diffusion tensor imaging in Attention Deficit/Hyperactivity Disorder: A systematic review and meta-analysis. *Neuroscience and Biobehavioral Reviews*, 36(4), 1093–1106.

Van Veen, M. M., Kooij, J. J. S., Boonstra, M., et al. (2010). Delayed circadian rhythm in adults with Attention-Deficit/Hyperactivity Disorder and chronic sleep-onset insomnia. *Biological Psychiatry*, 67, 1091–1096.

Vitiello, B., Elliott, G. R., Swanson, J. M., et al. (2012). Blood pressure and heart rate over 10 years in the multimodal treatment study of children with ADHD. *American Journal of Psychiatry*, 169(2), 167–177.

Vohs, K. D., & Baumeister, R. F. (2004). *Handbook of Self-Regulation*. New York: The Guilford Press.

Volkow, N. D., Ding, Y. S., Fowler, J., et al. (1996). Dopamine transporters decrease with age. *Journal of Nuclear Medicine*, 37(4), 554–559.

Volkow, N. D., Fowler, J. S., Wang, G., et al. (2002a). Mechanism of action of methylphenidate: Insights from PET imaging studies. *Journal of Attention Disorders*, 6 (Supplement), s31–s43.

Volkow, N. D., Fowler, J. S., Wang, G., et al. (2002b). Role of dopamine in the therapeutic and reinforcing effects of methylphenidate in humans: Results from imaging studies. *European Neuropsychopharmacology*, 12(6), 557–566.

Volkow, N. D., Logan, J., Fowler, J. S., et al. (2000). Association between age-related decline in brain dopamine activity and impairment in frontal and cingulate metabolism. *American Journal of Psychiatry*, 157(1), 75–80.

Volkow, N. D., Wang, G., Fowler, J. S., et al. (2004). Evidence that methylphenidate enhances the saliency of a mathematical task by increasing dopamine in the human brain. *American Journal of Psychiatry*, 161, 1173–1180.

Volkow, N. D., Wang, G. J., Kollins, S. H., et al. (2009). Evaluating dopamine reward pathway in ADHD, clinical implications. *JAMA*, 302(10), 1084–1091.

Volkow, N. D., Wang, G. J., Newcorn, J. H., et al. (2010). Motivation deficit in ADHD is associated with dysfunction of the dopamine reward pathway. *Molecular Psychiatry*, 16(11), 1147–1154.

Volkow, N. D., Wang, G. J., Tomasi, D., et al. (2012). Methylphenidate-elicited dopamine increases in ventral striatum are associated with long-term symptom improvement in adults with Attention Deficit Hyperactivity Disorder. *Journal of Neuroscience*, 32(3), 841–849

Waber, D. P., & Holmes, J. M. (1985). Assessing children's copy productions of the Rey Osterreith Complex Figure. *Journal of clinical and experimental neuropsychology*, 7, 264–280.

Wang, G. J., Volkow, N. D., Logan, J., et al. (1995). Evaluation of age related changes in serotonin 5-HT2 and dopamine D2 receptor availability in healthy human subjects. *Life Sciences*, 56(14), 249–253.

Weafer, J., Camarillo, D., Fillmore, M. T., et al. (2008). Simulated driving performance of adults with ADHD: Comparisons with alcohol intoxication. *Experimental and Clinical Psychopharmacology*, 16(3), 251–263.

Wechsler, D. (1997a). *Wechsler adult intelligence scale* (3rd edition). San Antonio, TX: The Psychological Corporation.

Wechsler, D. (1997b). *Wechsler memory scale* (3rd edition). San Antonio, TX: The Psychological Corporation.

Wechsler, D. (2003). *Wechsler intelligence scale for children* (4th edition). San Antonio, TX: The Psychological Corporation

Weiss, G., & Hechtman, L. T. (1993). *Hyperactive children grown up – 2nd edition*. New York: Guilford Press.

West, R., Murphy, K. J., Armilio, F., et al. (2002). Lapses of intention and performance variability reveal age-related increases in fluctuations of executive control. *Brain and Cognition*, 49, 402–419.

Willcutt, E. G., Doyle, A. E., Nigg, J. T., et al. (2005). Validity of the executive function theory of Attention-Deficit/Hyperactivity Disorder: A meta-analytic review. *Biological Psychiatry*, 57(11), 1336–1346.

Williams, N. M., Franke, B., Mick, E., et al. (2012). Genome-wide analysis of copy number variants in Attention Deficit Hyperactivity Disorder: The role of rare variants and duplications at 15q13.3. *American Journal of Psychiatry*, 169(2), 195–204.

Wong, C. G., & Stevens, M. C. (2012). The effects of stimulant medication on working memory functional connectivity in Attention-Deficit/Hyperactivity Disorder. *Biological Psychiatry*, 71, 458–466.

Yoshimasu, K., Barbaresi, W. J., Colligan, R. C., et al. (2012a). Childhood ADHD is strongly associated with a broad range of psychiatric disorders during adolescence: a population-based birth cohort study. *Journal of Child Psychology and Psychiatry*, 53(10), 1036–1043.

Yoshimasu, K., Barbaresi, W. J., Colligan, R. C., et al. (2012b). Written-language disorder among children with and without ADHD in a population-based birth cohort. *Pediatrics*, 128, e605–e612.

Zoega, H., Rothman, K. J., Huybrechts, K. F., et al. (2012). A population-based study of stimulant drug treatment of ADHD and academic progress in children. *Pediatrics*, 130 (1), e53–e62.

Zuo, X. N., DiMartino, A., Kelly, C., et al. (2010). The oscillating brain: Complex and reliable. *Neuroimage*, 49, 1432–1445.

INDEX